КУЛИНАРНЫЕ РЕЦЕПТЫ

ИЗДАТЕЛЬСТВО
ПИЩЕВАЯ
ПРОМЫШЛЕННОСТЬ

МОСКВА

RUSSIAN COOKING

TRANSLATED FROM
THE RUSSIAN
BY
F. SIEGEL

MIR
PUBLISHERS
MOSCOW

First published 1974

На английском языке

5

Contents

Foreword

Russian cookery today has come to include the favourite recipes from the kitchens of other nationalities inhabiting the USSR. Traditional Russian foods vary as greatly as the climatic zones through which the country stretches. Many basic recipes are similar in remotely situated areas, but each has its own local variation.

Pelmeni, for instance, are Russian poached pasties that have a meat filling. In the Ukraine, they are known as vareniki and usually have a sour cherry or cottage cheese filling. However, Siberian pelmeni are practically proverbial. Neighbours gather after the frosts set in for special "sessions" or "bees" where pelmeni are made in quantities running into the thousands. They are laid out on huge doughboards and carried outside to freeze, after which they are dumped into sacks like so many pebbles and stored away until needed.

The long and severe winters make it necessary to preserve every possible kind of produce in large quantities. Through the centuries resourcefulness and fantasy have been put to the test to discover suitable ways to pickle, spice, cure or dry vegetables, fruits, berries, mushrooms and meat.

Hence Russian cookery is noted for its abundance of appetizers, soups and other dishes in which the main ingredient is spiced, pickled or cured.

Russian cooking has also been influenced by the design of the Russian oven. This rectangular, box-shaped structure made of brick and mortar was usually about half the height of the ceiling and occupied about a quarter of the kitchen space (if the old peasant hut had a kitchen). If the hut was a one-room affair, the oven served numerous purposes from a facility inside which food was cooked and water was heated for the animals to a winter playpen for the younger children and/or a bed for the older generation.

Since the old Russian village consisted of thatched huts, all fires had to be out and dampers closed by sunrise. Thus the oven served as a sort of thermos jug where in summer meals were kept hot from 4 or 5 am till evening, and sometimes till the following day. The food acquired a peculiar sapid flavour.

Although the Russian oven is today somewhat of a museum piece, the recipes that originated in this oven remain popular, and with slight modifications in method of cooking they can be made in the modern range.

Russian cookery today also abounds in new recipes that are in keeping with contemporary concepts of food and advanced kitchen facilities.

The close association and friendship between the Russian people and the numerous other nationalities inhabiting the USSR could not but influence Russian cookery. Favourite Georgian, Armenian, Kazakh, Uzbek and Ukrainian dishes have won such wide popularity that their origin is sometimes disputed.

The recipes in this book are for 4-5 servings unless otherwise indicated.

Weights and Measures

All recipes in this book are based on metric weights and measures.
The measuring cup used for recipes in this book contains 250 millilitres (250 cu cm). In the table of weight and measurement equivalents given below the dry ingredients are measured in heaping spoonsful, or as much as the spoon will hold. Measurements of ground spices are level.

Weight and Measurement Equivalents

Ingredient	cup	tblsp	tsp	piece
Flour and Cereals				
Wheat flour	160	25	10	—
Potato flour	200	30	10	—
Dry bread crumbs	125	15	5	—
Buckwheat groats	210	25	—	—
Rolled oats	90	12	—	—
Mannacroup (semolina)	200	25	8	—
Pearl barley	230	25	—	—
Pot barley	180	20	—	—
Rice	230	25	—	—
Millet	220	25	—	—
Beans	220	—	—	—
Split peas	230	—	—	—
Lentils	210	—	—	—
Dairy Products				
Butter (melted)	245	20	5	—
Milk	250	20	—	—
Sour Cream	250	25	10	—
Vegetables				
Carrot, medium	—	—	—	75
Potato, medium	—	—	—	100

Ingredient	cup	tblsp	tsp	piece
Onion, medium	—	—	—	75
Cucumber, medium	—	—	—	100
Tomato paste	—	30	10	—
Tomato puree	220	25	8	—
Parsley root	—	—	—	50
Miscellaneous				
Granulated sugar	200	25	10	—
Salt	325	30	10	—
Vinegar	250	15	5	—
Gelatine, powdered	—	15	5	—

Oven Temperatures

	Fahrenheit	Centigrade
Very cool	225°-275°	107°-135°
Slow	275°-300°	135°-149°
Moderate	325°-375°	163°-190°
Hot	400°-450°	205°-232°
Very hot	450° and over	232° and over

APPETIZERS

lettuce - and - egg salad
with sour cream dressing

1 egg

300 g lettuce

parsley...

1 cucumber

+ ½ cupful sour cream
and vinegar dressing

Zakuski

Russian "zakuski" are usually a hearty introduction to a still heartier meal. They begin with several kinds of salted and pickled fruits, vegetables and mushrooms and are followed by copious hot or cold savouries.

Salads

Lettuce-and-Egg Salad with Sour Cream Dressing

300 g lettuce, washed and drained
1 cucumber
1 hard-cooked egg

1/2 cupful sour cream and vinegar dressing
Dill or parsley

Cut the lettuce. Chop the hard-cooked egg and combine with sour cream and vinegar dressing (see p. 24). Pour the dressing over the lettuce, toss, decorate with sliced cucumber, sprinkle with minced dill or parsley. Serve immediately.

Lettuce Salad with Vinegar-and-Oil Dressing

300 g lettuce, washed and drained
White bread crust rubbed with garlic (optional)

1 cucumber (optional)
1/4 cupful vinegar and salad oil dressing
Dill or parsley

Cut the lettuce leaves crosswise. Pour the dressing (see p. 25) over the lettuce just before serving, toss and sprinkle with finely minced dill or parsley. Cucumber, sliced thin, may be added; decorate with bread crusts rubbed with garlic and cut into diamonds. Serve with any roast, fried or boiled meat or fried fish.

Health Salad

2 cucumbers
2 raw carrots
2 apples
2 tomatoes

100 g lettuce
1/2 cupful sour cream
Juice of 1/4 lemon
Salt and sugar

Wash and shred the cucumbers, carrots, apples and lettuce. Mix with sour cream and lemon juice; add salt and sugar to taste. Garnish with sliced tomatoes.

Cucumber Salad with Sour Cream

3 cucumbers
1/4 cupful sour cream
1/2 tblsp vinegar

Salt
Pepper
Dill

Wash and peel the cucumbers. Cut into thin slices and arrange in a salad bowl. Before serving sprinkle with a dash of salt and pepper, pour over the sour cream mixed with the vinegar. Salt to taste. Sprinkle with minced dill.

Radish Salad with Sour Cream

2-3 bunches of radishes
1 hard-cooked egg

1/2 cupful sour cream
Salt

Wash and slice 25-30 radishes thin. Mash the egg yolk, add sour cream and salt. Combine with radishes and white of egg chopped fine.

Tomato and Cucumber Salad

5-6 tomatoes
2-3 cucumbers
2 tblsps salad oil

3-4 tblsps vinegar
Salt, pepper, sugar
Minced dill or parsley

Wash and slice the tomatoes and cucumbers crosswise. Sprinkle with salt, a dash of pepper and sugar to taste. Before serving pour over the vinegar mixed with salad oil. Sprinkle with minced dill or parsley. Tomatoes or cucumbers may be prepared separately in the same manner. If desired, onion sliced in thin rings or minced green onions may be added.

Beetroot Salad

2-3 beetroots	Salt, pepper
2 tblsps salad oil	Minced dill
1/4 cupful vinegar	or passley

Boil or bake the beetroots until tender. Peel and shred, sprinkle with salt and a dash of pepper. Moisten with the oil and vinegar. Sprinkle with minced dill or parsley.

Beetroot and Potato Salad

Follow the directions for beetroot salad using an equal amount of beets and potatoes.

Potato Salad

500 g boiled potatoes	1/4 cupful vinegar
50 g minced green onions	Salt and pepper
	Dill or parsley
2 tblsps salad oil	

Peel and dice the potatoes; salt and pepper to taste; moisten with vinegar and salad oil. Heap in a bowl and sprinkle with minced dill, parsley or green onions. This salad is especially good if the potatoes are freshly cooked and still warm. Serve with hot or cold veal, mutton, pork or fish or as a separate course.

Red Cabbage Salad

I

500 g red cabbage	1 tsp salt
1/4 cupful vinegar	1 tblsp salad oil
1/2 tblsp sugar	(optional)

Wash and clean the cabbage; cut into four parts, remove the runt; shred with a sharp knife or shredder. Pour over boiling-hot water, cover and let stand for 20-30 minutes. Drain in a colander. Pour cold water over the cabbage, drain again and squeeze. Transfer into a salad bowl and moisten with vinegar. Add sugar and salt to taste, toss and set aside for 20-30 minutes. If desired, pour over salad oil and toss again. Serve with meat, wild fowl, poultry or fish.

II

Follow the directions given for the previous salad. Instead of pouring over boiling-hot water, salt the cabbage lightly and rub it until soft and a dark juice appears; squeeze and drain. Pour over vinegar, add sugar and toss. In a few minutes the cabbage will become bright. Serve with meat, wild fowl, poultry or fish.

Cabbage Salad

I

500 g white cabbage	Salt
1/4 cupful vinegar	2 tblsps salad oil
1/2 tblsp sugar	(optional)

Clean and wash the cabbage, remove the runt. Shred finely, sprinkle lightly with salt and rub until the cabbage becomes soft. Squeeze and drain off the juice. Combine the vinegar and sugar and pour over the cabbage. Set aside for 30-40 minutes. Add salad oil if desired.

II

500 g white cabbage	Salt
1/4 cupful vinegar	2 tblsps salad oil
1/2 tblsp sugar	

Clean and wash the cabbage, remove the runt and shred. Add salt and vinegar. Stirring constantly warm over low heat until the cabbage becomes soft and settles. Chill, sprinkle with sugar and pour over oil.

Cabbage, Apple and Celery Salad

500 g white cabbage	1 apple
1 stalk of celery or	1/4 cupful vinegar
equal amount of	1/2 tblsp sugar
celeriac	

Prepare the cabbage as directed for plain cabbage salad. Pare and dice the apple; shred the celery. Mix together cabbage, apple and celery. Add sugar and pour over vinegar. Serve with roast or boiled meat, fried or boiled fish or with cold meat or fish.

Sauerkraut Salad

500 g sauerkraut	Fresh or pickled apple
1 tblsp salad oil	Celery and red
1-2 tblsps sugar	bilberries (optional)

Mix the sauerkraut with sugar and salad oil. Should the sauerkraut be too sour, wash in cold water and squeeze. If desired, slices of fresh or pickled apples (see p. 179), diced celery, fresh or soaked red bilberries may be added. Serve with sausages, roast pork or boiled fowl.

Fruit Salad

3 apples	1/4 cupful mayonnaise
1 pear	Juice of 1/4 lemon
1 orange	1 tsp powdered sugar
1 tangerine	Salt

Wash and peel the fruit, remove the core and seeds and dice. Before serving sprinkle the fruit with powdered sugar and a dash of salt. Combine lemon juice and mayonnaise and moisten the fruit. Arrange in a salad bowl; sprinkle with finely shredded orange rind. Reserve some of the fruit for garnishing. Stewed prunes, grapes or berries may also be used as garnishing. All the ingredients except the apples can be varied in season (peaches, apricots, stewed quince, strawberries, etc.). Serve with cold roast or boiled meat, veal, mutton, poultry or wild fowl, or as a separate course.

Meat Salad

200 g boiled or roast meat	1/2 tblsp Yuzhny sauce[1]
4-5 boiled potatoes	1/2 cupful mayonnaise
2 pickled cucumbers	Lettuce leaves
	Salt, pepper

Dice the meat, potatoes and pickled cucumbers; combine Yuzhny sauce with mayonnaise, salt and black pepper. Heap in a salad bowl and garnish with lettuce leaves, pickles sliced lengthwise and pieces of meat.

Sausage or Ham Salad

200 g sausage or ham	1 apple
3 or 4 boiled potatoes	1/2 head lettuce
50 g celery	1 cupful mayonnaise
75 g gherkins or sweetsour pickles	Parsley
	Tarragon
	Salt

Dice the sausage or ham, potatoes, celery, gherkins or pickles and apples. Cut the lettuce. Combine the mayonnaise with minced parsley and tarragon and salt to taste. Pour dressing over the salad and toss. Garnish with sliced cold boiled beets, apples and onion rings.

Hazel Hen or Partridge Salad

1 boned boiled (or roast) hazel hen or partridge	1 apple
4 or 5 boiled potatoes	1/2 cupful mayonnaise
2 cucumbers or pickled cucumbers	1/2 tblsp Yuzhny sauce[1]
100 g lettuce	1 tblsp vinegar or lemon juice
2 hard-cooked eggs	1/2 tsp powdered sugar
	Salt

Dice the boned fowl, potatoes, cucumbers (or gherkins), one egg and the apple; cut the lettuce into large pieces. Combine the mayonnaise with the lemon juice and powdered sugar. Pour dressing over the salad and salt to taste. Heap in a salad bowl and garnish with the lettuce, wedges of hard-cooked eggs, sliced tomatoes and cucumbers.

Hazel Hen and Vegetable Salad

1 boned roast or boiled hazel hen	100 g string beans or green peas
2 or 3 potatoes	1 tomato
1 cucumber	1/3 cupful salad oil and vinegar dressing
100 g asparagus or cauliflower	Lettuce
1 boiled carrot	Sprig of celery
Salt	

Cut the lettuce. Arrange the vegetables on the lettuce. Cut the hazel hen meat into wide thin slices and arrange in a pyramid over the lettuce. Garnish with sprigs of celery or lettuce leaves. Before serving, sprinkle with salt and moisten with salad oil and vinegar dressing (see p. 25).

Poultry and Vegetable Salad

Any poultry may be substituted in the above recipe. Out of season, canned asparagus, cauliflower, green peas, string beans, tomatoes, etc., may be used.

Fish and Tomato Salad

200 g fillet of fish	1 pickled cucumber
1 tomato	1/2 cupful mayonnaise
1 cucumber	1 tblsp vinegar
3 boiled potatoes	Salt
1/2 head lettuce	50 g minced onion or green onions (optional)
75 g gherkins or	

Fresh sturgeon, sevruga, beluga, zander or salmon are all suitable for this salad. Thoroughly mix the fish, gherkins, sliced tomato, lettuce, peeled and diced potatoes and cucumbers. If desired, minced onion or green onions may be added. Just before serving salt lightly and blend with the mayonnaise and vinegar. Heap in a salad dish and garnish with lettuce leaves, sliced tomato and cucumber. The salad may also be garnished with pressed, soft or red caviar, strips of salmon or sturgeon and pitted olives.

Fish Satsivi

500 g fish	and cinnamon
1 cupful walnut kernels	1 tsp kindza[10] seeds
3/4 cupful grape	2 bay leaves
vinegar	8 whole allspics
3-4 onions	1 whole pepper
2-4 buttons of garlic	Ground black pepper
1 tsp ground cloves	and salt to taste

Cut cleaned fish into pieces, place in a saucepan and add just enough water to cover. Put in the bay leaves and allspice and cook for 30-40 minutes. When tender arrange the fish in a serving platter.

Crush the walnuts or put them through the food grinder together with the garlic, the whole pepper and salt. Add the kindza[10] seeds which have been crushed, mix thoroughly, pour in the fish liquor and transfer the mixture to a clean saucepan. Add finely minced onion and cook for 10 minutes. Add the cinnamon, cloves and black pepper which have been combined with vinegar. Continue to cook 10 minutes longer. Pour the hot satsivi over the fish, cool and serve.

Pomegranate or sour grape juice may be substituted for the vinegar.

Codfish Salad with Horseradish

250 g fillet of codfish	1/2 cupful mayonnaise
4 or 5 boiled potatoes	2 tsps vinegar
2 pickled cucumbers	50 g green onions
20 g horseradish	Parsley

Dice chilled boiled codfish, potatoes and pickles. Grate the horseradish, add mayonnaise, salt and vinegar. Blend with fish, horseradish and sprigs of parsley. cucumbers, minced green onions, grated potatoes and pickles. Garnish with sliced

Codfish Salad with Mayonnaise

200 g fillet of	1 pickled cucumber
codfish	1/2 cupful mayonnaise
50 g celery	1 tblsp vinegar
1 apple	Lettuce leaves
1 bunch radishes	Salt

Chill the radishes, cucumber and apple before slicing. Bone the chilled, boiled fish, remove the skin and cut into portions. Pour vinegar over the fish and set aside in cold place. Before serving salt the vegetables lightly and combine with two or three tablespoonsful of mayonnaise. Drain the lettuce and arrange on salad plates. Heap the vegetables on the lettuce and top with a piece of fish. Pour the remaining dressing over the fish. For variety, different combinations of vegetables may be used.

Marinated Fish Salad

300 g fillet of fish	150 g canned peas
200 g potatoes	150 g mayonnaise
150 g pickled	2 tsps (20 g) Yuzhny
cucumbers	sauce[1]
1 carrot	1 egg

Marinade

2 tblsps (20 g)	1 tblsp (20 g) sugar
vegetable oil	1 tblsp 3% vinegar
40 g minced parsley	Salt

Fillet of conger eel, sole, scad, eel-pout, bluefish or black cod may be used. Cook the fish in a small quantity of hot water, adding the spices and salt after the water begins to boil. Chill and then remove the fish from the liquor. Cut up the fish, reserving a few large pieces for garnishing. Combine the ingredients of the marinade and pour over the fish. Allow the fish to marinate for 1 hour in the refrigerator; this will make it juicier. Slice the pickled (or spiced) cucumbers, boiled potatoes and carrot, combine with mayonnaise to which the Yuzhny sauce[1] has been added. Toss and heap in a salad plate. Arrange the large pieces of fish on the salad and dress with mayonnaise. Garnish with greens and a hard-cooked egg.

Boiled Fish Salad

300 g fillet of fish	100 g greens
200 g potatoes	150 g mayonnaise
150 g cucumbers	1 tsp Yuzhny sauce[1]
100 g tomatoes	Marinated sweet red
150 g canned pease	pepper for garnishing

Boil and then chill and flake the fish. Reserve several pieces for garnishing. Slice thinly the boiled potatoes, cucumbers and tomatoes, add the peas and then combine with the mayonnaise to which the Yuzhny sauce[1] has been added. Mix gently but thoroughly with the fish. Heap in a salad bowl and garnish with ingredients which have been reserved and also herbs and marinated sweet red pepper.

Crab Salad

1 can crabmeat	100 g canned green
1 boiled turnip	peas or string beans
1 boiled carrot	1/2 head lettuce
2 or 3 boiled potatoes	1/3 cupful mayonnaise
1 cucumber	1 tblsp salad oil
1 tomato	2 tblsps vinegar
	Salt

Dice the vegetables; cut the tomato into round slices. Cut up the lettuce and heap in a salad dish; reserve lettuce leaves for garnishing. Arrange each vegetable in a separate "bouquet" around the lettuce.

Put the drained and picked crabmeat in the centre of the lettuce. Just before serving, sprinkle a dash of salt over the vegetables, moisten with salad oil and vinegar dressing which has been blended with a little crabmeat juice. Pour the mayonnaise over the crabmeat and garnish with lettuce leaves.

Crayfish Salad

Substitute crayfish meat in the above recipe.

Russian Vegetable Salad

(Vinegret)

4-5 potatoes	100 g sauerkraut
1 beetroot	1 carrot
2 pickled cucumbers	50 g green onions
1 fresh or pickled apple	100 g mustard dressing
	Minced dill

Separately boil the potatoes, beetroot and carrot until tender, drain and chill. Peel and dice, slice or shoestring the ingredients. Mix with sauerkraut. Before serving pour over mustard dressing and toss. Garnish with sliced beetroot, minced green onions and dill, or cucumbers and tomatoes.

Mushroom Vinegret

Add to the above recipe 100 g any kind of pickled mushrooms (see p. 180).

Russian Herring Salad

1 medium-sized herring	1 or 2 hard-cooked
2 boiled potatoes	eggs
1 apple	3 tblsps salad oil
1 pickled cucumber	2 tblsps vinegar
1 onion	1 tsp mustard
1 boiled beetroot	Parsley or dill

Clean, bone and dice the herring. Thinly slice the vegetables and apple. To make the dressing mash the egg yolk with a fork, add to it salt and mustard, gradually stir in oil enough to make a thick paste and then add the vinegar. Combine the salad and dressing, add the minced onion and parsley or dill. Garnish with slices of beet, pieces of herring and chopped egg whites.

Russian Fruit and Vegetable Salad

1 apple	Celery and parsley
1 pear	greens (50 g each)
1 tangerine	1/2 head lettuce
1 orange	50 g green peas
3-4 boiled potatoes	1/2 cupful mayonnaise
1 boiled carrot	Juice of 1 lemon
1 cucumber	Salt
2 tsps sugar	

Peel and slice the apple, pear, potatoes, carrot and cucumber. Add the peas, minced celery and parsley. Before serving sprinkle with a dash of salt and sugar and combine with the mayonnaise and lemon juice. Garnish with sliced orange, tangerine and lettuce.

Russian Vegetable Salad with Fish

250 g fillet of fish	1 (100 g) onion
1 (100 g) beet	150 g fresh cabbage
2 (200 g) carrots	or sauerkraut
3 (150 g) potatoes	50 g salad dressing
100 g green onions	100 g canned peas
150 g pickled	100 g pickled plums
cucumbers	Greens

Either boiled or fried fish may be used in this salad. Boil the beet, carrot and potatoes chill and cut up along with the pickled cucumber. Slice the onion into half rings. Mince the green onions and

slice the tomatoes. Squeeze the sauerkraut, but if it is too sour, wash in cold water, squeeze and then add. Cut the fish into little chunks. Combine with vinegar and oil dressing (see p. 25) or mayonnaise. If boiled fish is used, add the green peas and pickled plums. Garnish with greens.

Bean Salad

1 cupful beans	200 g lettuce
2-3 carrots	2 tblsps salad oil
1/2 cupful shredded	200 g mustard dressing
celery	

Soak the beans for 4-5 hours in cold water, then cook, drain and chill. Cook, cool and dice the carrots. Mix beans and carrots with shredded celery and lettuce. Pour over mustard dressing (see p. 25). Arrange in a heap and garnish with lettuce leaves, carrots and, if desired, sliced apple.

Beans with Salad Oil

1 cupful beans	Pepper
1 onion	Salt
3 tblsps vegetable oil	Minced herbs

Soak the beans in cold water for 4 hours, then cook until tender, drain and fry in oil until browned. Fry the onion separately and add to the beans. Add salt and pepper to taste. Mix thoroughly and chill. Before serving sprinkle with minced herbs.

Mushroom "Caviar"

250 g pickled	Pepper
mushrooms or 50 g	Lemon or vinegar
dried mushrooms	Minced green onions
1 onion	1 or 2 tblsps vegetable
	oil

Any pickled mushrooms or cooked dried mushrooms may be used. Wash and drain the pickled mushrooms and chop fine. Mince the onion and sauté in oil, cool and add to the mushrooms. Add pepper to taste. After cooking the dried mushrooms, prepare as directed above. Add salt and pepper to taste. Add a little lemon juice or vinegar. Sprinkle with minced green onions.

Eggplant "Caviar"

300 g eggplant	1 tomato
1-2 onions	Salt, pepper
2 tblsps vegetable oil	Vinegar

Bake or boil the eggplant. Peel and chop fine. Add the tomato and slightly browned fried onion. Salt, pepper, oil and vinegar to taste. Mix thoroughly, warm over low heat to eliminate any extra moisture. Chill before serving.

Beetroot "Caviar"

500 g beetroots	2 tblsps butter
2-3 tblsps sugar	1/2 lemon

Wash and cook the beetroots until tender. Peel and mince in a food chopper. Add sugar, butter, a bit of lemon rind and lemon juice. Mix thoroughly and heat in a saucepan for 5 to 10 minutes, stirring constantly. Chill before serving.

Fish

Herring with Garnishing

Soak the skinned herring fillets in water, weak tea or milk for 3 or 4 hours.
To clean and skin the herring cut off the edge of the belly, the head and tail; remove the viscera; slit the skin from head to tail along the backbone; remove the skin beginning at the head and working towards the belly and tail. Cut the flesh from the backbone and remove the rib bones on both sides. Put the two fillets together, cut into pieces of the desired size and arrange in an oblong herring plate. Put the head (gills removed) at one end and the tail at the other. Garnish with cucumbers, tomatoes, gherkins, pickled mushrooms (for edible brown mushrooms or milk mushrooms see p. 180), finely diced boiled beets, potatoes, carrots, onion or green onions, capers and hard-cooked eggs. Before serving moisten the herring and garnish with dressing.

Vegetable Oil and Vinegar Dressing

Combine 2 or 3 tablespoonsful vinegar with salt, sugar and pepper to taste. Stir in 1 to $1^1/_2$ tablespoonsful vegetable oil.

Mustard and Egg Dressing

Combine the yolk of one egg with one teaspoonful prepared mustard and one teaspoonful vegetable oil, 2 or 3 tablespoonsful vinegar and salt to taste. Mix the ingredients thoroughly.

Salmon, Chum Salmon

Skin, bone and thinly slice the salt salmon. Garnish with parsley or lettuce leaves and lemon slices. If too salty, soak the salmon in water for 3 or 4 hours before slicing. Then wipe it dry with a towel, brush with salad oil, refrigerate for 1 — 1 $1/_2$ hours and then slice.

Lamprey Eels
(Minogi)

Cut prepared eels into pieces 3 or 4 cm long. Cover with thinly sliced onions. Add 1 or 2 teaspoonsful freshly grated horseradish to salad oil and vinegar dressing and pour over the eels.

Sturgeon and Red Caviar

Serve soft and red caviar in small bowls. Pass minced green onions separately. Shape pressed caviar into a little cake and garnish with a sprig of parsley and a slice of lemon; pass butter in a separate dish. Serve with small rasstegai[2] with viziga[3] or rice and fish filling.

Sturgeon, Beluga, Sevruga, Catfish

Boil and chill the fish before removing the cartilage and rib bones. Slice and serve garnished according to season and preference with sliced tomatoes, cucumbers or gherkins, a salad of plain or red cabbage, greens or potatoes, carrots and peas. Moisten the garnishing with vinegar and oil dressing. Serve immediately. Pass horseradish and vinegar, mayonnaise, green sauce and pickles separately.

Chopped Herring

200 g filleted herring	2 tblsps unsalted butter
100 g white bread	1 onion
1 large apple	Nutmeg

Mince the herring, apple and onion and press through a sieve together with the bread which has been soaked and squeezed dry. Combine with the butter and mix thoroughly with a paddle or spoon.

Add a dash of ground nutmeg if desired. Serve in an oblong dish. Put the herring head at one end and the tail at the other. Garnish with sliced apple and sprigs of parsley. For variety, finely grated apple may be added. Serve in a butter dish or spread on slices of deep fried bread.

Anchovies and Potatoes

1 can anchovies	2 tblsps vinegar
5-6 potatoes	Green onions
1 tblsp salad oil	Salt, pepper

Rice the freshly boiled potatoes and arrange in a heap. Roll the boned anchovies into rings and place them around the potatoes alternately with minced green onions. Make a dressing of salad oil, vinegar, salt and pepper. Pour over the potatoes.

Sprats and Potatoes

Substitute sprats in the above recipe.

Fried Fish in Marinade

500 g sturgeon, zander, pike, smelt, navaga or cod	300 g marinade (see below)
1 tblsp flour	50 g green parsley or dill
1 tblsp vegetable oil	

Prepare one of these or another similar fish as directed in the section "Fish". Cut large fish into portions of the desired size; small fish can be marinated whole. Slash the skin, sprinkle with salt and pepper, then roll in flour. Fry in hot vegetable oil until golden brown then bake until tender. Chill and pour over marinade. Set aside in refrigerator for 2-3 hours. Before serving sprinkle with parsley or dill.

Marinade

150 g carrots	2-3 cloves
20 g parsley root	1 piece stick cinnamon
100 g onion or leeks	1/2 cupful weak (3%)
2 1/2 tblsps vegetable	vinegar
oil (40 g)	8 peppercorns
5 tblsps tomato puree	1 tblsp sugar
4 bay leaves	Salt to taste

Scrape and wash the carrots and parsley, clean the onions, then slice or shred them. Sauté slightly in vegetable oil for 10 to 15 minutes. Add tomato puree and spices, cover and sauté for 10 to 15 minutes. Pour in vinegar and fish liquor, add salt and condiment and boil for 10 minutes longer. Chill, remove the bay leaves, cloves, peppercorns and cinnamon.

Boiled Zander with Mayonnaise

800 g fish	150 g potatoes
150 g mayonnaise	1 cucumber
3 tblsps salad dressing	2 tomatoes
100 g carrots	1 small can of peas

Boil the fish till tender then chill and cut into portions. Boil, peel and then dice the potatoes and carrots. Add sliced cucumber and tomatoes and green peas (reserve 1/3 for garnishing). Combine the vegetables with mayonnaise and heap in the centre of each individual plate. Place a piece of fish on top. Arrange the cucumber, tomato and peas which have been reserved for garnishing in contrasting colours around the edge and pour over salad dressing. Dress the pieces of fish with mayonnaise.

Boiled Fish with Horseradish

300 g fillet of fish	600 g garnishing
2 tblsps salad dressing	(potatoes, carrots,
(50 g)	cucumbers, green peas
100 g prepared	or coleslaw)
horseradish	

Cut unskinned fillet of fish into portions and cook in hot water to which herbs, carrot and condiments have been added. The fish may be cooked in hot spiced fish liquor. Cool the fish in the liquor then remove and drain. Dice the boiled and peeled carrots and potatoes, slice fresh or pickled cucumbers and arrange them and peas and coleslaw around the fish. Pour over oil and vinegar dressing (see p. 25). Pass horseradish separately.

Fish in Mayonnaise and Aspic

1 kg fillet of fish	Salt and herbs to taste
200 g mayonnaise	Vegetables for
1 tblsp powdered	garnishing
gelatin	

Cook the fish and vegetables. Drain off the stock and strain. Cook until 2/3 of the amount are left. Chill, add gelatin and set aside for 40 minutes till the gelatin swells. Heat until the gelatin is completely dissolved but do not bring to the boil. Flake the cold fish, add minced greens and combine thoroughly with the cold stock which has been mixed with mayonnaise. (Reserve 1/3 of the stock and mayonnaise mixture for garnishing). Transfer to a deep platter. Chill slightly in the refrigerator, then pour the remaining mayonnaise and aspic mixture over the fish. Garnish with bright coloured vegetables and chill. Cut into portions before serving. Pass pickled cucumbers. The fish stock will be stronger if the trimmings are cooked in it.

Any lean fish or fish with a specific smell may be used.

Jellied Zander

1 zander	1 parsley root and
(1000-1200 g)	leaves
1 tblsp gelatin	1 or 2 bay leaves
1 carrot	Salt to taste
1 onion	Lemon

Clean, wash and cut the fish. Remove the gills. Cook the bones, trimmings, roe and head with the vegetable roots. Add bay leaves and salt and water to cover. Boil for 15 to 20 minutes. Add the fish and cook whole. When "done" cool and then cut. Arrange on a platter in the shape of a whole fish, leaving spaces between the pieces. Set aside to chill. Soak the gelatin in 1/2 cupful of stock for 40 min, then dissolve in the remaining stock and make 2 to 2 1/2 cupsful of aspic. Strain through a double cheesecloth. Decorate each piece of fish with a slice of lemon, a star-shaped piece of carrot and parsley leaves. Fix the decorations by pouring the aspic in layers, allowing each layer to congeal before adding the next. Refrigerate. Serve with red cabbage or potato salad, cucumbers or pickles. Pass mayonnaise separately.

Jellied Sturgeon

1000 g sturgeon	1 onion
25-30 g gelatin	Parsley leaves
1 carrot	Salt
1 parsley root	Lemon

Cook the sturgeon (sevruga or beluga), carrot, parsley and onion in water enough to make 3 or 4 cupsful of stock for a clear aspic.

Slice the cooked sturgeon and lay in a mould leaving space for aspic between the pieces. Decorate with the parsley leaves, slices of the carrot or cucumber. Pieces of crab or crayfish meat and capers may also be used. Fix the decorations by pouring over aspic in two or three layers. When jellied, cut into portions. Garnish with bouquets of cooked carrot, turnips, potatoes sand green peas; moisten with vegetable oil and vinegar. Pass horseradish with vinegar and mayonnaise separately.

Jellied Sterlet

1000 g sterlet	1 carrot
15-20 g gelatin (for	1 parsley root
4 cupsful aspic)	1 onion
25 g caviar	Salt

Clean and wash the sterlet and then cook as directed in the recipe for jellied zander. When tender remove from the stock, cover with a cloth and set aside. Add the soaked gelatin to the stock and stir until completely dissolved. Clarify the aspic with pressed or soft caviar as directed in the recipe for ukha[5] (see p. 46), strain and cool. Decorate with parsley leaves, crayfish tails or crab meat before pouring the aspic over.

Cold Meat

A goodly number of "cold zakuski" can be obtained ready-to-serve; these include ham, roast beef, pork and veal, roast poultry and wildfowl. There is a large assortment of boiled, smoked and semi-smoked sausage liver sausage and paste. These can all be used in making up combination meat platters garnished with fresh, pickled or spiced fruits and vegetables.

Given below are recipes of favourite appetizers that may be made at home.

Liver Paste

500 g calf or beef liver	1 egg
50 g salt pork	Salt, pepper
2 tblsps butter	Nutmeg
2 carrots	2 tblsps stock or milk
2 onions	

Dice the salt pork and render in a hot frying pan. Add the finely cut up carrots and onions. When slightly browned, add the liver which has been cut into medium size pieces and sprinkled with salt and pepper. Cover with a lid and sauté until done. (**Do not fry the liver too long or it will be dry**). Remove from the heat and cool. Put the liver, vegetables and pork through a mincer two or three times. Combine with creamed butter and a dash of grated nutmeg. Taste to correct seasoning then transfer to plates or a serving dish. Decorate with butter shaped with a bag or tube, hard-cooked eggs, green onions or deep fried onions. Put the yolks of the eggs through the ricer and chop up the whites.

Sucking Pig with Horseradish

Prepare and cook the sucking pig as directed in the recipe for jellied sucking pig (see below).

Before serving chill and cut into portions. Decorate with sprigs of parsley or lettuce leaves.

Pass horseradish and sour cream sauce or horseradish and vinegar separately.

Jellied Sucking Pig

1 sucking pig (2 to	1 parsley root
2 1/2 kg)	1 onion
30 g gelatin	Salt, pepper, bay leaf,
1 carrot	cloves

If necessary, singe the sucking pig over a spirit flame to remove any bristles and then wash it. Cut off the head and cut the creature in half at the middle (each half may be chopped down the backbone). If cooked whole, begin at the neck and chop down the backbone lengthwise on the inside to the flesh. Add the carrot, parsley, onion, water to cover and salt. Bring to the boil, skim and then simmer for 40 to 50 minutes. When tender, put the meat on a platter, cover with a moist cloth and refrigerate.

Heat the stock, add pepper, bay leaf and cloves; bring to the boil. Add the gelatin which has been soaked in cold water. Stir and bring to the boil; strain through a double layer of cheesecloth. Cut the chilled meat into portions; arrange on a platter leaving about 1/2 cm between the pieces. Decorate with half slices of hard-cooked eggs, sprigs of parsley, sliced cooked carrot and lemon. Pour the aspic over as directed in the recipe for jellied zander. Pass horseradish and sour cream sauce or horseradish and vinegar separately.

Jellied Tongue

1 tongue (about 1 kg)	1 carrot
20-25 g gelatin (for	1 parsley root
2-2 1/2 cupsful aspic)	1 onion

Cook, chill and slice the tongue. Cover with aspic as directed in the recipe for jellied sturgeon. Skim the fat from the stock and make the aspic. Decorate with sliced hard-cooked eggs, cucumber, gherkins and parsley leaves. Pour over the aspic. Set aside to jell. Before serving cut around each piece with a knife and unmould. Garnish with plain or red cabbage salad, sliced tomatoes and cucumbers, spiced cherries, plums or grapes, lettuce and sprigs of parsley. Pass Ostry sauce[1], mayonnaise, horseradish and sour cream sauce or horseradish and vinegar.

Jellied Ham

Substitute lean ham in the above recipe.

Jellied Beef

Singe, cut and soak the lip and feet in cold water for 3 or 4 hours. Scrub with a brush and rinse in clean water. Add water until it is 8 or 10 cm above the meat. For each kilogram of meat and bones add 1 or 2 carrots, an onion, parsley. Cover and cook over low heat for 6 to 7 hours or until the meat easily comes away from the bone. Skim all the fat. Bone the meat and put it through the

meat mincer; combine with the strained stock. Add a bay leaf and a dash of pepper, salt to taste, and bring to the boil. Add one crushed button of garlic. Pour into the mould. Sliced hard-cooked eggs may be added after pouring 1/3 the aspic. After the aspic sets, add another layer of sliced eggs, cover with more aspic and jell. Before serving, unmould and garnish with parsley leaves, sliced cucumbers, plain or red cabbage salad. Pass a sauce of horseradish and vinegar or horseradish and sour cream, and mustard.

Jellied Veal

4 calf's feet	1 parsley root
5-6 eggs	2-3 bay leaves
2 onions	Salt
2 carrots	Pepper
	Button of garlic

Scald the feet and dry with a cloth. Rub with flour and over a spirit burner singe off any hair. Cut the feet lengthwise and cut the meat from the bone. Chop and wash the bones. Add water to cover the bones and meat by 4-5 cm. Add the carrots, parsley and onions; bring to the boil and simmer for 3-4 hours. Skim the fat, remove the carrots and parsley, remove the bones and cut up the meat or put it through the mincer. Return the bones to the stock, add bay leaves and pepper. Bring to the boil and cook for 3-4 hours. Strain and remove the bay leaves. Add the meat. Salt to taste. Pour into mould, alternating layers of aspic and hard-cooked eggs, and then chill. Serve with horseradish and sour cream sauce, mustard, horseradish and vinegar sauce or grated horseradish. Separately pass lettuce salad with sour cream and vinegar dressing or cucumbers.

Jellied Pig's Knuckles

Substitute pig's knuckles in the above recipe.

Jellied Pig's Head

Substitute pig's head in the above recipe. Add 1-1 1/2 tsps gelatin to the stock.

Sauces and Salad Dressing

Numerous commercial derivatives of mayonnaise and tomato sauce are available. The tomato sauces include Yuzhny, Ostry, Kubansky and Lyubitelsky[1]. With these, numerous derivative sauces can be made at home.

Mayonnaise and Sour Cream Dressing

1 1/4 cupsful (250 g) mayonnaise	Lyubitelsky sauce[1] (optional)
150 g sour cream	Salt, pepper
1 tsp Yuzhny or	Sugar

Combine the mayonnaise with thick chilled sour cream, and pepper, salt and sugar to taste. Mix until smooth. If desired, Yuzhny or Lyubitelsky sauce may be added.

Mayonnaise and Gherkin Dressing

1 1/2 cupsful (300 g) mayonnaise	1 tblsp Yuzhny sauce[1]
	100 g gherkins or mixed pickles

Mince the gherkins or pickles, squeeze slightly and mix with the mayonnaise. Add the Yuzhny sauce and combine thoroughly. Serve with cold roast beef, veal, lamb, boiled meat or hot fried crumbed fish.

Green Dressing

300 g mayonnaise	1/2 tsp mustard
2 tblsps spinach puree	3/4 tsp sugar
15 g terragon	1 tblsp vinegar
10 g parsley	Salt
5 g dill	

Parboil the spinach, terragon, parsley and dill for 2-3 minutes. Cool, sift and combine with mayonnaise, add 1 tblsp Yuzhny sauce, sugar, mustard and salt to taste and blend thoroughly. Serve with cold boiled fish or fried crumbed fish.

Mustard and Capers Sauce

2 hard-cooked eggs	3-4 tblsps vinegar
2 tblsps vegetable oil	1 tblsp small capers
1/2 tblsp mustard	1/2 tsp sugar

Press the egg yolks through a strainer. Blend with the mustard, sugar and salt until light in colour. Stirring constantly, gradually add the oil and vinegar. Add the capers and then minced egg whites.

Horseradish and Vinegar Sauce

Scrape, wash and grate a horseradish root. Pour over boiling water to cover and close with a lid. When cool add vinegar, salt and sugar. Mix thoroughly.

Sour Cream and Vinegar Dressing

I

1/4 cupful sour cream	1 tsp powdered sugar
1/4 cupful vinegar	Salt and pepper to taste

Thoroughly blend the sour cream, salt, pepper, vinegar and sugar.

II

1/2 cupful sour cream
1-1 1/2 tblsps vinegar
Sugar to taste

Thoroughly blend the ingredients.

Sour Cream and Horseradish Sauce

Scrape, wash and grate a horseradish root. Mix with one cupful of sour cream, add salt and sugar to taste.

Oil and Vinegar Dressing

I

1/4 cupful vinegar
1-2 tblsps vegetable oil

1 tsp powdered sugar
Salt and pepper to taste

Thoroughly blend the ingredients. Use immediately.

II

2 tblsps vinegar
4-5 tblsps vegetable oil

1/2 tsp powdered sugar
Salt and pepper to taste

Blend the ingredients thoroughly.

Mustard dressing

4 tblsps vegetable oil
4 tsps prepared mustard
4 tblsps 3⁰/₀ vinegar

1 tsp sugar
Dash of salt and
pepper

Blend the mustard, salt, sugar and ground pepper with the vegetable oil then add the vinegar. Stir until thoroughly blended.

Hot Snacks

These may be briefly defined as miniature main course dishes minus the garnishing. They may consist of meat or fish, mushrooms in sour cream, pirozhki[6], pirogi[7], kulebyaki[8] or rasstegayi[2], with almost any kind of filling, and numerous other savouries.

Forcemeat Cakes in Sour Cream

Prepare the meat as directed in the recipe for forcemeat cutlets (see p. 101), shape into round cakes 3 to 4 cm in diameter. Dredge with flour and fry in a deep skillet. Pour sour cream over and simmer for 5 to 7 minutes. Before serving pour over the sauce and sprinkle with finely minced greens.

Meat and Herring Forcemeat Pudding
(Forshmak)

250 g boiled or roast meat (beef, veal, lamb or fowl)
1/2 herring
2 or 3 boiled potatoes
1 onion
1 tsp vegetable oil

1 1/2 tblsps butter
2 or 3 tblsps thick sour cream
2 or 3 eggs
1 tblsp grated cheese
Salt, pepper

Put the boiled or roast beef, veal or lamb and the fillet of soaked herring through a fine mincer. Mash the potatoes and mix with onion sautéed in oil. Combine the ingredients and blend thoroughly. Add the creamed butter and sour cream and put through the mincer again. Add the raw egg yolks, salt and pepper to taste and mix; carefully fold in the egg whites beaten stiff. Transfer to a buttered pan and smooth the top. Sprinkle with grated cheese and melted butter. Bake for 30 to 40 minutes at about 150°C (300°F) or until the forshmak shrinks and leaves the sides of the pan. Serve on a platter with red sauce or sour cream poured over. The sauce may also be passed in a sauceboat.

SOUPS

summer borshsh

1 bunsh of beets

salt, pepper, cloves, bay leaf

1 carrot

50-75g green onions

1 stalk of celery

200 g marrow

3-4 potatoes

1-2 tomatoes

It is doubtful whether any kitchen in the world can claim a variety of soups as large as that known in Russian cooking. Through the centuries the assortment of traditional Russian soups has undergone little change and in the dinner menu the term "first course" still means soup. The word itself appeared in the Russian vocabulary in the time of Peter the Great when it was used in reference to foreign liquid dishes. Russian dishes of this type were called **pokhlebka.** The classification of traditional Russian soups, as known today, has been traced back to 16th and 17th century annals. And today as in those times they are **shchi,** cabbage soup, **borshch,** beet soup, **rassolnik,** cucumber pickle and brine soup, **ukha,** fresh-water fish soup; **solyanka** was originally applied to any food eaten by the peasantry. Today solyanka denotes a savoury, tart food in which sauerkraut or pickled cucumbers are one of the main ingredients.

Reinforced Soups

Reinforced soups are made with a meat, fish, mushroom or vegetable stock.
The vegetables used should be pared and cut to conform in size and shape with the other ingredients. For instance, the roots for a potato soup with cereal should be finely diced; for a noodle soup they should be cut in strips. The cabbage for shchi[28] is usually shredded with a knife.

Tomato puree and fresh tomatoes are used in most reinforced soups, but they are not used in rassolnik[22], green shchi[28] and soups containing sorrel or spinach. The vegetables will retain their flavour and fragrance if they are sautéed in a small amount of fat; do not allow them to become dark.
The vegetables may be cut in any shape but they must all be of the same thickness. The more finely the vegetables are cut the more easily the fat extracts the colouring matter (of carrots in particular) and the aromatic volatile oils of the onion.
Each vegetable and the tomato puree should be sautéed separately in vegetable oil or boiled butter. The layer of vegetables in the frying pan should be not more than 30 mm (about 1/6 of an inch) thick, otherwise they will steam instead of fry and the volatile oils will escape. To preserve the volatile oils in the sliced onion, it is sufficient to mix it with the melted fat.
Put the carrots in the pan first and when they are slightly browned add the onion and mix it with the carrot. In a few minutes add the parsley or celery. Fry the vegetables stirring from time to time until they are soft but not brown. The sauerkraut added to shchi will be tastier if stewed beforehand.
Pearl barley, peas, beans and lentils will cook quicker if they are soaked: soak pearl barley for 2-3 hours and legumes, for 4 to 6 hours. Do not soak split peas. Pearl barley soup sometimes acquires an unpleasant bluish colour. To prevent this,

cook the pearl barley separately until nearly done, drain and then add it to the soup.

The ingredients must be added to the soup in a definite order so that they are all done at the same time. The sequence to be observed is given in the respective recipes. A little pepper, bay leaf or other spices make some soups more savoury; the taste of other soups is improved by thickening them with flour.

The thickening is made by rubbing together flour and butter (1 tblsp flour: 1 tblsp butter). Stir continuously and brown it over a low heat (5 to 10 minutes); stir in a little stock and then pour the thickening into the soup. Cook the soup for another 10 to 15 minutes. Browning of the flour eliminates the moisture it may contain and also the specific undesirable flavour and smell of moist flour. For such soups as green shchi[28] the flour may be browned together with the root vegetables.

The flavour and nutritive value of vegetable soups can be improved by adding milk, cream, sour cream or sour milk. The addition of minced aromatic herbs will improve the flavour and appearance of the soups. They also add vitamine C. Since vitamine C is highly volatile, vegetable soups should be cooked as close as possible to the serving time. Remember that three hours after cabbage or potato soup have been cooked, only half the original amount of vitamine C is left.

A two-day supply of soup stock kept in the refrigerator will simplify soup making, and make it easier to vary your menu. Fresh frozen vegetables are great time savers in soup making. Pour a little hot soup stock over these vegetables and stew them until they are tender. Stir in tomato puree which has been heated with a little fat; then add the hot stock and bring to the boil.

Canned soups are also great times savers. By adding them to the soups stock or combining with canned meat, a tasty meat soup can be made.

A soup can be quickly prepared by using canned meat or fish. Cook all the ingredients in water until tender, then add the canned meat or fish and bring to the boil.

Meat Stock

Any grade of meat, including the thick flank, shank or hock may be used to make the stock for soups, shchi[28] and borshch[17] (500 g meat, 2 1/2-3 litres water). Wash the meat in a stream of cold water, crack the bones and put the meat and bones in a saucepan. Add the cold water, cover the saucepan with a lid and rapidly bring to a boil. Turn down the heat, skim and remove the fat. Carrots, turnips, parsley root and onion may be added. Except for the onion, these vegetables may be served in the soup. Boil gently for 1 1/2 hours and then add salt to taste. When the meat is tender, remove it to another saucepan and strain the stock.

Bone Stock

The nutritive value and flavour of bone stock is inferior to that of meat stock since bones do not contain meat extracts. Bones contain mainly gelatinous matter and fat and therefore the stock is chiefly used for potato soups. Make this stock with the bones left after the meat has been cut away for the main course (cutlets, fricassee, etc.). For each 500 g of bones use 1 carrot, 1 parsley root, 1 onion and 2 1/2 to 3 litres cold water. Wash and chop up the bones as small as possible. Cover with water and cook as directed for meat stock. Do not allow it to boil rapidly. From time to time skim the fat and waste matter. Cook for 2 hours keeping covered; add the vegetables and salt. Cook for another 1/2 or 1 hour and then strain.

Quick Meat Stock

500 g meat	1 parsley or celery root
1 carrot	1 1/2 to 2 litres water
1 onion	Salt

The most inexpensive cuts of meat may be used. Wash and put the meat through the mincer; chop up the bones. Pour cold water over the meat and bones and set aside for 20-30 minutes. Cook without changing the water. Clean and cut the vegetables and add half to the stock. Slightly sauté the remaining vegetables before adding to the stock. Cook for 20 minutes then add salt. Boil gently for another 30-40 minutes, then strain and use as plain bouillon. The meat may be used as filling for pirozhki[6] or meat zapekanka[21].

Fish Stock

500-600 g fish	1 onion
2-2 1/2 litres water	1 parsley root

Use either small white fish (zander, bass, etc.) or red fish (sturgeon, sevruga, beluga, salmon, etc.). White fish stock is made as follows:

Clean and trim the fish. Place the whole fish and trimmings in a saucepan and cover with cold water. Boil gently for 25-30 minutes. Remove the fish. Cook the head and other trimmings for another 15-20 minutes. The fish meat may be served in the fish soup or as the main course. Fish stock may be made of trimmings or small fish. Use the fish fillet for the main course. Chop up the bones, remove the gills from the head, add the fins and tail; wash thoroughly, pour over cold water or cold spiced liquor (see below). Add the greens and parsley root, celery, onion, carrot, bay leaf and peppercorns. Bring to the boil and skim. Turn down the heat and boil gently for about one hour removing the scum and fat from time to time. Should the scum settle to the bottom of the pot, add one cupful of cold water; most of the scum will then rise to the top and the stock will become clear.

If the fish stock is allowed to boil rapidly or too long, it will not be clear and acquire a fatty taste and unpleasant flavour.

When the fish has a specific undesirable smell and taste, cook it in spiced stock and add pickled cucumber brine (200-800 g per litre of water) or the peelings of pickled cucumbers; this will reduce the "fishy" smell and taste. Instead of brine a little vinegar may be used. In this case the fish flesh acquires a pleasant colour.

Spiced Liquor

1 litre cold water	15 g carrots
15 g (1 1/2 tsps) salt	15 g onion
0.1 g (2-3) peppercorns	15 g parsley or celery root
1 bay leaf	

Boil the above ingredients gently for 5-7 minutes. Cool liquor before cooking fish in it.

Strain the fish stock and use it to make soups, sauces and solyanka[20]. If the stock is to be used in the future to make sauce or aspic, it should be salted very slightly.

Cabbage Soup

(Shchi[28])

300 g meat	Pepper, salt and bay leaf
800 g plain cabbage	Flour for thickening
200 g vegetable roots and onion	Potatoes (optional)
200 g tomatoes	2 tblsps butter

Cook the meat in 1 1/2 litres water for 1 1/2 to 2 hours to make a stock. Remove the meat. Clean, slice and brown the roots and onion. Strain the stock onto the roots and onion. Add the meat and shredded cabbage. Cook for 25 to 30 minutes. Add pepper, bay leaf and salt to taste. Cook another 5 to 10 minutes. If desired, potatoes may be added after the cabbage has been cooked for 10 to 15 minutes. Add sliced tomatoes at the end and cook together with the condiment. If made without potatoes, thicken the shchi with browned flour.

Sauerkraut Shchi[28]

300 g meat	1 tblsp flour
800 g sauerkraut	2 tblsps butter
1 carrot	2 tblsps tomato puree
1 parsley root	Salt, pepper, bay leaf
1 onion	

I

Prepare a meat stock (1 1/2 litres). Put the sauerkraut in the soup kettle (if too sour, wash and drain). Add 1 to 1 1/2 cupsful of water and 1 tblsp butter. Cover and simmer for about an hour. Pour 1 litre of meat stock over the sauerkraut. Brown the vegetable roots, then add the onion and together with the tomato pouree cook until tender. Add the bay leaf, pepper and salt. Stir in the flour thickening.

II

Wash the meat. Boil gently in 1 1/2 litres water together with the sauerkraut for 1 to 1 1/2 hours. Add the carrot, parsley and onion which have been browned and the tomato puree. Cook for another 20 to 30 minutes. Add the bay leaf, pepper and salt. Thicken with browned flour.

Sauerkraut Shchi[28] with Head of Fish

1 kg head of sturgeon	2 tblsps butter
800 g sauerkraut	1 tblsp flour
200 g vegetable roots and onion	1 1/2 litres water
2 tblsps tomato puree	Salt, pepper, bay leaf

Chop up the fish head, remove the gills and wash. Scald with hot water for 1 or 2 minutes and then wash again. Add water to cover and simmer for 1 hour.

Strain the stock, bone the head and return the flesh and cartilage to the stock. Cook for two hours. Add the sauerkraut prepared as directed in the recipe for sauerkraut shchi. Brown the roots, add the tomato puree and add to the stock. Thicken with flour, add salt, pepper and bay leaf.

Cabbage Sprout Shchi

300 g meat	2 tblsps butter
800 g cabbage sprouts	1 tblsp flour
200 g vegetable roots	Sour cream
and onion	Minced dill or parsley

Prepare 1 1/2 litres meat stock. Pare and slice the root vegetables and onions; sauté in butter in the soup kettle. Discard the roots of the sprouts and cut the leaves into two or three pieces. Wash, scald and drain in a strainer. Pour cold water over, drain and add to the vegetables. Add meat stock, bay leaf, pepper and salt. Cook for 25 to 30 minutes. Put a piece of meat in each plate. Top with a teaspoonful of sour cream and sprinkle with minced dill or parsley before serving.

Summer Shchi with Potatoes

300 g meat	500 g potatoes
500 g early cabbage	200 g tomatoes
2 or 3 carrots	Salt
1 parsley root	Minced dill or parsley
1 or 2 onions	

Prepare a meat stock 1 1/2 litres water. Add scraped and sliced carrots and parsley, onion and cabbage, the cabbage runts cut into 4 to 6 chunks and whole potatoes. Boil for 15-20 minutes. Salt to

taste. Add tomatoes cut in quarters. Bring to the boil. Serve immediately, putting a piece of cabbage runt, 2 or 3 potatoes and a piece of tomato into each plate and sprikling with minced dill or parsley.

Spinach and Sorrel Soup

300 g meat	1 parsley root
500 g spinach (or	1 tblsp flour
nettles)	2 tblsps butter
200 g sorrel	Salt, pepper, bay leaf
1 carrot	Sour cream
1 onion	Hard-cooked eggs

Make a meat stock with 1 1/2 litres water. Wash the spinach thoroughly and cook in boiling water till tender. Drain and sift. Wash the sorrel and cut up the large leaves. Sauté the diced roots and onion in butter in the soup kettle. Add the flour and brown for another 1 or 2 minutes. Add the sifted spinach and stir. Gradually pour in the meat and spinach stock. Add bay leaf and pepper. Cook for 10 to 15 minutes. Add the sorrel leaves and salt. Cook for 5 to 10 minutes more. Before serving put half a hard-cooked egg and a teaspoonful of sour cream in each plate.

Borshch

(Beet Soup)

300 g meat	1 tblsp vinegar
400 g beets	1 tblsp sugar
400 g fresh cabbage	1 tblsp boiled butter
200 g vegetable roots	Bay leaf
and onion	Salt, pepper
2 tblsps tomato puree	Potatoes
or 100 g tomatoes	1 tblsp flour

Prepare a meat stock. Wash and shoestring the beets. Add one cupful of hot meat stock, vinegar, tomato puree and boiled butter. Bring to the boil, turn the heat down, cover and simmer for 1-1 1/2 hours; stir every 15-20 minutes. Shoestring and sauté the carrots and parsley; add onion, continue to sauté and then add to the beets. Cook for 10-15 minutes. Stir in the sugar.

Strain the meat stock, bring to the boil and add the shredded cabbage. Cook for 5 minutes and then add the beets and other vegetables and bring to the boil. Thicken with flour as directed or with white stock sauce. Add peppercorns, bay leaf and salt to taste. Cook for 5 minutes.

Fresh tomatoes may be added five minutes before the borshch is ready to be served. In addition to meat, boiled ham or sausages may be added.

Add beet stock to make the borshch a bright red. Serve with a spoonful of sour cream in each plate.

Beet Stock

Wash and cut up one beet. Cover with boiling stock or water. Add a little of vinegar and bring to the boil. Set aside for 15-20 minutes, strain and add to the borshch before serving.

Sauerkraut Borshch

Substitute sauerkraut in the above recipe. Stew it with tomato puree in a little stock. Add the other vegetables which have been stewed separately and cook in the boiling meat stock.

Summer Borshch

1 bunch of beets	Salt, pepper, cloves,
3-4 potatoes	bay leaf
1 carrot	Sour cream, cold
1-2 tomatoes	scalded milk or sour
50-75 g green onions	milk
1 stalk of celery	1 1/2 litre water or
200 g marrow	mushroom stock

Shoestring the beetroots and carrot and cook in boiling water or mushroom stock for 10 to 15 minutes. Add the beet leaves and stems which have been cut into pieces 2 to 3 cm long and scalded, the marrow, tomatoes, potatoes, green onions, celery and condiments. Cook until the vegetables are tender. Add sour cream, scalded milk or sour milk before serving.

Ukrainian Borshch

500 g meat	20 g salt pork
400 g cabbage	1 tblsp butter
400 g potatoes	4 cloves of garlic
250 g beets	2 tblsps 3% vinegar
1/2 cupful tomato puree	or 1 tblsp lemon juice
1/2 cupful sour cream	1 tblsp flour
1 carrot	Bay leaf, allspice,
1 parsley root	peppercorns, salt
1 onion	Minced parsley

Prepare the meat stock and strain. Shoestring the vegetable roots. Separately stew the beets for 20 to 30 minutes, add fat, tomato puree, vinegar and stock (beetroot or bread kvass[14] may be substituted). Sauté the roots and onion in butter, add flour, stir in a little stock and bring to the boil. Add to the prepared stock chunks of potato and shredded cabbage. Bring to the boil and add the stewed beetroot. Salt to taste. Cook for another 15 minutes and then add the sautéed vegetables, the flour rubbed together with butter and browned, and condiments. Cook until the potatoes and cabbage are tender. Add garlic cloves rubbed together with the salt pork and tomatoes cut into quarters. Quickly bring to the boil. Remove from the heat and set aside for 15 to 20 minutes. Top each plate with a spoonful of sour cream. Sprinkle with the minced parsley.

Mushroom Borshch with Prunes

Follow the directions for plain borshch substituting mushroom stock for meat stock. Wash 200 g of prunes and add them to the sautéed vegetables. Pour in the mushroom stock and cook for 25 to 30 minutes.

Sorrel Soup

300 g meat	2 tblsps flour
400 g sorrel	Salt
200 g vegetable roots	Eggs
and onion	Sour cream
2 tblsps butter	Minced dill or parsley

Prepare a meat stock with 1 1/2 litres water. Clean and finely dice the vegetable roots and onion. Slightly sauté the vegetables in the butter or drippings. Sprinkle with flour and brown. Wash the sorrel; cover and simmer separately in a little water for 10 minutes. Drain and sift through a sieve. Add browned vebetables, stock and salt; stir and cook for 15 to 20 minutes. Serve with soft-boiled egg in each plate. Top with a spoonful of sour cream and sprinkle with the minced dill or parsley. If served with meat, put half a hard-cooked egg in each plate.

Pickled Cucumber Soup
(Rassolnik)

500 g beef kidney	2 tblsps butter
2 pickled cucumbers	100 g sorrel or lettuce
2 parsley roots	Pickle brine
1 celery stalk	Sour cream or cream
1 onion	Minced dill or parsley
4 potatoes	

Core and skin the kidney. Cut each kidney into 3 or 4 pieces, wash, cover with water and bring to the boil. Drain, wash the kidney again, cover with cold water and cook for 1-1 1/2 hours. Clean and shoestring the vegetable roots and onion and sauté in butter in the soup kettle. Remove from the heat. Peel, slice and cook the pickles separately. Cut the potatoes into chunks and add to the vegetables. Pour in the strained stock and simmer for 20-25 minutes. Add the pickles and strained pickle brine (for savouriness) and shredded sorrel (or lettuce). Salt to taste. Cook for 5 to 10 minutes. Before serving put pieces of kidney and a spoonful of sour cream or cream in each plate. Sprinkle with the minced parsley or dill.

Rassolnik may also be made with meat or chicken stock and served with pieces of veal, lamb or chicken. Giblets of any domestic fowl (goose, duck, turkey, chicken) may be used instead of kidneys.

Pickled Cucumber Soup with Fish

300 g fish	1 parsley or celery
500 g potatoes	root
4 tblsps cereal (rice	2 pickled cucumbers
or pearl barley)	(200) g
1 carrot	2 bay leaves
1 onion	5-6 peppercorns
2 tblsps vegetable oil	

Peel the cucumbers, remove the seeds and cut into shoestrings. Cook the cucumbers in fish stock.

Sauté the sliced onion, carrot and parsley or celery cut into shoestrings. Cut the potatoes into chunks and add them and the sautéed vegetables to the boiling fish stock. Cook for 15 minutes. Add the pickled cucumbers, peppercorns, bay leaf and salt and cook for another 5 minutes. Serve sprinkled with minced herbs.

Should the rassolnik lack savouriness, add strained and boiled brine.

If desired the rassolnik may be made with pearl barley. The pearl barley should be added to the stock first. Soak the pearl barley for 2-3 hours, then drain. Put it in the upper part of a double boiler, cover with boiling water and steam for 50 minutes over a slow fire. Add the remaining ingredients as directed above.

Pickled Cucumber Soup with Fish Balls

Prepare pickled cucumber soup according to the above recipe and serve with fish balls made as follows:

Fish Balls

300 g filleted fish	Salt and pepper to
1/2 egg	taste
Herbs	1-2 onions
1 tblsp butter	

Put the fish through the meat chopper twice. Add the minced herbs and onion rubbed together with butter, raw egg, salt and pepper. Shape into balls the size of a walnut and arrange in one layer in a saucepan. Pour over hot salt water and cook. When done the fish balls will rise to the top. Remove the balls and serve with fish bouillon.

Cauliflower Soup

800 g cauliflower	1 1/2-2 tblsps rice
1 carrot	(optional)
1 stalk of celery	1 or 2 parsley roots
1 1/2 litres meat stock	Salt

Wash and cut or break up the flower clusters, scrape and slice the carrot. Add to strained meat stock. Add the celery. Salt to taste. If desired, add rice. Cook for 20 to 30 minutes. Remove the celery a few minutes before the soup is done. Serve with pirozhki[6] or pirogi[7] with meat filling.

Brussels Sprout Soup

600 g Brussels sprouts	2 tblsps butter
6-7 cupsful mushroom	1/2 cupful sour cream
stock (or hot water)	Salt to taste
3-4 potatoes	

Cut the heads from the stock and clean. Parboil 2 minutes and drain, sauté slightly in butter. Add mushroom stock or hot water. Add sliced potatoes and salt to taste. Cook 20 to 30 minutes. Top each plate with a spoonful of sour cream. Serve immediately.

Mushroom Stock

50 g dried mushrooms	1 onion
2-3 litres water	

Wash the mushrooms in warm water. Clean and cut the onion in half. Add cold water, bring to the boil and simmer for 2-2 1/2 hours. To reduce cooking time, soak the mushrooms in cold water to 2 hours and cook in the same water until tender. Strain. Rinse the mushrooms in cold water, drain and shred. Add them to the soup made with the stock.

Vegetable Soup with Meat Stock

300 g meat	1 1/2 litres water
500 g potatoes	2 tblsps butter
200 g cabbage	100 g lettuce or
200 g tomatoes	spinach
200 g vegetable roots	Pepper, salt, bay leaf
and onion	Sour cream

Prepare a meat stock. Clean and slice the root vegetables and onion; brown slightly in butter in the soup kettle. Add the cabbage and the stock. Bring to the boil, add the diced potatoes and cook for 20 to 25 minutes. Shred the spinach or lettuce, slice the tomatoes and add together with bay leaf. Add pepper and salt to taste. Top each plate with a spoonful of sour cream.

Vegetable Soup with Mushroom Stock

Use mushroom stock instead of meat stock in the above recipe.

Plain Vegetable Soup

Substitute vegetable stock for the meat stock in the above recipe.

Potato Soup

300 g meat	1 1/2 litres water
800 g potatoes	2 tblsps butter
200 g vegetable roots	Salt, pepper, bay leaf
and onion	Minced dill or parsley

Prepare a meat stock. Pare and slice the vegetable roots and onion. Sauté in butter or drippings. Add to boiling stock together with diced potatoes and sautéed vegetables. Add bay leaf; salt and

pepper to taste. Cook for 25 to 30 minutes. Before serving sprinkle each plate with minced dill or parsley.

Potato Soup with Mushroom Stock

Substitute mushroom stock (see p. 36) for the meat stock in the above recipe. Put shredded mushrooms in each plate before serving.

Potato Soup with Fish

300 g fish	Parsley or celery
1 kg potatoes	2 onions (100 g)
4 tblsps cereal	2 tblsps vegetable oil
(optional)	4 tsps tomato puree
1 carrot (100 g)	5-6 peppercorns
2 bay leaves	1 1/2 litres water

Dice the potatoes and add them to the boiling fish stock. Bring to the boil again and add the sautéed sliced onion, carrot, parsley root and tomato puree. Bring to the boil and add the pepper corns, bay leaves and salt to taste. Cook till the vegetables are tender. Remove the bay leaves and peppercorns. Serve with a piece of fish in each plate and sprinkle with herbs.
If desired cereal may be added.

Potato Soup with Fresh Mushrooms

500 g mushrooms	Salt, pepper, bay leaf
800 g potatoes	Sour cream
200 g vegetable roots	Minced green onions
and onion	and dill
2 tblsps butter	

Clean and wash edible boletus mushrooms or butter mushrooms (the latter should be peeled). Chop up the stems and sauté in butter. Separately sauté the sliced vegetable roots and onion. Slice the mushroom caps. Blanch, drain thoroughly, add water to cover. Cook for 40 minutes. Add diced potatoes, mushroom stems, vegetables, and a bay leaf. Salt and pepper to taste. Simmer for 20 to 25 minutes. Top each plate with a spoonful of sour cream and sprinkle with minced green onions and dill.

Veal and Mushroom Soup

800 g veal	Celery, parsley, dill
16 medium-size potatoes	4 carrots
	1/2 litre kvass[14]
20 boletus or cultured mushrooms	2 tblsps vegetable oil
	1 hot pepper
4 onions	Salt

Wash the meat, pour over cold water and cook over low heat for 30 minutes, then add salt, mushrooms and potatoes. When the potatoes are almost "done", noodles may be added if desired. After cooking for another 10-15 minutes, add the kvass[14] and the carrot and onion which have been minced and sautéed in vegetable oil. Cook for another 5-10 minutes. Before serving sprinkle with finely minced herbs and drop in the pepper. Cultured (meadow) mushrooms should be peeled immediately before cooking. Drop them in cold water so that they do not turn dark.
Dried mushrooms may be substituted. Rinse the mushrooms in warm water, then soak them in cold water for 1-2 hours. Remove the mushrooms from the water and cook the veal in it. Slice and return the mushrooms to the kettle.

Chanterelle Mushroom Soup

500 g chanterelle mushrooms	3 litres water
	1 tsp flour
100 g salt pork	2 tblsps sour cream
1 onion	Salt, pepper

Dice and render the salt pork and sauté sliced onion for 10 minutes. Wash mushrooms and add to the onion; sauté another 45 minutes. Add water and salt. Simmer for 30 minutes. Blend flour and sour cream and thicken the soup. Add pepper and salt to taste.

Potato and Vermicelli Soup

500 g meat	200 g vegetable roots and onion
100 g vermicelli	
500 g potatoes	2 tblsps butter
1 1/2 litres water	Salt, pepper, bay leaf

Shred the vegetable roots and onion; sauté in butter. Cut up the potatoes and add to the boiling meat stock together with browned vegetables. Simmer for 15 minutes, then add the vermicelli and a bay leaf. Add salt and pepper to taste. Cook for 12 to 15 minutes.

Potato Soup with Sturgeon Head

1 kg head of sturgeon or similar fish	200 g vegetable roots and onion
800 g potatoes	Salt, pepper, bay leaf
2 tblsps butter	Minced dill or parsley

Cook the fish head as directed in recipe for sauerkraut shchi with fish head (see p. 32). Clean and slice the vegetable roots and onion, sauté in butter. Pare and dice the potatoes and add to the strained and boiling fish stock. Add the slightly browned vegetables and a bay leaf. Add salt and pepper to taste. Cook for 25 to 30 minutes. Sprinkle minced dill or parsley in each plate.

Potato Soup with Cereal

300 g meat	2 tblsps butter
1/2 cupful cereal	Salt, pepper
500 g potatoes	Bay leaf
200 g vegetable roots and onion	Minced dill or parsley

While the stock is cooking, soak the pearl borely in 1/2 cupsful of cold water and set aside to swell for 2 hours. Drain the pearl barley and add to the stock. Boil gently 10 to 15 minutes, then add the diced potatoes. Sauté the vegetable roots and onion in the butter and add to the stock. Cook until tender. Add a bay leaf, salt and pepper to taste. Before serving sprinkle with minced dill or parsley.

Potato Soup with Rice, Millet or Mannacroup[9]

Cook as directed in recipe for potato soup with cereal. If rice or millet are used, do not soak. Add mannacroup[9] after cooking the other ingredients for 10 to 15 minutes.

Noodles Cooked in Broth

(Lapsha)

500 g meat	1 onion
150 g noodles or vermicelli	2 tblsps butter
1 carrot	Salt, pepper, bay leaf
1 parsley root	Minced dill or parsley

Prepare a meat or chicken stock. Clean and shred the vegetables and onion; sauté slightly in butter. Add to the strained stock and bring to the boil. Add the noodles (see below). Add a bay leaf; salt and pepper to taste. Bring to the boil and cook for 15 to 20 minutes. Before serving sprinkle with minced dill or parsley.

Noodles

1 cupful flour	2 tblsps water
1 egg	1/3 tsp salt

Break the egg into a small mixing bowl, beat slightly and add water. Stir in salt. Gradually work in flour to make a heavy dough. Turn onto a dough board, knead slightly. Roll into thin sheets 5-6 cm wide. Sprinkle with flour, cover and let stand for 30 minutes or more to dry. Roll up and cut into thin strips with a sharp knife.

Vermicelli, Shells or Stars Cooked in Broth

Any of these or other similar paste can be used in the above recipe for noodles cooked in broth.
Boil in salt water till half done, drain and then add to the broth.

Dried Pea Soup

500 g meat, ham or bacon	200 g vegetable roots and onion
250 g dried peas	2 tblsps butter
Croutons	Salt

Soak the peas in cold water for 4-5 hours. Prepare the meat stock and strain. Drain the peas and cook in the stock for 1 1/2 hours. Wash, clean and dice the vegetables; sauté slightly in butter and add to the soup 15 to 20 minutes before serving. Salt to taste. Instead of meat, ham or bacon may be used. Serve with croutons.

Dried Bean Soup

1/2 cupful dried beans	2 tblsps butter
1 carrot	Salt, pepper, bay leaf
1 parsley	Minced parsley or dill
1 onion	Sour cream
1 tblsp tomato puree	

Soak the beans in cold water for 4-5 hours. Cook for 20 to 30 minutes. Add first the vegetables, which have been finely diced and sautéed in butter, and then tomato puree. Add a bay leaf; salt and pepper to taste. Cook until beans are tender.
Before serving sprinkle with minced parsley or dill. Top each plate with a spoonful of sour cream.

Dried Bean Soup with Potatoes

1 cupful dried beans	1 onion
5 or 6 potatoes	2 tblsps butter
1 carrot	

Soak the beans in cold water for 4-5 hours and then cook until tender. Shred the vegetables, sauté in butter and add to the beans together with a bay leaf.
Add salt and pepper to taste. Cook until done.

Dried Bean Soup with Noodles

1 1/2 cupsful dried beans	2 1/2 litres cold soup stock or cold water
1 onion	Salt and pepper to taste
100 g noodles	
2 tblsps butter	Minced parsley

Soak the beans for 3 to 4 hours in cold water. Drain and add to the cold stock or water. Bring to the boil and simmer until tender. Add the onion browned in butter; salt and pepper to taste. Add the noodles. Cook for another 20 minutes. Sprinkle with the minced parsley before serving.

Kidney Bean Soup

1 1/2 cupsful kidney beans	2 litres water
1 or 2 onions	2 tblsps butter
50 g shelled walnuts	Red pepper to taste
1/2 tblsp flour	1 tsp salt
	Minced parsley

Wash the beans and cook in 2 litres cold water. Bring to the boil and skim. Simmer for 1 1/2 hours. Brown the chopped onion in butter, add the red pepper and flour and brown for another 1 or 2 minutes. Add to the beans along with the crushed or ground walnuts. Salt to taste. Cook for another 15 to 20 minutes. Before serving sprinkle with the minced parsley.

Tart Meat Solyanka[20]

500 g meat for stock	1/4 lemon
300 g any boiled or roast meat	1 tblsp capers
4 pickled cucumbers	3 tblsps butter
2 onions	Olives
2 tblsps tomato puree	Bay leaf
100 g sour cream	Salt to taste
	Minced parsley or dill

Prepare the soup stock. Slice the onion and sauté in butter, add the tomato puree, a little stock and braise. Peel the pickles, cut in half, slice and boil for 20-25 minutes. Dice the meat (boiled or roast beef, ham, veal, kidneys, tongue, sausages or sausage meat) and add to the onion together with cooked pickle, capers and a bay leaf. Add the stock and boil gently for 5 to 10 minutes. If desired, sliced tomato may be added. Salt to taste. Put an olive, 1/4 slice of lemon (peeled) in each plate and top with a spoonful of sour cream. Sprinkle with minced parsley or dill.

Tart Fish Solyanka[20]

500 g fish	1 tblsp capers
4 or 5 pickled	Olives
cucumbers	2 tblsps butter
1 or 2 onions	Bay leaf, salt, pepper
2 or 3 tomatoes or	1/4 lemon
2 tblsps tomato puree	Minced parsley or dill

Sturgeon, sevruga, beluga or sterlet are best for this soup but any fish that is not small and bony can be used. Cut the fillet to have 2 or 3 pieces per plate. Make a fish stock with the bones and head. Clean, slice and slightly brown the onion in butter in the soup kettle. Add the tomato puree and simmer for 5 or 6 minunutes, then add the pieces of fish, sliced cooked pickles, capers, a bay leaf, dash of pepper. Stir in hot fish stock, add salt to taste, and simmer for 10 to 15 minutes. Put an olive and a quarter slice of lemon (peeled) in each plate. Sprinkle with the minced parsley or dill.

Georgian Mutton Soup

(Chikhirtma)

500 g mutton	1/2 tsp saffron
2 onions	2 tblsps grape vinegar
1 tblsp flour	Kindza[10]
1 tblsp butter	Salt
2 eggs	

Wash the mutton in cold water. Cut so

as to have 3 or 4 pieces per plate. Bring to the boil and skim. Remove the mutton when tender; strain the stock through a cheesecloth. Chop the onion, sauté in butter, sprinkle with flour and continue to brown. Return the mutton to the stock, thicken with browned flour and onion. Add saffron, salt and pepper to taste. Bring to the boil. Separately boil the light grape vinegar, add it to the soup, bring to the boil again and remove from the heat. Beat the egg yolks, combine with a little of stock and then stir into the soup; heat but do not bring to the boiling point otherwise the yolk will curdle. Sprinkle with kindza[10] and serve immediately.

Chicken may be substituted for mutton.

Georgian Beef Soup

(Kharcho)

500 g brisket	1/2 cupful tart plums
2 onions	Salt, pepper
2 or 3 cloves of garlic	Butter or drippings
2 tblsps tomato puree	Minced kindza[10]
or 100 g tomatoes	Parsley or dill
1/2 cupful rice	

Wash and cut the meat so as to have 3 or 4 pieces per plate. Cover with cold water, bring to the boil and skim. Simmer for 1 1/2 to 2 hours, add finely sliced onion, crushed garlic, rice and plums. Add salt and pepper to taste. Simmer for 25 minutes. Sauté tomatoes or tomato puree in butter or drippings. Add to the kharcho and cook for another 5 to 10 minutes. Serve sprinkled with minced kindza[10], parsley or dill.

Mutton may be substituted for beef.

Turkmenian Mutton Soup
(Shurpa)

500 g mutton	2 tblsps tomato puree
750 g potatoes	2 tblsps butter
2 onions	Salt
2 carrots	Pepper

Prepare a mutton stock. Slice the onions and sauté in the butter or drippings. Cut the meat into 25- to 30-g pieces, sear and mix with the browned onions. Add diced carrots and tomato puree; brown for another 5 to 6 minutes. Pour the stock over the meat and other ingredients and bring to the boil. Add chunks of potato. Salt and pepper to taste. Cook for 15 to 20 minutes.

Armenian Mutton Soup
(Bozbash)

500 g mutton	2 tblsps tomato puree
1 cupful split peas	2 tblsps butter
500 g potatoes	Salt
2 apples	Pepper
2 onions	Minced parsley

Wash and cut the mutton into 30- to 40-g pieces. Add water to cover and salt. Cover the kettle with a lid and simmer. Pick and wash the peas, add 2 or 3 cupful of cold water and bring to the boil. Cook over low heat for 1 to 1 1/2 hours. Bone the mutton. Add the peas to the meat. Strain and add the mutton broth, the finely sliced onion sautéed in butter, the potatoes and apples cut into chunks and the tomato puree. Salt and pepper to taste. Cover and simmer for 20 to 25 minutes. Serve sprinkled with the minced parsley.

Clear Soups and Broths

The foundation of all clear soups is a broth made of beef, wildfowl or chicken. The accompaniments, such as rice, eggs, kletski[11], vermicelli and various vegetables are generally cooked separately and put in the plate just before service.

Beef Broth

500 g beef (rump or shank)	1 onion
1 carrot	1 1/2 to 2 litres water
1 parsley or celery root	Salt

Wash the meat and add cold water to cover. Cover the saucepan with a lid. Bring to the boil and skim. Simmer for 1 1/2 hours then add half the vegetable roots and onion. Brown the remaining vegetables and onion without turning in a hot skillet and add to the broth. Salt to taste.
A clear broth cooks from 2 to 2 1/2 hours. Remove the meat when tender. Cool the broth and skim off the fat; strain through a fine cheesecloth. The broth may be additionally clarified as follows:
Put 300 g ground meat in a separate saucepan and combine with beaten egg white and one cupful of stock. Set aside for 20-30 minutes. Heat the strained broth but do not boil. Add the clarifier, raw celery and the carrot and onion which have been browned without fat. Simmer for 30-40 minutes. When the clarifier

curdles and settles, carefully strain the broth. Serve with croutons or pirozhki[6]. This broth may be used to make a clear soup.

Wildfowl Broth

1 pheasant	1 or 2 celery stocks
(1 heath-cock or	(or several slices of
4 hazel-hens)	celeriac)
1 carrot	Salt
1 parsley	2 or 3 litres water
1 onion	

This broth may be made when the cooked fowl meat is needed for salad or any other dish, or to use the bones and sundries left after boning fowls. Chop up the bones and sundries. Add the carrot, parsley and onion browned on a dry skillet. Then add celery (or celeriac) and water. Bring to the boil and skim; simmer for about an hour. Add salt to taste just before removing from the heat; strain.

Chicken Broth

1 chicken (1 kg)	1 onion
1 carrot	2 1/2 to 3 litres
1 parsley	water

Wipe the chicken dry and singe over a spirit or gas flame. Chop off neck and feet; remove the giblets and wash thoroughly. Clean out and remove lining of the gizzard. Scald the feet, remove the skin and chop off the claws. Scald the head. Carefully cut the gall away from the liver. Wash the giblets thoroughly.
Make two slashes in the skin just below the breast and fit the ends of the drumsticks into them. Bend the ends of the wings back over the spine.

Place the bird and giblets in a soup kettle, add cleaned and cut vegetables and cover with cold water. Bring to the boil, skim and then cover with a lid. A chicken cooks from 1 to 2 hours depending on its size and age. Try the leg with a fork; if tender, remove the bird and giblets. Strain the broth.

Clear Beet Soup
(Borshchok)

1 1/2 litres stock	2 or 3 tblsps grape
500 g beets	vinegar
	1 tblsp sugar

Make a clear meat, chicken or wildfowl broth. Add thinly sliced beets, grape vinegar and sugar. Cook for 10 to 15 minutes. Strain and serve in bouillon cups. Pass croutons and cheese.

Broth with Drop Dumplings
(Kletski)

When the meat or chicken broth is nearly ready, prepare the batter for the kletski. Drop pieces of batter into the broth with a teaspoon that has been dipped in water. Cook for 1 or 2 minutes after the dumplings rise to the top. A batter made with 1/2 cupful of flour, mannacroup[9] or 3 potatoes will be sufficient for 2 litres of broth.

Boiled Batter Kletski

1/2 cupful flour or	2 eggs
mannacroup[9]	1/2 tsp salt
2 tblsps butter	1/3 cupful broth

Bring the broth, butter and salt to the boil, stir in the flour (mannacroup[9]). Mix steadily with a whisk. Cook for 1 or 2 minutes if flour is used, and for 5 to 6 minutes if mannacroup[9] is used. Remove from the heat, add eggs and mix thoroughly.

Plain Batter Kletski

1/2 cupful flour	1/4 cupful broth
1 egg	1/2 tsp salt
1/2 tblsp butter	

Mix the broth, butter, egg and salt. Stir in the flour and beat until smooth.

Potato Kletski

3 potatoes	2 eggs
3 to 4 tblsps flour	1/2 tsp salt

Pare and boil the potatoes, press through a strainer. Add raw egg yolks and mix thoroughly. Fold in whites of eggs beaten stiff.

Broth with Pelmeni[29]

This dish can quickly be prepared with ready-to-cook pelmeni[29] obtainable in the shops. Put the pelmeni in boiling broth and continue to boil until all the pelmeni rise to the surface. This will take about 10 minutes. Pelmeni may be made at home as follows (for 1 1/2 litres of broth):

Filling

300 to 400 g meat	Pepper
1 or 2 onions	2 tblsps cold
1/2 tsp salt	water

A filling made with equal amounts of beef and pork is the best. Put the meat through the mincer twice together with the onion. Add 2 tablespoonsful of cold water, salt and pepper. Mix thoroughly.

Dough

1 1/2 cupful flour	1/4 cupful water
1 egg	Salt

Sift the flour and salt. Heap it on the moulding board, make a hollow in the centre, pour in the egg and water beaten together and knead into a stiff dough. Roll out thin (about 0.1 cm) and cut into 5 or 6 cm rounds. Put a ball of meat filling on one half of the round, moisten the edges with beaten egg and fold over into a half moon. Pinch the edges. Before laying the pelmeni in the broth, dip them in hot salt water for a few seconds to wash off the extra flour.

Serve the broth sprinkled with minced parsley or dill.

Broth with Cake Bread

2 to 2 1/2 litres broth	2 or 3 eggs
100 g flour	1/2 cupful water
3 tblsps butter	Salt

Heat the water, butter and salt in a saucepan. As soon as it begins to boil stir in the flour and beat steadily with a whisk for 1 or 2 minutes. Remove from the heat, cool slightly, add the eggs one at a time and beat. Mix until the batter is smooth. With a teaspoon or a dough bag with a 1/2 cm tube drop pieces of batter half the size of a hazelnut onto a greased cookie sheet. Bake for 10 to 15 minutes at 200°C (395°F). When baked, the cake breads should be dry and two and a half times their original bulk. Put the cake breads in each plate of broth and serve immediately.

Broth with Vegetables and Rice

1 1/2 litres clear broth	50 g string beans or
1 carrot	green peas in pods
1 onion	1 tblsp butter
1 turnip	3 tblsps rice or pearl
1 parsley root	barley
50 g sorrel	Minced parsley

Scrape and dice the vegetable roots. Sauté slightly in a saucepan and add 2 cupsful bouillon. Cover with a lid, simmer for 5 to 10 minutes, add the peas or beans which have been cut up. Simmer for another 10 minutes and add the sorrel which has also been cut up. Simmer for 2 or 3 minutes. Salt to taste.

Cook the rice separately. Put cooked rice and vegetables into each plate, pour in the bouillon, sprinkle with parsley and serve.

Broth with Baked Rice

1 1/2 litres clear broth	1 tblsp dry bread
1/2 cupful rice	crumbs
2 eggs	Salt
2 tblsps butter	50 g cheese, grated

Boil the rice in salt water until tender. Drain thoroughly in a sieve or strainer. Add raw eggs, 1 tblsp butter, half the grated cheese and salt and mix thoroughly. Pour into a well-greased baking pan sprinkled with bread crumbs. Level the top with a knife, sprinkle with the remaining grated cheese and melted butter. Bake for 15 to 20 minutes at 150°C (300°F). Cool the baked rice slightly, turn out onto a board. Put a piece into each plate of meat or chicken broth.

Broth with Custard

Prepare 1 1/2 litres broth.

Custard

1/2 cupful milk	Parsley leaves
1 tblsp butter	(optional)
4 eggs	150 g spinach or 15 g
Salt	tomato paste
	(optional)

Break the eggs into a mixing bowl and beat well with a whisk. Add salt. Beating continuously, gradually add the cold milk or broth. Strain into well-oiled custard cups or one large mould, cover and steam in a hot water bath until the custard sets, (10 to 15 minutes for custard cups and 30 to 40 minutes for a large mould). Keep the water in the bath close to boiling point. Cool slightly (10 to 15 minutes) and unmould. If the custard is made in a large mould, cut into squares after unmoulding. Serve the broth with a piece of custard in each plate.

Before serving, parsley leaves may be added to the broth.

Spinach or Tomato Custard

Substitute 150 g cooked or fresh spinach for the milk in the above recipe. If fresh spinach is used, wash, stew and sift it before adding.

Instead of spinach 15 g tomato paste may be used.

Broth with Meat Balls

1 1/2 litres clear broth	Salt
200 g beef (boned)	Pepper
2 tblsps cold water	Minced parsley

Force the meat through the mincer two or three times. Add salt, pepper and cold water and mix thoroughly. Roll into balls about the size of a large hazelnut. Cook in a saucepan in a small amount of broth. Put 8 to 10 meat balls in each plate, pour over broth and sprinkle with minced parsley.

Forcemeat balls may also be made of veal or lamb. If lamb is used, cut away all fat and substitute a little butter.

Broth with Chicken Drop Dumplings

1 1/2 litres clear broth	1/4 cupful milk
100 g chicken meat	1 slice white bread
1 egg white	Salt
	Minced parsley

Mince the chicken meat, add egg white, bread, which has been soaked in milk and squeezed, and salt to taste. Mix thoroughly and force through the mincer again, once or twice. Add milk a tablespoonful at a time mixing continuously, blend. Beat with a paddle and sift through a strainer. With a spoon drop little balls into hot salt water. When cooked, the dumplings will rise to the top. Put dumplings in each plate. Pour over broth and sprinkle with the parsley before serving.

Fish Soup

(Ukha)

1 kg fish	1 stalk of celery
1 onion	2 1/2 to 3 litres water
1 leek	Salt
1 parsley root	

Sterlet or fresh-water perch are best for ukha but zander and various small fish (except tench) may be used. The soup will be stronger if the scales are not scraped from such small fish as ruff and perch. Remove the intestines or viscera and wash thoroughly. Remove the gills of perch. Add the cleaned vegetables, salt and pour water to cover. Simmer for 40 to 60 minutes, strain. Clarify the stock with soft or pressed caviar as follows: Rub 50 g of caviar in a mortar, add water gradually until it is like heavy cream. Blend with one cupful of cold water, then add one cupful of hot stock and mix. Stir half the mixture into the hot fish stock, bring to the boil and add the remaining clarifying mixture. When the soup begins to boil, uncover and simmer for 15 to 20 minutes. Stand until the clarifier settles (10 to 15 minutes). Strain carefully. Serve with a piece of fish in each plate. Pass kulebyaka[8] or rasstegai[2].

Angler's Fish Soup

(Ukha Rybatskaya)

500 g small fish	2 tblsps butter
1 kg potatoes	5-6 peppercorns
2 onions (120 g)	2 bay leaves
1 parsley root (30 g)	1 tblsp minced herbs

This soup is best when different kinds of fish are cooked together. Add to the fish stock parsley or celery roots, whole small potatoes, onion and pieces of fish. Bring to the boil, skim and simmer for 25 minutes. Add the peppercorns, bay leaves and salt to taste. Put a piece of butter in each plate before serving and sprinkle with minced herbs.

Cream Soups

All cream soups are served with white bread croutons browned in the oven or fried in butter. Pirozhki[6] with a meat or cabbage and egg filling may be served with meat or vegetable cream soups; ras-stegai[2] with a viziga[3] or fish filling may be served with fish cream soup.

Cream of Potato Soup

1 kg potatoes	Garnishing: 2 egg
2 to 3 cupsful milk	yolks 3/4 cupful
3 tblsps butter	milk
3 leeks	Salt

Clean, wash and cut up the leeks; brown slightly in butter, then add washed pared and sliced potatoes. Salt and boil in 5 cupsful of water for 25 to 30 minutes. Sift the potatoes and stock through a strainer, stir in hot milk. Before serving garnish with butter or thicken with egg yolks and milk that have been blended in a separate bowl. Pass croutons.

Cream of Pumpkin Soup

800 g pumpkin	4 or 5 cupsful milk
150 g croutons or	3 tblsps butter
2 tblsps flour	2 tsps sugar
300 g potatoes	Salt

Pare, wash and slice the pumpkin and potatoes. Cook in 3 or 4 cupsful of water. Add salt, sugar and a tablespoonful of butter. Simmer for 25 to 30 minutes. Add croutons (fried in butter or toasted), stir and bring to the boil. Sift and rub through a sieve. Add hot milk until it is the thickness of cream. Top with butter.
This soup may also be made as follows:
Cut up the pumpkin and cook in 2 cupsful of water. In a separate saucepan blend 2 tblsps flour and 2 tblsps butter, brown slightly then stir in 4 cupsful of milk and 2 cupsful of water. Bring to the boil and

combine with the pumpkin. Cook for 15 to 20 minutes. Sift the soup and rub through a sieve; add salt to taste. Stir in 1 to 2 cupsful of hot milk and butter. Pass croutons separately.

Cream of Carrot Soup

800 g carrots	2 cupsful milk
1/2 cupful rice	1 tsp sugar
3 tblsps butter	1 tsp salt

Scrape, wash and slice the carrots. Simmer for 5-10 minutes in 1/4 cupful of water; add salt and sugar. Add washed rice and 5 cupsful of water. Cover with a lid and cook over low heat for 40 to 50 minutes. Sift the soup and rub through a sieve. Reserve 2 tablespoonsful cooked rice (without carrot) for garnishing.
Blend the puree with hot milk; add salt to taste. Before serving, season with butter and add the rice reserved for garnishing. Pass croutons.

Cream of String Bean Soup

600 to 700 g fresh or	2 cupsful milk
canned string beans	Salt
3 tblsps butter	Croutons
500 g potatoes	

Wash the fresh string beans and remove the strings. Cut about a quarter of them into diamonds. Put the rest through the food chopper. Pare, wash and cut the potatoes. Add the minced string beans, salt, 1 or 2 tablespoonsful butter, and 4 or 5 cupsful of hot water. Cook covered. When the potatoes are tender, sift through a sieve. Blend the puree with hot milk; add the butter. Garnish with the cut string beans which have been cooked separately. Pass croutons.

If canned string beans are used, reserve part of them for garnishing, add the remainder (including juice) to the potatoes and continue as directed above.

Cream of Cauliflower Soup

600 g fresh or canned cauliflower (or 750 g plain cabbage)	2 cupsful milk
	3 tblsps butter
	Salt
500 g potatoes	

Reserve one quarter of the small flower clusters for garnishing; cook them separately in salt water. Cook the rest of the cauliflower and pared and sliced potatoes for 25 to 30 minutes in 4 cupsful of water to which 2 teaspoonsful salt have been added. Rub through a sieve and stir in the hot milk. Garnish with cream or butter, and the flower clusters cooked separately. Pass croutons.

If canned cauliflower is used, cook the soup for 10 to 15 minutes.

Cream of Cabbage Soup

Discard the bad leaves; wash the cabbage. Cook for 15 to 20 minutes and then add the potatoes, and proceed as directed above.

Cream of Vegetable Soup

150 g carrots	100 g peas
150 g turnips	3 tblsps butter
200 g potatoes	2 cupsful milk
100 g leek	Salt
3/4 cupful rice	Croutons

Wash and cut up finely the carrots, turnips and white portion of the leek. Add 2 tblsps of butter and braise for 10

to 15 minutes. Stir in 4 cupsful of water, add pared and sliced potatoes and washed rice. Cover with a lid and cook over low heat for 30 to 35 minutes. Strain and rub through a sieve. Stir in 2 cupsful of hot milk, add salt to taste and butter. Serve garnished with fresh or canned peas. Pass croutons.

Lettuce Cream Soup

800 g lettuce	5 to 6 cupsful milk
3 tblsps butter	1 cupful cream
2 tblsps flour	Salt

Wash the lettuce leaves and dip into boiling water for 1 or 2 minutes. Drain in a strainer and then put through a fine mincer. In a separate saucepan sauté the flour using 2 tablespoonsful of butter; gradually stir in 5 to 6 cupsful of hot milk. Bring to the boil and blend with the lettuce. Cook for 15 to 20 minutes. Add salt to taste and butter. Stir in another cupful of hot milk or cream. Separately serve croutons.

Mushroom Cream Soup

600 g fresh mushrooms	1 onion
2 tblsps flour	2 egg yolks
4 cupsful milk	1 cupful cream or milk
4 tblsps butter	(additional)
1 carrot	Salt

The champignon (common meadow mushroom), the morel and the edible boletus are preferred. Clean and wash the mushrooms. Pass them through the mincer. Put the carrot cut in half lengthwise and the whole onion into a saucepan, add one tablespoonful of butter and simmer covered with a lid for 40 to

45 minutes. Add one cupful of water. Bring to the boil. In a separate saucepan blend 2 tablespoonsful of flour with 2 tablespoonsful of butter. Stir in 4 cupsful of hot milk and 1 cupful of vegetable stock or water. Bring to the boil. Add the braised mushrooms (remove the carrot and onion). Cook for 15 to 20 minutes. Add salt to taste. Garnish with butter and the egg yolks blended with cream or milk (and heated to 70°C (160°F) in the top part of a double boiler). Serve croutons separately.

Cream of Pea Soup

1 can or 800 g fresh frozen green peas	2 egg yolks
	4 cupsful milk
3 tblsps butter	Salt
2 tblsps flour	Water

Rub the canned or cooked fresh frozen peas through a sieve and stir in milk sauce made as follows. Blend the flour and 2 tablespoonsful of butter and stir in hot milk. Simmer for 10 to 15 minutes, strain and add hot water. Salt to taste and add egg yolks blended with cream or milk and heated to 70°C (160°F) in the top part of a double boiler. Before serving add a tablespoonful of butter and garnish with 2 or 3 tablespoonsful of whole peas. Serve croutons separately.

Dried Bean Cream Soup

400 g dried beans	4-5 cupsful water
1 carrot	Salt
1 onion	Croutons
2 cloves	4 tblsps butter
2 cupsful milk	

Wash and soak the beans in cold water for 5-6 hours. Drain and then cover with

4-5 cupsful of water. Add the carrot cut in half and the whole onion into which the cloves have been inserted. Cover and simmer for 40 to 50 minutes. Remove the carrot and onion. Strain the stock and rub the beans through a sieve. Stir in the hot milk; add salt to taste. Serve garnished with butter. Pass croutons on a separate plate.

Dried Pea Cream Soup

Substitute dried peas and prepare as directed above; do not use cloves.

Liver Cream Soup

400 g veal or beef liver	1 carrot
	1 parsley root
500-600 g meat for stock	1 leek
	2 egg yolks
4 tblsps butter	1 cupful cream or milk
2 tblsps flour	Salt

Peel the skin off the liver and remove any gall ducts. Cut the liver into small chunks and sauté slightly in 2 tablespoonsful of butter together with the thinly sliced carrot, parsley and leek. Cover and simmer in 1/2 cupful of water or stock for 30 to 40 minutes. Pass the liver through the mincer 2 or 3 times and then rub through a sieve. In a separate saucepan, make a white stock sauce by blending 2 tablespoonsful of flour and 2 tablespoonsful of butter. Stir in 4 cupsful of stock, simmer for 20-30 minutes and then strain. Stir in the sifted liver and bring to the boil. If the soup is too thick, add stock. Combine slightly beaten egg yolks with hot cream or milk; heat in a heavy saucepan but do not boil. Before serving garnish the soup with this mixture. Separately pass small croutons.

Chicken Cream Soup

1 fowl	2 eggs
4 tblsps butter	1 cupful cream or milk
2 tblsps flour	Salt

Cook the fowl and bone it. Reserve the breast for garnishing. Pass the rest of the meat through a mincer 2 or 3 times and then rub through a sieve adding 2 or 3 tablespoonsful of cold broth. Blend the flour and 2 tablespoonsful of butter and stir in 4 cupsful of hot broth. Cook for 20 to 30 minutes. Strain this sauce and stir in the chicken puree. If the soup is too thick, add hot broth and bring to the boil. Remove from the heat. Salt to taste. Combine slightly beaten egg yolks with hot cream or milk; heat in a heavy saucepan but do not boil. Add this mixture to the soup. Before serving put a piece of butter and diced breast of chicken in each plate. Pass croutons in a separate plate.

Rabbit Cream Soup

Substitute rabbit for the fowl and prepare as directed in the recipe for chicken cream soup.

Wildfowl Cream Soup

1 pheasant or grouse (2 hazel hens or partridges)	1 carrot
	1 parsley
	1 leek
500 to 600 g meat for stock	2 eggs
	1 cupful cream or milk
4 tblsps butter	Salt
2 tblsps flour	

Make a meat stock. Prepare the fowl. Brown it and braise for 20 to 30 minutes in meat stock along with carrot, parsley and leek; when tender, bone the fowl. Reserve the breast meat for garnishing. Pass the rest of the meat through the mincer 2 or 3 times. Add 2 or 3 tablespoonsful of cold meat stock, mix and rub through a strainer. From here follow the directions for chicken cream soup.

Fish Cream Soup

750 g fish (carp, navaga, cod, zander, salmon, smelt, etc.)	1 carrot
	1 parsley root
	2 onions
2 tblsps flour	Salt
4 tblsps butter	1 egg yolk
2 cupsful milk	

Clean, wash and fillet the fish. Make a fish stock with the bones, vegetable roots and one onion. In a separate saucepan braise the fish which has been cut into pieces and the onion chopped fine in 2 tablespoonsful of butter. Blend flour with 2 tablespoonsful of butter and stir in 4 cupsful of fish stock. Bring to the boil and add the fish. Simmer for 15 to 20 minutes. Strain and rub the ingredients through a sieve. Cool the soup slightly. Beat the egg yolk and combine with hot milk. Add this mixture to the soup. Salt to taste. Garnish with butter and pieces of fish or fish balls. (Reserve 100 g of fish for fish balls). Pass croutons separately.

Crabmeat Cream Soup

1 can crabmeat	4 cupsful milk
4 tblsps butter	2 egg yolks
2 tblsps flour	1 cupful cream or milk
1 cupful stock or water	Salt

Reserve several large pieces of crabmeat for garnishing. Pass the rest through a mincer. Put the crabmeat and one cupful of stock or water in a saucepan. Simmer for 5 to 10 minutes. In a separate saucepan blend the flour with 2 tablespoonsful of butter and stir in hot milk. Bring to the boil. Add the crabmeat and simmer for 15-20 minutes, then rub through a sieve. Add salt to taste and butter. Beat the egg yolks and combine with the cream which has been heated (**do not boil**) in a heavy saucepan. Stir this mixture into the soup. Add the diced crabmeat reserved for garnishing. Serve croutons separately.

Milk Soups

Milk soups are simple to make. Fresh or canned milk may be used. Use a heavy saucepan and cook over low heat to avoid burning. Foodstuffs of vegetable origin cook longer when boiled in milk. To save time, first cook them in salt water until almost tender then add to the milk.

Milk Soup with Rice

1 litre milk	1 tsp sugar
4 tblsps rice	Salt
1 tblsp butter	

Wash and drain the rice. Boil in salt water till almost soft then drain and add to the boiling milk. When the rice is soft, add salt and sugar to taste. Add the butter just before serving.

Milk Soup with Noodles

1 litre milk	1 tblsp butter
50 g noodles or	1 tsp sugar
vermicelli	Salt

Bring the milk to the boil. Add the noodles, salt and sugar. Simmer for 20 to 25 minutes. Add the butter just before serving. If vermicelli is substituted for noodles, cook for 12 to 15 minutes. For home-made noodles see the recipe on p. 39. Cook for 15 to 20 minutes.

Milk Soup with Baked Rice

1 litre milk	25 g cheese
3 tblsps rice	2 tsps dried bread
1 egg	crumbs
1 tblsp butter	Salt

Make baked rice as directed in the recipe for broth with baked rice (see p. 45). Put pieces of baked rice in plates and pour over boiling milk.

Milk Soup with Pearl Barley

1 litre milk	1 tblsp butter
4 to 5 tblsps pearl	1 tsp sugar
barley	Salt

Wash pearl barley and soak in cold water for 2 hours. Drain and pour over hot water. Boil for 10 minutes and then drain the pearl barley thoroughly. Add to boiling milk. Simmer over low heat for 40 to 50 minutes. Add salt, sugar and butter and serve.

Milk Soup with Potato Drop Dumplings

1 litre milk	3 or 4 tblsps flour
3 or 4 potatoes	1 tblsp butter
2 eggs	Salt

Boil the potatoes and rub through strainer. Combine with raw egg yolks, flour and salt. Fold in egg whites beaten stiff. Drop into the hot milk with a teaspoon that has been dipped in hot water. Cook uncovered over low heat for 10 to 12 minutes. Add salt and butter.

Plain or mannacroup kletski (see p. 44) may be substituted for potato kletski.

Fruit and Berry Soups

Cherry Soup with Poached Dumplings
(Vareniki[13])

600 g cherries	Salt
1 cupful flour	1/2 cupful sugar
2 eggs	

Divide the cherries. Stone one half and crush the other. Boil the cherry pits, sugar and crushed cherries in 4 or 5 cupsful of hot water and then strain. Make a dough as directed in the recipe for pelmeni (see p. 44). Roll out thin and cut rounds. Put 1 or 2 stoned cherries on each round and fold over into a half moon. Pinch the edges. Cook the vareniki for 5 to 10 minutes in the hot cherry stock and serve at once.

Cherry Soup with Rice

300 g cherries
4 or 5 tblsps rice
1/2 cupful sugar

Wash and stone the cherries. Boil the pits in 4 or 5 cupsful of hot water. Add the sugar, bring to the boil and strain.

Cook the rice till half done, drain and add to the cherry stock. Cook until the rice is soft, add the stoned cherries and boil 5 minutes longer.

Cranberry and Apple Soup

300 g cranberries	1 cupful sugar
500 g apples	1 tblsp potato flour

Pick, wash and crush the berries in an enameled saucepan. Squeeze out the juice. Pour 5 cupsful of boiling water over the skins, stir, cover with a lid and let stand for 10-15 minutes. After this strain the liquor through a cheesecloth; add the sugar, pared and sliced apples and bring to the boil. Pour in the potato flour which has been mixed with 5 tablespoonsful of water and boil for 2-3 minutes. Cool to 60°C, (140°F) and carefully stir in the cranberry juice.

Currant and Peach Soup

300 g black or red currants	1 cupful sugar
500 g peaches	1 tblsp potato flour

Follow the directions for cranberry and apple soup. Before slicing the peaches remove the pits.

Oatmeal and Prune Soup

Wash 1/2 cupful of oatmeal with cold water, pour 2 litres hot water onto the oatmeal. Add 1 tablespoonful of butter and cook until the oatmeal is done. Rub the oatmeal through a strainer and add another spoonful of butter. Stone 200 g prunes, cover with water, add 1/4 cupful sugar and cook. When the prunes are soft, stir in the cooked oatmeal. Bring to the boil and serve.

Apricot and Apple Soup

500 g fresh ripe apricots	3 tblsps sugar
500 g apples	2 tsps potato flour

Wash and stone the apricots. Simmer in 2 cupsful of water until soft. Rub through a sieve or strainer. To this puree add 3 cupsful of hot water, sugar and apples which have been pared and sliced or cut into strips. Bring to the boil and, stirring constantly, add the potato flour which has been combined with about 3 tblsps of cold water. Bring to the boil. If desired, lemon juice may be added.

Fresh Berry Puree

500 g berries	150 g vanilla rusks
1/2 cupful sugar	1/2 cupful sour cream

Wash and drain the berries (strawberries, wild strawberries, raspberries). Rub them through a sieve. Add sugar to 2 cupsful of boiling water. Stirring continuously, cook until sugar dissolves and then strain. Cool this syrup and combine with the berry puree. Chill before serving. Pass sour cream and vanilla rusks.

Apricot Puree

400 g apricots	1/2 cupful rice
1/2 cupful sugar	4 tblsps sour cream
1 tblsp potato flour	

Wash ripe apricots and cook in 6 cupsful of water then rub through a sieve together with stock. (Canned apricot puree may be used instead of fresh fruit). Add the sugar to the puree and bring to the boil. Stir in the potato flour which has been mixed with 1/2 cupful of cold water.

Bring to the boil, remove from the heat and chill. Boil the rice until done, drain and add to the puree. Garnish with sour cream or cream.

Peach Puree

Substitute peaches for apricots in the above recipe.

Mixed Dried Fruit Soup

200 g mixed dried fruit	100 g rice, sago or paste
50 g potato flour	1/2 cupful sugar
Cinnamon	Sour cream

Wash the dried fruit. Cover the apples and pears with water and cook until tender. Add sugar, the remaining fruit and a dash of cinnamon. Cook over a low heat for 10 to 15 minutes. Stir in the potato flour combined with 1 cupful of water and bring to the boil. This soup may be garnished with boiled rice, sago or paste. Put a spoonful of sour cream in each plate before serving.

Dried Fruit Soup with Macaroni

Wash 200 g mixed dried fruit. Cover with 3 litres of cold water and set aside for 2 to 3 hours. Add 1/2 cupful of sugar, a dash of cinnamon and cloves. Cover with a lid and cook over high heat for 10 minutes then set on the hob. When the fruit is soft, remove from the range and cool. Separately cook 100 g macaroni in salt water until tender. Drain and wash off with boiled water. Put the macaroni in a tureen and mix with 1/2 cupful of sour cream. Pour the fruit stock over the macaroni.

Fruit Soup Garnished with Paste or Cereal

Prepare a fruit or berry soup as directed above. Separately cook one of the following for garnishing.
1. Vermicelli (or rice) boiled in water. Drain in a sieve and add to the soup after removing it from the heat.
2. Small-sized vareniki[13] (flour or manna-croup kletski[11]) cooked in water and added to the soup after chilling it.
This soup is served cold. Sour cream may be passed separately.

Apple Puree

500 g apples	2 tblsps rice
200 g white bread	Lemon rind or stick of
1/2 cupful sugar	cinnamon

The antonovka, a tart apple, is best. Wash, pare and slice the apples. Add white bread (without crust) and a piece of lemon rind or a few pieces of stick cinnamon. Add 4 cupsful of hot water, cover with a lid and cook until the apples are mushy. Remove from the heat, take out the lemon rind or cinnamon and rub the apples through a sieve. Add sugar and hot water until the puree is like heavy sour cream. Bring to the boil. Cook the rice separately. Serve the puree with a spoonful of rice in each plate and sour cream if desired.

Currant or Cranberry Soup with Mannacroup[9]

300 g currants or 200 g cranberries	1 cupful milk
2 tblsps mannacroup[9]	1/2 cupful sugar

Stem, wash and crush the berries with a wooden spoon. Stir in 4 or 5 cupsful water; add sugar. Bring to the boil, strain and cool. Cook the mannacroup in the milk and pour into a plate that has been wet with water. Chill and cut into squares or diamonds. Put pieces in each plate and pour over the berry liquor.

Chilled Soups Made with Bread Kvass[14] or Beet Broth

Bread kvass[14] or beet broth are the foundation for okroshka[15], botvinnya[16], borshch[17], and jellied soups. The ingredients of these soups must be chilled. A piece of ice may be put into each plate. Like the fruit and berry soups, iced okroshka, botvinnya and borshch are especially good in spring and summer.

Cold Kvass[14] Soup with Vegetables
(Okroshka)

1 litre bread kvass[14]	2 tblsps sour cream
1 or 2 potatoes	1 tsp sugar
1 carrot	1 tsp mustard
1 or 2 cucumbers	Salt
50 to 75 g green onions	Minced dill
2 hard-cooked eggs	

Dice the cooked and chilled carrot and the cucumber. Grate the boiled potato. Mince the green onion finely, sprinkle with salt and rub with a spoon until soft and juice appears. Separate the egg white from the yolk. Chop up the egg

55

white. Rub together the egg yolk and a little mustard. Mix the green onion, potatoes, yolks, sugar and salt. Stir in the kvass. Add the cucumber, carrot and egg whites. Sprinkle each plate with minced dill. Garnish with a spoonful of sour cream.

Boiled turnip or cauliflower may be substituted for the carrot.

Cold Kvass[14] Soup with Meat

1 litre bread kvass[14]	2 hard-cooked
250 g boiled beef, ham	eggs
and tongue	1/2 cupful sour cream
2 cucumbers	1 tsp sugar
75 g green onions	Minced dill
2 diced boiled potatoes	Salt

Cut into small dice the boiled beef, ham, tongue and peeled cucumbers. Mince the green onions, sprinkle with salt and rub with a spoon till soft. Chop up the egg whites. Rub together and thoroughly combine the egg yolks with a little mustard, sugar and salt. Stir in the kvass. Add the other ingredients. Sprinkle each plate with minced dill and garnish with a spoonful of sour cream.

Cold Fish-and-Vegetable Soup

(Botvinya)

1 litre kvass[14]	50 g horseradish
250 g spinach	250 g fish (sturgeon,
250 g sorrel	zander, etc.)
1 tsp sugar	Dill
75 g green onions	2 cucumbers

Wash the spinach and sorrel thoroughly. Cook the spinach in boiling water. Separately cook the sorrel in a covered saucepan. Then sift the spinach and sor-

rel and rub through a sieve. To this puree add sugar, salt and a little of mustard. Stir in the bread kvass.[14] Add the diced cucumber, minced green onions and dill. Before serving, put a little grated horseradish and a piece of boiled fish in each plate. If desired, the fish may be passed separately. Botvinnya may also be served with cured fillet of white fish, fillet of beluga or dried salt whitefish. Young nettles may be substituted for spinach.

Cold Beet Soup
(Cold Borshch)

500 g beets	2 tblsps sour cream
200 g potatoes	1 tsp sugar
2 cucumbers	Vinegar
75 g green onions	Dill or parsley
2 hard-cooked eggs	Salt, mustard

Peel and dice the beets, add boiling water (2 cupsful per plate) and 1 teaspoonful of vinegar. Simmer for 20 to 30 minutes. Strain the beet broth and chill. Put the beets in a saucepan, add the diced boiled potatoes and cucumber, chopped eggs and minced green onions, salt, sugar and mustard. Stir in the chilled beet broth. Add the sour cream and combine thoroughly. Before serving sprinkle each plate with minced parsley or dill.

Sorrel and Beet Top Soup

Wash 1 kg beet tops. Add 2 litres hot water. Simmer for 10 to 15 minutes. Add 200 g washed sorrel and simmer for another 10 minutes. Remove the greens with a skimmer. Pass them through a food mincer. Stir into the strained and cooled broth. Cut up cucumbers, onions and radishes, dill and hard-cooked egg. Add sour cream and mustard. Combine the ingredients and pour over and stir in the cold broth and greens.

Chilled Beet Soup

1 1/2 litre bread kvass[14]	2 hard-cooked eggs
500 g young beets and tops	2 tblsps sour cream
2 cucumbers	1 tsp sugar
75 g green onions	1 tsp salt
	Minced parsley or dill

Wash the young beets and tops. Peel the beetroots, add 2 cupsful of water per portion and simmer for 10 to 20 minutes. Add the beet tops and cook for another 10 minutes. Strain the broth through a strainer or sieve. Chop the beets and tops fine. Add sliced cucumbers, eggs, green onions, sour cream, sugar, and pour the kvass and chilled beet broth over. Before serving sprinkle with parsley or dill.

FISH AND SEA FOODS

sole in tomato sauce

40g crabmeat

10g parsley

60g mushrooms

60g sole

10g onion

pepper

300g sauce

Live, fresh, frozen or salt fish and ready-to-cook or ready-to-eat fish products are all easily available. Fresh frozen fillet of carp, zander, codfish, bream and other fish can be purchased in the shops. This is a great time saver and simplifies cooking immeasureably.

Thaw frozen fish or fillets in cold water so that it does not dry. After thawing wash in fresh water.

Soak salt fish in cold water to cover for 30 to 40 minutes. Remove the scales, cut the fish and then soak again for 4 to 6 hours, depending on the saltiness. Change the water every hour or two.

Methods of Cooking Fish

In cooking fish the nutritive matter of the raw product must be preserved and if possible its value should be increased while improving its flavour and digestibility.

The choice of manner of cooking is most important for the proper use of any food, fish included.

Fish should be cooked for no more than 15 to 25 minutes. Over-cooking like undercooking makes fish hard to digest.

In the process of cooking, complex chemical changes take place. Part of the soluble substances such as protein, carbohydrates, mineral salts, extractives and vitamines pass from the flesh into the liquid. To prevent as much of the soluble protein as possible from passing from the fish into the water, do not add salt before the water begins to boil.

In the different methods of cooking, moisture leaves the fish (or meat) in different ways. When fish is boiled, all the moisture and nutritive matter leave the flesh in a liquid state. The soluble substances leave the fish mainly along with the water. Fish looses the greatest amount of soluble nutritive matter when it is cooked in water.

Less liquid moisture leaves the fish when it is steamed on a rack over boiling liquid or parboiled in just enough water to half cover the fish.

The least amount of soluble substances is lost when fish is cooked in hot fat in a frying pan; when it is "done" it is jucier and more sapid. The little moisture that does leave the fish forms a juice. However, the greater part of this moisture evaporates and very little of the soluble substances leave the fish.

Less soluble substances will leave the fish if it is cooked in a small amount of water at a high temperature and if the pieces are not small.

If the fish to be cooked has an undesirable pungent smell, condiments and berbs should be added to the broth. The quantity and combination of spices and herbs used will depend on the natural flavour and smell of the fish.

Regardless of whether fish is boiled whole, filleted or cut into portions, it must be completely submerged in the water. A piece of fish weighing 100-150 g will require an average of 150-200 g water. Remember, if cooked in too much water, there will be a great loss of soluble substances and, consequently, the fish will be less tasty, nutritious and lack juiciness.

Boiled Fish

Almost any fish may be boiled. The less water used, the tastier the fish will be. To each litre of water add one teaspoonful of salt, 1/2 carrot, parsley, 1 onion, 1 or 2 bay leaves and a dash of pepper. Slice the onion and vegetable roots. When cooking cod, sole, catfish or pike, add one half cupful of pickled cucumber brine per litre of water. This will eliminate their specific "fishiness". Pieces of fish weighing 500 g or over should be put in cold water; when cooking small fish, pour boiling water over them. When the water begins to boil, the heat is turned down and the fish simmers until tender. All fish must be well cooked. Small pieces of sturgeon, sevruga or beluga should be boiled for 20-30 minutes; pieces weighing over 500 g, for 1 1/2 hours. Zander, carp or pike weighing 1-1 1/2 kg cook for 50-60 minutes, while 100-150 g pieces cook for 15-20 minutes.

Test the fish with a toothpick. The fish stock may be used to make white stock sauce or tomato sauce to be served with the fish or to make soup.

Salt fish should be soaked. After soaking, drain and pour over cold water. Cook without salt.

Boiled fish may be served hot or cold. When served hot, garnish with boiled potatoes and when served cold, garnish with Russian salad, coleslaw, pickled beets, cucumbers or green salad.

Parboiled fish is cooked in a small amount of water or stock to which aromatic herbs, mushrooms, pickled cucumber brine or grape wine have been added; cover the saucepan and simmer.

Boiled Fish with Potatoes

500 g fish	1 tsp salt
800 g potatoes	Minced parsley
200 g sauce	

Cut the prepared fish (zander, pike, catfish, tench, etc.) into pieces. Separately boil whole potatoes. Place the fish on a platter, garnish with the boiled potatoes, sprinkle with minced parsley. Separately pass egg-and-butter sauce or horseradish-and-vinegar sauce. Instead of sauce, parsley butter may be served.

Boiled Beluga, Sevruga or Sturgeon

500 g fish	1 tblsp butter
800 g potatoes	Salt, minced parsley

Cook beluga, other sturgeon fish or catfish in large pieces and slice immediately before serving. Cover with water until about 2 cm above the fish; bring to the boil over high heat then turn the heat down, cover and simmer for 30 to 40 minutes.

Cut and serve the fish garnished with buttered boiled potatoes sprinkled with the minced parsley. Pass horseradish and vinegar separately.

Boiled Zander and Vegetables

1 kg fish	800 g potatoes
1 carrot	1 tblsp butter
1 beetroot	1/2 cupful milk
1 onion	Salt, pepper, bay leaf

Prepare and cut the zander into pieces of the desired size. Clean, wash and slice the carrot, beet and onion. Pare and cut the potato into chunks, spread the carrot, beet and onion on the bottom of the saucepan, then put in the potatoes. Add 1 1/2 cupsful of water and salt. Sprinkle the fish with salt and arrange on the vegetables. Add pepper and a bay leaf. Cover with a lid, bring to the boil and cook over low heat for one hour. Do not stir; shake the saucepan every 10 minutes to keep the vegetables from sticking to the bottom and burning. When the fish and vegetables are almost done, add the milk and butter. Simmer for 15 to 20 minutes longer. Remove from the heat and baste the fish with the sauce taken from the bottom of the saucepan. Leave the saucepan covered until service.

Fish Boiled in Oiled Paper

500 g fish (bream,	1 tblsp lemon juice
zander or codfish)	2 tblsps butter
1 carrot	Salt, pepper
1 onion	Minced greens

Cut fillets of bream (zander or codfish) into pieces of the desired size and stand in salt water for five minutes (1 tablespoonful of salt per cupful of cold water). Drain off the water and put the fish on a sheet of buttered oil paper or foil. Combine the remaining butter, pepper, grated carrot and onion and spread over the fish. Sprinkle with lemon juice and minced greens. Gather up the edges of the paper with a string tie like a pouch and lower into a saucepan 2/3 filled with boiling water. Cook for 15 to 20 minutes

over low heat. Serve with a side dish of buttered boiled potatoes, and fresh-salted cucumbers.

Boiled Fish with Potatoes and Salt Pork

750 g fish	100 g salt pork
800 g potatoes	Salt, pepper
1-2 onions	Minced parsley

Dice the pork, add sliced onion and fry. Add the pared and sliced potatoes, salt, pepper and one cupful of water. Cover and simmer for 5 minutes. Cut the fish into pieces and add to the potatoes. Simmer until tender. Sprinkle with the minced parsley; serve with potatoes.

Boiled Sole with Butter

500 g fish	Vinegar
800 g potatoes	Minced parsley
2 tblsps butter	

Cut the boiled fish into pieces. Arrange on a platter with garnishing of boiled potatoes. Dry the parsley in a towel. Heat the butter to a golden colour. Add the minced parsley and vinegar (1 tsp for 3 or 4 portions). Before pouring the butter over the potatoes, drain off any fish stock on the bottom of the platter.

Boiled Codfish

800 g codfish	600 g boiled
200 g sauce or 40 g	potatoes
butter	

Cut the fish into portions with or without skin, ribs and backbone. Arrange in the boiling savoury stock (see below) in a single layer, skin upward. Cook for 12-15 minutes. Serve with a garnishing of boiled potatoes. Pour over egg sauce (or egg-and-butter sauce, tomato sauce, capers sauce, melted butter) or pass the sauce separately.

Savoury Stock
Ingredients for 1 lit of savoury stock:

15 g salt	15 g onions
2 whole allspice	15 g parsley or celery
3 peppercorns	Dash of thyme or
1 bay leaf	savoury
15 g carrots	

The strong specific flavour and smell of seafish (cod, sole, halibut, mackerel) or fresh-water fish (catfish, carp, tench) can be reduced by adding 200 g of cucumber pickle brine (or the peelings of pickles) to each litre of savoury stock.

Boiled Zander, Pike, Catfish or Burbot
Substitute any of these fish in the above recipe.

Pike Boiled in Brine

500 g pike	200 g pickled
Savoury stock (see	cucumber brine
above)	200 g brine sauce

Add the brine to the boiling savoury stock. Lay the fish skin upward in a saucepan in one layer, pour over savoury stock to cover. Cook for 12-15 minutes. Garnish with boiled potatoes. Serves four.

Zander Parboiled in Brine

800 g zander	mushrooms
300 g pickled	120 g fishhead
cucumber brine	(sturgeon, etc.)
2 pickled cucumbers	300 g brine sauce
(about 50 g)	600 g boiled potatoes
15-20 g dried	Minced parsley or dill

Cut the fish into portions and parboil for 25 minutes in savoury stock (300 g per kg of fish) to which the brine has been added. Peel the pickles; cut small ones in half and large ones into quarters, remove the seeds, slice and cook. Soak the mushrooms (boletus) in cold water for 2 hours then slice and cook until tender. Cut up the cartilage of the cooked sturgeon, add it to the mushrooms and cooked pickles, mix in a little hot brine sauce and set aside. Garnish the cooked fish with boiled potatoes, pickles, the cooked cartilage and mushrooms. Pour over the brine sauce made with the fish liquor, sprinkle with minced parsley or dill. Serves four.

Codfish, Pike, Catfish or Burbot Parboiled in Brine
Substitute any of these fish in the above recipe.

Parboiled Fish with Steamed Sauce

1 kg fish	600 g boiled potatoes
1 onion	1 1/2 cupsful steamed
1 carrot	sauce
2 bay leaves	1 lemon
5 peppercorns	Herbs
40 g parsley	

Fillet the fish but do not skin. Cut into portions. Parboil in water, add salt, condiments and vegetables as directed in the recipe for boiled fish. Garnish with chunks of boiled potatoes. Pour over steamed sauce and heat. Decorate with slices of lemon and parsley greens. Pass tomato sauce separately if desired.

Catfish in Tomato Sauce with Vegetables

600 g catfish	120 g mushrooms
20 g onion	40 g crabmeat
20 g parsley	300 g greens
20 g carrot	Salt

Cut the fillets of catfish into portions. Steam together with the onion, carrot and parsley. Use the fish stock to make the sauce. Serve garnished with boiled potatoes, mushrooms and crabmeat. Pour over tomato sauce with vegetables (see p. 88). Sprinkle with minced parsley.

Zander, Pike, Codfish, Burbot, Sole, Halibut or Sturgeon in Tomato Sauce with Vegetables

Any of these fish may be substituted in the above recipe.

Stuffed Zander

400 g zander	8 crayfish tails
350 g stuffing	300 g sauce
120 g mushrooms	

Cut the fillets (skinned and boned) into strips 3 to 4 cm wide and 20 to 25 cm long. Spread raw stuffing over each strip and roll it up. Put the roll in a casserole and add a little stock. Cover the casserole with oiled paper or foil and steam in the oven. Before serving, garnish with mushrooms, crayfish tails and boiled potatoes. Pour over boiled fish sauce (see p. 88) or capers sauce (see p. 108).

Stuffing

1 kg filleted fish	500 g milk or cream
100 g dry white bread	4 egg whites
(without crust)	Salt

Put through the food chopper two or three times the skinned and boned fillets of fish and the bread which has been soaked in milk. Add the egg whites. Beat well and gradually pour in the milk or cream. Beat until light. Add salt last.

Stuffed Codfish

Substitute codfish and follow the above directions.

Boiled Sole or Halibut in Sauce

500 g sole or	40 g vegetables and
halibut	spices for savoury
200 g sauce	stock

Cut the fish into portions and boil in savoury stock. Garnish with boiled potatoes.

Serve with egg-and-butter, tomato or capers sauce, or cold horseradish and vinegar sauce.

Boiled Sole or Halibut with Anchovy Butter

600 g sole or halibut	20 g anchovies or
40 g vegetables and	herring
spices for savoury stock	Boiled potatoes
40 g butter	

Boil the fish in savoury stock. Put a piece of anchovy or herring butter on each piece of fish. Serve garnished with boiled potatoes.

Sole or Halibut in Tomato Sauce

500 g sole or halibut	40 g crabmeat
10 g onion	60 g mushrooms
10 g parsley	300 g sauce
Boiled potatoes	Pepper

Cut the fish into portions. Steam till tender in stock to which onion and parsley have been added. Garnish with cooked mushrooms, crabmeat and boiled potatoes. Pour over tomato sauce.

Sole or Halibut with Leek and Celery in Boiled Fish Sauce

600 g sole or halibut	300 g boiled fish sauce
100 g leek	40 g butter or butter
100 g celery	margarine
40 g white wine	1 tsp lemon juice
120 g mushrooms	Salt
40 g crabmeat	Pepper

Spread the finely shredded leek and celery on the bottom of a saucepan and put in the fish cut into portions. Sprinkle with salt and pepper. Add fish stock and white wine. Cover with a lid and steam over low heat. Serve the fish and vegetables garnished with cooked mushrooms and crabmeat. Boil the stock until one half remains. Add the boiled fish sauce (see p. 87) to the stock and bring to the boil. Add the butter and lemon juice; taste to correct seasoning. Serve the fish with sauce poured over.

Fillet of Sole or Halibut in Boiled Fish Sauce

600 g fillet of sole or halibut	40 g white wine
20 g onion	40 g crabmeat
20 g parsley	4 oysters
120 g mushrooms	320 g boiled fish sauce
	1 tsp salt

Butter a saucepan and put the fish in. Add stock, white wine, onion and parsley. Cover with a lid and steam. When tender serve garnished with mushrooms, crabmeat and oysters, and boiled potatoes. Add the boiled fish sauce to the fish liquor. Bring to the boil and simmer until it is of the required thickness and taste. Strain and pour over fish.

Sole or Halibut in Boiled Fish Sauce with Terragon

600 g sole or halibut	320 g boiled fish sauce
20 g onion	60 g butter
20 g parsley	40 g terragon
40 g white wine	1 tsp lemon juice
120 g mushrooms	Pepper
40 g crabmeat	

Steam the fish in stock to which onion, celery and white wine have been added. Serve garnished with the cooked mushrooms, crabmeat and boiled potatoes. Boil the stock until one half remains, then add to it the boiled fish sauce (see p. 87). Bring to the boil and strain, bring to the boil again and add the minced terragon and the lemon juice. Taste to correct seasoning. Pour over the fish before serving.

Sole or Halibut with Apples and Leeks

600 g sole or halibut	200 g sour cream or
400 g apples	80 g butter
80 g leek	Salt
40 g white wine	Pepper

Pare and slice the apples (antonovka or any other tart apples), slice the white part of the leek. Put them in a buttered saucepan. Lay the pieces of fish on top. Sprinkle with salt and pepper. Pour in a little stock and add white wine. Steam, basting from time to time. When tender, remove the fish. Boil the stock until one half remains. Add to it the sour cream or butter. Salt to taste. Pour over the fish.

Hot-Smoked Sea Bass with Potatoes

600 g hot-smoked sea bass	600 g potatoes
	40 g butter

Put the whole fish or portions in a saucepan. Add a little stock, cover and simmer until hot. Pour melted butter over and serve with boiled potatoes.

Sea Bass in Tomato Sauce

600 g fillet of sea bass	120 g mushrooms
40 g carrot, onion, and parsley	300 g tomato sauce
4 crayfish or 40 g crabmeat	1/2 lemon
	Greens
	Potatoes (optional)

Cut the fillet into portions and steam. Garnish with boiled potatoes, boiled mushrooms and pieces of crabmeat. Pour over tomato sauce (see p. 88). Put a slice of lemon on each piece of fish. Sprinkle with minced parsley.

Codfish, Burbot, Zander, Pike or Catfish with Tomato Sauce

Substitute any of these fish in the above recipe.

Stuffed Fish Cutlets in Don Manner

500 g sea bass	Pepper
120 g mushrooms	Greens
120 g onion	40 g vegetable fat
400 g sauce	

Cut the filleted fish (skinned and boned) into rectangular pieces (2 pieces per portion) and pound slightly with a chopper. Put some stuffing (see below) on each piece of fish, fold over and shape into a cutlet. Lay the cutlets in a buttered casserole overlapping side down. Add stock, cover with a lid and simmer over low heat. Before serving pour over white wine sauce (see p. 88) or tomato sauce with mushrooms. Serve with a garnishing of boiled potatoes.

Stuffing

Finely chop the mushrooms and fish trimmings. Sauté slightly together with the minced green parsley and onion. Season with salt and pepper.

Stuffed Salmon or Sole Cutlets

Substitute salmon or sole in the above recipe.

Sprat Balls and Vegetables

320 g fillets of sprat	40 g parsley
60 g white bread	400 g stock
20 g flour	1 small egg
60 g carrot	Salt, pepper
120 g onion	Dill

Put the filleted sprats through the mincer twice together with the bread which has been soaked in water. Add the egg, flour, salt and pepper. Mix thoroughly and shape into round balls the size of a walnut. Put a layer of finely sliced carrots, onions and parsley on the bottom of a casserole and the balls on the vegetables. Add hot fish stock or water to cover. Season with salt and simmer for 1 to 1 1/2 hours.

Serve with the broth and vegetables and a garnishing of boiled potatoes, green peas or stewed beetroots. Sprinkle with minced dill.

Steamed Sprat Pudding

400 g filleted sprats	60 g sour cream
60 g white bread	40 g butter or 300 g sauce
4 eggs	
50 g milk or water	Salt, pepper

Put the filleted sprats (boned) through the mincer together with the bread which has been soaked in milk and squeezed dry. Add the egg yolk, salt, pepper and sour cream. Mix thoroughly. Fold in the egg white beaten stiff. Transfer to a buttered mould, set in a water bath and cover. Bring the water to the boil and cook for 35 to 40 minutes. Unmould and cut into portions. Serve with melted butter or tomato sauce poured over. Tomato sauce may be passed separately.

Smoked Sprats in Sour Cream

320 g smoked sprats	100 g onion
200 g sour cream	Allspice

Remove the heads, skin and intestines of the sprats and wash. Bring the sour cream to the boil and add grated onion, a dash of ground allspice and pepper. Heat the sour cream to the boiling point again, add the sprats and simmer for 8 to 10 minutes. Serve with mashed potatoes.

Herring in Tomato Sauce with Pickled Cucumbers

500 g fresh herring	400 g stock
120 g pickled	20 g flour
cucumbers	40 g butter
60 g tomato puree or	Minced parsley
300 g fresh tomatoes	

Bone the portions of filleted herring and arrange in one layer in a buttered casserole. Add thinly sliced pickles, tomato puree or fresh tomatoes (peeled, seeded and cut into small pieces). Add fish stock to cover just half the fish. Cover with a lid and simmer for 25 to 30 minutes. Carefully drain off the stock or transfer the fish to another saucepan. Make a sauce by gradually adding to the stock the flour which has been combined with an equal amount of butter. Stirring continuously, heat until the sauce thickens. Add salt, pepper and butter to taste.

Strain, pour over the fish, bring to the boil. Serve together with the pickle and the sauce poured over. Garnish with boiled potatoes. Sprinkle with minced parsley.

Boiled Salt Roach

600 g salt roach	10 g celery
20 g onion	Bay leaf
20 g carrot	10 g parsley root
1 egg	Minced green parsley
300 g sauce	

Soak (3-4 hours) and then skin the fish. Lay in a saucepan in one layer. Add cold water to cover, the bay leaf, dry or fresh parsley root, celery, carrot and onion sliced thin or shredded. Simmer for 12 to 15 minutes. Before serving pour over boiled fish sauce with minced green parsley, hard-cooked chopped egg, butter or capers. Horseradish and vinegar sauce may be served separately instead of boiled fish sauce. Garnish with boiled or mashed potatoes.

Boiled Salt Zander, Bream, Cod or Sole

Substitute any of these fish in the above recipe.

Steamed Fish

The fish best for steaming are zander, catfish, pike, burbot, salmon, pieces of sturgeon, sevruga, beluga and sterlet. If a rack is used, cook the bones, head (without gills), tail and fins in the stock. The bones must be washed thoroughly and boiled for 40 to 50 minutes with onion and parsley and then strained. Use the fish liquor to make the sauces served with fish.

Lay the fish in one layer in a shallow pan or on the rack of a fish pan. Add salt and pepper and just enough liquor to cover 2/3 of the fish. Cook covered with a lid.

Steamed Sturgeon

500 g sturgeon	1 tblsp flour
200 g fresh mushrooms	2 tblsps butter
3 tblsps white table	Salt
wine or 1 tsp lemon	Pepper
juice	

Clean, scald, wash and cut the fish into pieces of the desired size. Put the fish in a shallow saucepan with the mushrooms between the pieces. Sprinkle with salt and pepper. Add white wine, a cupful of stock (or water), cover with a lid and simmer for 15 to 20 minutes. When the fish is tender, drain off the liquor and boil until a cupful remains. Blend one scant tablespoonful of flour with one tablespoonful butter and combine with the liquor. Boil for 3 to 4 minutes stirring constantly. Remove the sauce from the heat, add a piece of butter and stir until thoroughly blended. Add salt to taste; strain. If wine is not used, add lemon juice to the sauce when it is done. Arrange the fish on a heated platter, top with the mushrooms and pour over the sauce. Serve with a garnishing of boiled potatoes, cucumbers or salad, and lemon slices.

Beluga in Brine

500 g fresh beluga	1 tblsp pickle brine
2 pickled cucumbers	1 tblsp flour
200 g fresh mushrooms	2 tblsps butter
or 100 g pickled	Salt, pepper
mushrooms	

Prepare and cut the fish into pieces of the desired size. Peel and cut the pickles lengthwise; remove the seeds and cut each half into three pieces. Cut up the mushrooms. Put the mushrooms and pickles between the pieces of fish. Sprinkle with salt and pepper. Add 1 1/2 cupsful of stock (or water) and the brine. Cover with a lid and simmer for 15 to 25 minutes. Drain the stock into another saucepan and boil until about a cupful remains. Prepare the sauce as directed in the recipe for steamed sturgeon but do not add lemon juice. Serve on a heated platter with the mushrooms, a slice of lemon and pickles on each piece of fish. Pour over strained sauce. Garnish with boiled potatoes.

Sturgeon, Sevruga, Sterlet or Catfish in Brine

Substitute any of these fish in the above recipe.

Sevruga in Tomato Sauce with Mushrooms

500 g sevruga	1 tsp flour
200 g fresh mushrooms	2 tblsps butter
3 tblsps white wine	Salt, pepper
3 tblsps tomato puree	

Cut the prepared fish into pieces of the desired size, scald and rinse in cold water. Add cut champignon or boletus mushrooms. Sprinkle with salt and pepper. Add white wine and a cupful of stock (or water) combined with the tomato puree. Cover the saucepan with a lid and simmer for 15 to 25 minutes. When the fish is tender, drain the stock into another saucepan and make the sauce as directed in the recipe for steamed sturgeon. Serve garnished with boiled potatoes and fresh-salted cucumbers.

Zander in White Wine

750 g fish or 500 g	1 raw egg
fillet of zander	200 g white bread
1/2 cupful table wine	4 tblsps butter
200 g fresh mushrooms	Salt, pepper
1 tblsp flour	

Put the pieces of fish and champignon or boletus mushrooms into a shallow saucepan. Sprinkle with salt and pepper. Add the wine and 3/4 cupful of stock (or water). Simmer for 15 to 25 minutes. Cut the crust off the bread and fry one slice for each piece of fish. When the fish is tender, drain off the stock into another saucepan. Make the sauce as directed in the recipe for steamed sturgeon (see p. 67). Remove the sauce from the heat, salt to taste and stir in the egg yolk which has been combined with a tablespoonful of butter. Mix thoroughly. Serve on the fried bread on a heated platter. Put mushrooms on each piece of fish. Pour the strained sauce over the fish. Garnish with little pieces of fried bread, asparagus, string beans or peas.

Pike with Potatoes and Onions

750 g pike	4 tblsps butter
2 onions	Salt
800 g potatoes	Minced parsley
300 g tomatoes	

Clean, wash and thinly slice the onions. Sauté slightly in butter. Add the pieces of fish which have been sprinkled with salt. Cover with the sliced tomatoes. Add 3 or 4 tblsps water. Sprinkle the tomatoes with salt and pepper. Slice and fry the potatoes and put them around the fish. Dot with butter. Cover the skillet with a lid and bake for 20 to 30 minutes at 150°C (300°F). Before serving sprinkle with the minced parsley.

Barbel, Sole, Codfish or Eels with Potatoes and Onions

Substitute any of these fish in the above recipe.

Sole in Red Wine

500-750 g sole	1 onion
1 cupful red table wine	2 tblsps butter
1 tblsp flour	4 cloves
800 g potatoes	Bay leaf
1 parsley root	Salt, pepper

Wash, clean and slice the parsley and onion. Put them in a saucepan, add the cloves, a dash of pepper and a bay leaf. Put in the pieces of fish, add salt, the wine and a cupful of stock (or water). Cover and simmer for 15 to 20 minutes. When the fish is tender, drain the stock into another saucepan and make a sauce as directed in the recipe for steamed sturgeon (see p. 77). Serve garnished with whole boiled potatoes. Pour over the strained sauce.

Zander, Pike or Eels in Red Wine

Substitute any of these fish in the above recipe.

Canned Sturgeon in Sour Cream with Potatoes

1 can (350 g) sturgeon in tomato sauce	2 tblsps butter
	800 g potatoes
1/2 cupful sour cream	Minced greens

Cut the fish into pieces, put it in a shallow saucepan together with the sauce and add the sour cream. Cover with a lid and simmer for 5 or 6 minutes. Serve on a hot platter garnished with buttered boiled potatoes. Pour the sauce over the fish and sprinkle with the minced greens. Pass cucumbers or pickles.

Canned Beluga or Sevruga in Sour Cream with Potatoes

Substitute beluga or sevruga in the above recipe.

Canned Salmon or White Salmon in White Wine

1 can (350 g) salmon, white salmon or zander in natural juice	1 tblsp flour
	200 g white bread
	1 egg
1 cupful white table wine	4 tblsps butter
	Salt
200 g fresh mushrooms	800 g boiled potatoes

Put the fish in a saucepan. Add the cooked and cut mushrooms, the fish juice and white wine. Cover and heat for 5 or 6 minutes. Transfer the fish to a hot platter. Bring the stock to the boil. Stir in the flour which has been combined with a tablespoonful of butter and mix until thoroughly blended. Boil for 3 to 5 minutes, then remove from the heat and add the egg yolk blended with 1 to 1 1/2 tablespoonful butter. Mix and add salt to taste; strain. Before serving pour the sauce over the fish and garnish with

pieces of bread fried in butter or boiled potatoes.

Steamed Fish Patties

750 g fish or 500 g filleted fish	200 g fresh mushrooms
	1 cupful white table wine
300 g string beans	
100 g white bread (without crust)	1 egg
	4 tblsps butter
1/2 cupful milk	Salt to taste

Prepare fish forcemeat (perferably zander, pike, burbot, catfish or cod) as directed in the recipe for fish cutlets (see p. 78). Shape into round patties and lay in a single layer in a buttered saucepan. Put the cut mushrooms into the spaces between the patties. Sprinkle with butter, pour in the white wine and add stock (made of fish bones) to cover 3/4 of the patties. Cover the saucepan with a lid and simmer for 15 to 20 minutes. When done, drain the stock into another saucepan and make a white wine sauce (see p. 88). Separately cook the string beans and season with butter; salt to taste. Serve the patties with mushrooms. Garnish with string beans; pour over the sauce.

Stuffed Fish

1 large pike, zander, carp or bream (2-3 kg)	3 carrots
	1 tblsp sugar
100 to 200 g white bread (without crust)	2 eggs
	1 tblsp vegetable oil
300 g onion	Salt, pepper
2 beets	

Remove the scales and cut off the head of the fish. Take out the viscera without cutting open the belly. Remove the gills. Wash the fish in cold water and cut it crosswise. Cut the flesh out of each piece without damaging the skin. Prepare the stuffing by mincing and mixing together the fish flesh, onions and dry bread which has been soaked and squeezed dry. Add the egg, sugar, vegetable oil, pepper and salt; mix thoroughly.

Fill the pieces of fish with the stuffing and smooth with a wet knife. Put the sliced beets, carrots and washed onion skins on the bottom of the kettle, then alternate layers of fish and vegetables. Add cold water to cover. Close the kettle with a lid. Bring to the boil and cook over low heat for 1 1/2 to 2 hours. See that the fish and vegetables do not burn. Baste the upper layer of fish from time to time with the stock. Transfer the fish and vegetables to a platter. Strain the liquor and pour over the fish. If desired, cook potatoes in the fish liquor and serve as garnishing.

Fish Stews

Fish stew is usually made with sautéed fish but stew may be made with raw or stuffed fish. The fish is cut into portions and braised with savoury vegetables, tomato paste or fresh tomatoes, green pepper, sorrel, milk and onion, and a variety of other ingredients.

Codfish Stewed in Milk

500 g codfish	2 cupsful milk
25 g flour	Salt
40 g vegetable oil	Pepper
250 g onion	Minced parsley or dill

Cut the unskinned fillet of codfish into 40-50 g pieces. Dredge with salt, pepper and flour; sauté in oil until golden brown. In a deep saucepan lay alternate layers of onion and fish, starting with sliced raw onion or leek. Add hot boiling milk to cover and simmer until the onion is tender. Serve hot garnished with boiled potatoes or rice; serve cold without garnishing.

Codfish and Horseradish Stew

500 g codfish	20 g flour
100 g horseradish	20 g butter or butter
3 cupsful fish stock	margarine
40 g weak (3%)	Minced greens
vinegar	Salt
120 g sour cream	

Butter a deep saucepan and sprinkle with a thin layer of grated horseradish then alternate layers of fish (cut into portions) and horseradish. Add vinegar and salt to the stock, heat and then pour over the fish. Cover with a lid and simmer for one hour. Carefully drain the stock into another saucepan. Add sour cream to the stock and bring to the boil. Gradually stir in the flour which has been combined with butter, blend thoroughly and bring to the boil. Pour the sauce over the fish and again bring to the boil. Simmer for 15 to 20 minutes. Remove from the saucepan with a skimmer. Serve with a garnishing of boiled potatoes. Pour over the pan sauce and sprinkle with the greens.

Sole, Catfish, Pike or Carp and Horseradish Stew

Substitute any of these fish in the recipe above.

Codfish and Cabbage Stew

500 g codfish	(or sauerkraut)
25 g flour	Caraway seed
40 g vegetable oil or	Pepper, salt
boiled butter	Minced parsley, dill or
200 g red sauce	green onions
600 g stewed cabbage	

Cut the unskinned fish (with or without bones) into portions. Sprinkle with salt, pepper and dredge with flour. Sauté in the oil or butter. Stew the cabbage, add red sauce and scalded caraway seed. Mix together. In a deep saucepan, lay alternate layers of cabbage and sautéed fish. Pour over the sauce. Braise for one hour. Serve each piece of fish topped with cabbage. Pour over sauce and sprinkle with the minced parsley, dill or green onions. If vegetable oil is used, this fish may be served cold.

Codfish and Sorrel Stew

500 g codfish	200 g onion or leek
25 g flour	3 cloves garlic
80 g vegetable or	60 g olives
olive oil	4 slices lemon
400 g sorrel	Salt
200 g tomatoes or	Pepper
40 g tomato puree	Minced parsley or dill

Cut the codfish into portions. Sprinkle with salt, pepper and dredge with flour. Sauté in vegetable or olive oil. Shred the onion or leek and stirring continuously bring to the boil in oil. Wash, stem and finely chop the sorrel leaves and add to the onion. Add garlic which has been crushed and rubbed together with salt, and the sliced tomatoes or tomato puree. Mix thoroughly and boil.
Put the sautéed fish in a deep saucepan

or skillet. Pour over the mixture of vegetables and greens, level off, cover with a lid and braise for one hour. Serve hot or cold. Top each piece of fish with the sorrel. Garnish with olives and a slice of lemon. Sprinkle with the minced parsley or dill.

Sole, Scad or Catfish and Sorrel Stew

Substitute any of these fish for cod in the above recipe. Scad is fried whole without head and tail.

Bass and Vegetables Stewed in Pickle Brine

600 g bass	1 tblsp butter
50 g celeriac	Dash of nutmeg
50 g parsley	(optional)
500 g pickle brine	4-5 peppercorns
120 g grape wine	4-5 whole allspice
1 tblsp flour	Herbs

Cut the unskinned fish into portions (with or without bones). Shred or dice the parsley and celeriac and spread on the bottom of a deep saucepan. Put in the fish and sprinkle with grated nutmeg, freshly ground black pepper and allspice. Add boiled and strained pickle brine and dry wine to barely cover the fish. Cover the saucepan and simmer from 25 to 30 minutes. Drain the stock into another saucepan, heat to the boiling point and stir in the flour which has been blended with creamed butter. Stir until smooth and heat until thick. Taste to correct seasoning with salt, pickle brine or wine. Pour the sauce onto the fish and heat but do not boil. Serve with boiled rice or potatoes; pour the sauce over the fish and sprinkle with minced parsley.

**Codfish, Scad, Sole or Catfish and Vegetables
Stewed in Pickle Brine**

Any of these fish may be substituted in
the above recipe.

Sole Stewed with Onion and Green Peppers

500 g sole	600 g fish stock
1 tblsp flour	(or water)
120 g onion	3 cloves garlic
120 g green peppers	Salt, pepper
3 tblsps vegetable oil	Herbs
200 g tomatoes	

Shred the onion and sauté in vegetable
oil. Add the peppers which have been
seeded and cut into strips. Sauté 5-10 minutes. Add the peeled, cut and seeded
tomatoes. Pour in the fish stock and bring
to the boil. Cut the fish into portions,
sprinkle with salt and pepper and dredge
with flour. Sauté the fish and then lay in
the stock and vegetables. Add the garlic
which has been crushed and rubbed together with salt, parsley and celery.
Simmer for 15 minutes. Serve with a
garnishing of boiled potatoes; pour over
pan sauce and sprinkle with the minced
herbs.
Lemon rind may be substituted for onion.
Shred the rind, scald it and sauté in
vegetable oil.

Stewed Sprats

500 g sprats	2 1/2 tblsps weak (3%)
2 1/2 tblsps vegetable oil	vinegar
	Salt

Prepare the sprats, sprinkle with salt and
arrange in a saucepan not more than three
deep (backs downward). Pour vinegar
and oil over each layer of sprats. Cover
the saucepan with a lid and cook in a
hot water bath for 2 to 3 hours. Serve hot
with boiled potatoes, or cold with vinegret or potato salad.

Sprats Stewed in Milk

500 g sprats	400 g milk
120 g onion	40 g vegetable oil

Clean the fresh sprats. Lay them in a
saucepan two deep alternating with layers of sliced onion. Pour over cold milk
and vegetable oil. Cover the saucepan
with a lid. Simmer for 1 to 1 1/2 hours.
Serve with the milk and onion. Garnish
with boiled potatoes.

Sprats Stewed Whole

600 g sprats	40 g weak vinegar
120 g onion	(2%)
40 g vegetable oil	200 g fish stock or
2 bay leaves	water
Salt	Dash of black pepper

Clean the sprats, remove the intestines
and wash thoroughly. Sprinkle with salt
and lay two deep (bellies upward) in a
buttered saucepan. Alternate each layer
with shredded onion; sprinkle with pepper and put in the bay leaves. Pour over
oil. Add water or fish stock and vinegar.
Cover with a lid and simmer for 1 to
1 1/2 hours. Garnish with boiled potatoes.

Sprats in Sorrel Sauce

500 g sprats	250 g sorrel
25 g flour	20 g parsley greens
80 g vegetable oil	or dill
100 g onion	20 g garlic
60 g tomato puree or	200 g fish stock
300 g fresh tomatoes	Salt

Prepare the sprats. Dredge with flour and sauté in oil. Lay one deep in a saucepan. Pour sorrel sauce over and braise for 40 to 50 minutes. Garnish with boiled or fried potatoes sprinkled with finely minced dill or parsley.

Sorrel Sauce

Add slightly browned onion, tomato puree, stemmed sorrel leaves, green parsley and the garlic (crushed and rubbed with salt) to the water or fish stock. Bring to the boil and simmer for 10 to 15 minutes.

Crucian Carp in Sour Cream

600 g crucian carp	Carrot
400 g fish forcemeat	Dill
300 g sour cream sauce	Salt, pepper
Onion	

Scale, remove the intestines, wash and sprinkle the fish with salt and stand for one hour. Put the fish, onion, carrot and condiment in the fish pot and pour over stock. Bring to the boil and cook for 15 to 20 minutes. Pour over sour cream sauce (see recipe for sturgeon baked in sour cream). Garnish with rounds of telnoye[27].

Salt Roach Stewed in Sour Cream

600 g salt roach	120 g sour cream
25 g flour	Green onions and
40 g vegetable oil	greens
400 g boiled fish sauce	

Wash the soaked salt roach and dry it with a towel. Dust with flour and fry in vegetable oil till brown and crisp on both sides. Bake in the oven till done. Arrange the fried fish slantwise in a single row in a casserole. Pour over boiled fish sauce and sour cream. Cover with a lid and braise for 20 to 25 minutes. Serve the fish with the sauce poured over and sprinkled with the minced parsley, dill and green onions. Garnish with wheat, barley or buckwheat cereal, boiled, fried or mashed potatoes.

Dried Roach and Onion Stewed in Milk

400 g dried roach	400 g milk
200 g onion or green onions	Minced greens

Skin the dried fish. Remove the head, fins and intestines. Wash and stand in cold water for 1 hour. Wash again. Put the roach in a saucepan, sprinkle with minced onion (or green onions), pour in hot milk and simmer for 30 to 40 minutes. Serve the fish together with the milk and onion. Sprinkle with minced green parsley. Garnish with buttered beans, boiled or mashed potatoes.

Fried Fish

Fish steaks for pan or deep frying should be cut no more than 3 cm thick; fry small fish whole. Before frying soak the steaks in milk to which salt and a dash of pepper have been added (1/4 cupful of milk, 1/2 tsp salt) for 15 to 20 minutes; then dredge with flour or bread crumbs.

Fried Fish

750 g fish or 500 g filleted fish	Flour
	Salt, pepper
2 tblsps vegetable oil	Minced parsley or dill

Prepare the fish, make a slit in the skin, sprinkle with salt and pepper and roll in flour. Fry the fish in the oil browning on both sides, then oven-fry 10 minutes. Before serving sprinkle with minced parsley or dill. Garnish with fried potatoes, buckwheat or barley kasha[18], salad of sauerkraut or red cabbage, cucumbers, pickles or tomatoes. Pass tomato sauce.

Fried Sturgeon with Tomatoes and Onions

750 g fish (500 g fillet of sturgeon)	2 tblsps flour
	3 tblsps butter
1/4 cupful milk	Salt, pepper
4 tomatoes	Minced parsley
1 onion	or dill

Dip the prepared fish in milk to which salt and pepper have been added. Roll in the flour. Fry the fish in butter. Wash and cut the tomatoes in half. Sprinkle with salt and pepper and fry separately. (Canned tomatoes may be used). Clean and cut the onion into rings and also fry separately. Serve the fish on a hot platter with fried onions heaped on each piece and the tomatoes on both sides. Pour the butter over the fish. Sprinkle with minced green parsley or dill. Garnish with boiled or fried potatoes or fried marrow.

Fried Breaded Fish

750 g fish (500 g filleted fish)	1/2 cupful bread crumbs
1/4 cupful milk	100 g frying fat
2 tblsps flour	Lemon
1 egg	Salt, pepper

Wash the prepared fish and wipe with a cloth. Sprinkle with salt and pepper and roll each piece in flour. Dip in slightly beaten egg to which the milk has been added and then roll in bread crumbs. Fry the fish for 10 to 15 minutes before serving. Serve on a hot platter garnished with lemon slices and parsley greens. Mayonnaise and gherkins sauce or hot tomato sauce may be substituted for lemon. Serve garnished with salad, apple pickles, or mashed potatoes.

Fried Breaded Zander, Bream, Carp, Crucian Carp, Navaga, Tench, Smelt or Sturgeon

Any of these or other fish may be used in the above recipe.

Fish Fried in Batter

500 g filleted fish	3 tblsps vegetable oil
2 eggs	Juice of 1/2 lemon
1/2 cupful milk or water	Salt, pepper
	Fat for frying
5 tblsps flour	Minced parsley or dill

In a bowl sift together flour and salt. Combine with 2 tblsps oil or melted butter, stir in water and mix until smooth. Cover the batter and set aside.
Cut the fillet into pieces 1 cm thick and 5 to 7 cm long. Sprinkle with salt, pepper and minced parsley (or dill); pour over the lemon juice and 1 tblsp oil, mix and set aside for about 1/2 hour to marinate.
Ten to fifteen minutes before service, beat the egg whites stiff and fold into the batter. Dip each piece of fish in the batter and fry in enough hot fat to completely cover the fish. When brown on both sides, remove to a rack to drain. Serve on a paper napkin. Decorate with parsley greens and lemon slices. Pass mayonnaise and gherkin sauce or hot to-

mato sauce separately. Garnish with salad or buttered boiled potatoes.

Fried Codfish with Green Peppers and Tomatoes

500 g codfish	200 g green peppers
25 g flour	20 g lemon rind
80 g vegetable oil	Salt, pepper
600 g fresh tomatoes	

Shred, scald and drain the lemon rind and sauté slightly in the vegetable oil. Add the peppers cut into thin strips. Slightly brown the tomato sliced 1 cm thick. Cut the filleted codfish into portions, sprinkle with salt and pepper, roll in flour and sauté in oil. Lay the fried fish on the fried tomatoes and the peppers and lemon rind, on the fish. Serve garnished with rice.

Codfish and Onion Fricassée

500 g filleted codfish	Salt, pepper, minced
200 g onion	greens
60 g vegetable oil	

Cut the filleted codfish into small pieces. Dredge with salt and pepper. Slice the onion thin and sauté in the oil until golden yellow. Add the fish and fry until tender. Serve garnished with fried potatoes; sprinkle with the minced greens.

Sautéed Codfish

800 g codfish	1 1/2 cupsful tomato
125 g vegetable oil	sauce
2 onions	60 g cheese
2 cloves garlic	1 tsp minced parsley
20 olives	greens
	Salt to taste

Cut the fish into steaks. Sauté in oil till golden yellow and transfer to a hot platter. Finely slice the onion and garlic and sauté in the oil. Add the tomato sauce and parsley. Bring to the boil and pour over the fish. Sprinkle with the grated cheese and garnish with the olives.

Stuffed Sole

1 kg sole	1/3 cupful crayfish tails
1 tsp minced parsley	1/2 lemon
3 tblsps bread crumbs	1 egg
3 tblsps butter	Salt, pepper, nutmeg

Clean the fish and slit down one side. Prepare the dressing as follows: mix together 2 tblsps butter, 2 tblsps crumbs, parsley, crayfish tails, slightly beaten egg, dash of grated nutmeg, salt and pepper. Reserve a little egg to brush the fish. Stuff the dressing into the fish beneath the fillet leaving the centre open. Melt the remaining butter in a skillet and put in the fish which has been brushed with egg and sprinkled with dry bread crumbs. Bake in moderate oven 7-10 minutes.

Sole or Halibut Fried with Tomatoes

500 g sole or halibut	600 g tomatoes
60 g vegetable oil or	Salt, pepper
boiled butter	Minced parsley
25 g flour	

Cut the skinned and boned fish into portions. Sprinkle with salt and pepper, and roll in flour. Fry in vegetable oil or boiled butter. Peel the tomatoes, cut in halves, remove the seeds and fry. Serve in the frying pan topped with the tomatoes.

Sole or Halibut Fricassée

600 g filleted sole or halibut	600 g fried potatoes
25 g flour	400 g tomatoes
120 g vegetable oil	4 g garlic
or boiled butter	Salt, pepper
200 g onion	Minced parsley

Cut the fillet of sole or halibut into large noodle-like strips. Sprinkle with salt and pepper, and roll in flour. Sauté in the vegetable oil or boiled butter. When the fish is done mix with the potatoes and onions which have been fried separately. Serve garnished with halves of fried tomatoes. Sprinkle with mixture of the minced parsley and garlic.

Sole or Halibut Fried with Onions, Mushrooms and Gherkins

600 g sole or halibut	30 g onion
25 g flour	20 g gherkins
100 g boiled butter	30 g mushrooms
or vegetable oil	Salt, pepper
15 g butter	Minced parsley

Chop the onion and mushrooms fine and slightly sauté each separately in the boiled butter or vegetable oil. Sprinkle the fish with salt and pepper, roll in flour and fry. Serve on sautéed onion. Garnish with boiled potatoes. Shoestring the gherkins and add to the mushrooms. Brown slightly in butter. While hot, spread over the fish. Sprinkle with the minced parsley.

Deep Fried Floured Sole or Halibut

500 g sole or halibut	2 slices of lemon
25 g flour	Salt, pepper
40 g milk	Minced parsley
Fat for deep frying	

Soak pieces of fish in milk. Sprinkle with salt and pepper and roll in flour. Fry in deep fat. Serve garnished with fried potatoes. Garnish with 2 slices of lemon. Sprinkle with the minced parsley.

Deep Fried Crumbed Sole or Halibut

500 g sole or halibut	200 g mayonnaise or
25 g flour	40 g tomato sauce or
80 g dry bread crumbs	2 slices of lemon
Fat for deep frying	Salt
1 egg	Pepper
1/3 cupful milk	

Cut the fish into portions. Sprinkle with salt and pepper and roll in flour. Dip into beaten egg which has been combined with milk, salt and pepper. Roll in dried bread crumbs and shake off any that do not adhere. Fry in deep fat till golden brown. Garnish with lemon and serve with fried potatoes. Instead of the lemon, tomato sauce or mayonnaise and gherkins may be served separately.

Fried Halibut

Cut the halibut into portions. Dampen with vinegar, sprinkle with salt and pepper and set aside for 2 hours. Roll in flour as directed in the above recipes and fry.

Deep Fried Crumbed Navaga

500 g navaga	80 g dry bread crumbs
25 g flour	Fat for deep frying
1 egg	2 slices of lemon

Crumb the fish as directed in the recipe for deep fried crumbed sole. Fry in deep fat until almost done, then put the fish into a well-heated oven for 2 or 3 minutes. Garnish with the lemon and serve with fried potatoes.

Sprats Fried with Tomato Paste

400 g filleted sprats	40 g vegetable oil
40 g tomato paste	25 g butter
25 g flour	Minced dill
1 egg	Salt
40 g dry bread crumbs	

Spread tomato paste on the inside of one fillet, sprinkle with salt and cover with the other fillet. Roll the two fillets in flour, dip in beaten egg and then roll in dry bread crumbs. Fry in the vegetable oil until done. Serve with garnishing of fried or boiled potatoes. Sprinkle with the minced dill.

Fried Sprats

500 g sprats	60 g vegetable oil
1 egg	or fat
15 g flour	300 g tomato sauce
Salt	

Clean, wash and dry the sprats with a cloth. Sprinkle with salt then dip in egg and flour batter. Melt the butter in a skillet and fry the sprats. Serve with boiled or mashed potatoes or stewed green peas. Separately pass tomato sauce.

Smoked Sprats and Egg

400 g hot smoked sprats	40 g butter or vegetable oil
4 eggs	

Remove the heads and intestines and skin the sprats. Heat the sprats in individual frying pans with butter. Pour beaten egg over the fish, cover with a lid and fry.

Broiled Sprats

600 g sprats	
20 g vegetable oil	
30 g butter	

Clean the sprats. Remove the intestines and gills; leave the head. Wash and dry with a cloth. Brush with oil. Put the fish on a hot grate over charcoals. Turn to brown evenly. Sprats may also be broiled strung on a wire by the head and hung over hot charcoals. When done, dip the sprats into hot salt water (120 g salt per litre of water) for a few seconds. Serve with fried potatoes.

Sprats Fried in Batter

350 g filleted sprats	2 eggs
20 g vegetable oil	1/2 cupful milk
10 g minced parsley	Fat for deep frying
120 g flour	300 g tomato sauce or
Lemon juice	200 g mayonnaise
4 g sugar	Salt, pepper

Sprinkle the boned fillets with salt and set aside for 10 to 15 minutes. Then sprinkle with lemon juice, pour over the vegetable oil, dredge with pepper and finely minced parsley. Stack the fillets and set aside to chill for at least half an hour. Before frying, roll up the fillets from the tail towards the head skin inward. Pin each roll with a wooden toothpick. Make a batter of milk, salt, sugar, 1 tsp vegetable oil and flour; mix until smooth. Fold in the egg whites beaten stiff. Dip the rolled fillets in the batter and fry in deep fat heated to 160°-170°C (320°-356°F) until the crust is golden brown. If the fish requires extra cooking, after frying put it in a hot oven to bake for a few minutes. Remove the toothpicks and serve at once on a platter lined with a paper napkin. Pass tomato sauce.

Salt Herring Cutlets

Soak in milk 4 medium-sized herrings then skin and bone them. Put the fillets through the meat grinder together with dry white bread that has been soaked in milk and squeezed dry. Add two slightly beaten raw eggs, two tblsps heavy sour cream and minced dill. Mix thoroughly. Shape into cutlets, brush with raw egg, roll in dried bread crumbs and fry in boiled butter. Serve with fried potatoes.

Fried Salt Roach

600 g salt roach	40 g vegetable oil
25 g flour	Minced parsley or dill

Soak the roach for 3-4 hours then wash, wipe and roll in flour. Fry in the oil, brown both sides. Put the pan in a hot oven and bake until tender. Serve garnished with fried potatoes, mashed potatoes, or stewed cabbage. Sprinkle with the minced parsley.

Fried Salt Cod, Zander, Bream or Carp-like Fish

Any of these fish may be substituted in the above recipe.

Fried Sprats with Onion

300 g sprats	80 g onion
40 g flour	Salt
60 g vegetable oil	

Wash the sprats in cold water and drain thoroughly in a colander. Sprinkle with salt.
Heat the oil in a skillet and fry the sliced onion. Roll the fish in flour and fry immediately. Stirring carefully, fry over high heat until done. Serve with fried potatoes or boiled potatoes, cucumber, tomato or sauerkraut.

Fried Anchovies or Sardelles

Either of these may be substituted in the above recipe for sprats.

Deep Fried Floured Anchovies

400 g anchovies	Fat for deep frying
40 g flour	Salt

Prepare the fish as directed in the recipe for sprats fried with onion. Heat the fat to 160-170°C. Roll the fish in the flour. Fry over high heat for 5 to 6 minutes then drain in a wire strainer. Serve immediately. Garnish with beans in tomato sauce or fried potatoes. Sauerkraut or pickled vegetables may be passed (beets, cabbage, tomatoes, watermelon, etc.).

Deep Fried Floured Sardelles, Sprats or Sparlings (Smelts)

Substitute any of these fish for anchovies in the above recipe.

Fish Cutlets or Patties

500 g fillet of zander, pike or cod	3 tblsps dried bread crumbs
125 g day-old white bread	4 tblsps vegetable oil
1/2 cupful milk	4 tblsps butter
50 g onion (optional)	1/8 tsp pepper

Grind the skinned and boned fillet. Mix with bread which has been soaked in milk and squeezed dry, add salt and pepper and, if desired, minced onion. Put through the mincer again once or twice. Cream the butter and combine thoroughly with the mixture. Shape into cutlets or round patties and roll or dust with bread crumbs. Fry in oil for 10-15 minutes or until golden brown on both sides then bake for 5-7 minutes in a hot oven. Serve on a hot platter. Garnish with buttered or creamed peas, beans, cauliflower or any other vegetable. Pass tomato, red or sour cream sauce with tomato paste and onion.

Stuffed Fish Cutlets

Prepare forcemeat as for fish cutlets (see above), divide, shape into rounds 1 cm thick and place on a wet cloth or towel. Put the stuffing on one half of the round, fold over the other half and pinch the edges together. With the towel, shape the cutlet into a half-moon. Brush with egg, roll in sifted white bread crumbs and fry.

Stuffing I

200 g fresh mushrooms or 50 g dried mushrooms	50 g bread crumbs
100 g onion	15 g parsley
	Salt to taste

Chop up and sauté the mushrooms, add fried onion, bread crumbs, salt and pepper to taste. If dried mushrooms are used, soak for 3-4 hours and cook until tender before using.

Stuffing II

75 g fresh mushrooms or 25 g dried mushrooms	1 hard-cooked egg
100 g cartilage or boiled fish	50 g butter
	15 g parsley
	Salt to taste
	175 g onion

Chop up the egg fine, add the fried onion, cooked mushrooms, cartilage of sturgeon fish or steamed fish cut up, parsley and salt to taste.

Stuffing III

2 hard-cooked eggs	15 g parsley
200 g onion	50 g butter
50 g bread crumbs	Salt

Shred the eggs, add bread crumbs, fried onion, parsley and salt to taste.
Serve stuffed fish cutlets garnished with green peas.

Forcemeat Fish Loaf

(Telnoye)

"Telnoye" in Russian cookery is the name for forcemeat made of fish. Reference to this dish is found in manuscripts that date back to the 16th and 17th century.

400 g filleted fish	1 tblsp butter
80 g bread	2 cloves garlic
1/2 cupful milk	1/2 egg
Salt, pepper	

Fillet of zander, catfish, pike, burbot, cod, salmon or any other fish that is not bony may be used. Put through the mincer the fish fillets, garlic and bread which has been soaked in milk and squeezed dry. Add salt, pepper, egg and creamed butter. Mix until thoroughly blended. Shape the forcemeat into a small loaf 5-6 cm thick, wrap in buttered celophane or foil and tie at the ends. Lay on the rack of a fishpan, pour over fish stock and cook for 30-40 minutes. Remove from the stock and when cold unwrap and slice. Heat in fish stock. Telnoye may be served with garnishing or as a garnishing.

Skewered Sturgeon

Cut the sturgeon into 40- to 50-g pieces. Wash in cold water and dredge with salt and pepper. Thread the pieces of sturgeon onto a metal skewer and broil over red hot coals for 6 to 10 minutes. Baste with butter. Turn so as to brown evenly. Remove from the skewer onto a hot plate, garnish with broiled tomatoes, onions and green onions and parsley.

Skewered Salmon

Substitute salmon in the above recipe.

Baked Fish

Regardless of whether the fish is put into the oven raw, fried or boiled, the oven must be well heated beforehand, otherwise the fish will turn pale yellow instead of golden brown, be dry and tasteless.

Baked Bream or Carp

500 g bream or carp	2 tblsps flour (or
1/4 cupful milk	bread crumbs)
2 tblsps butter	

Clean and wash the fish. Cut it along the backbone and then into pieces crosswise. Soak in salted milk for 2 or 3 minutes. Roll in flour or dry bread crumbs. Lay in a buttered baking pan skin upwards. Dot with butter and bake. Within 5 minutes the skin should begin to turn brown. Fish fillets will be done in 6 to 7 minutes; unboned fish, in 12 minutes. Serve in the baking dish or on a hot platter, pouring over the butter from the baking dish. Garnish with boiled or fried potatoes, cucumbers or green salad. This fish may be served cold garnished with cucumbers, tomatoes or any spiced fruits.

Zander Baked with Potatoes

600 g fillet of zander	2 tblsps dry bread
600 g potatoes	crumbs
1 tblsp flour	2-3 tblsps butter
Pepper	Salt

Cut the fish into portions, slit the skin, then sprinkle with pepper and lay in a buttered baking dish. Pare and shoestring the potatoes; wash in cold water, drain and spread over the fish. Line the sides of the baking dish with sliced potatoes. Sprinkle with salt and flour. Pour over fish stock or water, sprinkle with dry bread crumbs and melted butter. Bake for 20 to 35 minutes depending on the thickness of the layer of potatoes. Should the stock evaporate quickly, add more stock or boiled water. A layer of fried onion may be placed between the fish and the potatoes. Before serving sprinkle with minced parsley greens. Garnish with green salad with fruits and vegetables, cucumbers or pickles and sauerkraut.
If desired, sliced boiled potatoes may be used instead of raw potatoes and fish stock sauce used instead of fish stock or water.

Baked Sturgeon

500 g sturgeon	1 tblsp butter
1 tblsp sour cream	Salt, pepper

Wash the sturgeon; do not cut into pieces. Remove the cartilage and bonelike scales. Sprinkle with salt and pepper. Lay the fish in a buttered pan. Brush with sour cream and dot with butter. Pour 1/2 cupful of water into the bottom of the pan and bake for 25 to 30 minutes basting several times with the pan juice. Before serving, cut the fish into pieces crosswise and serve on a heated platter. Pour over the strained pan juice. Decorate with parsley greens. Garnish with buttered boiled potatoes or fried potatoes, a vegetable salad, cucumbers and slices of lemon. Pass mayonnaise and capers sauce.

Sturgeon, Sevruga, Beluga, Zander, Carp or Pike Baked in Sour Cream

750 g fish or 500 g	2 tblsps flour
filleted fish	4 tblsps butter
800 g potatoes	Salt, pepper
1 cupful sour cream	Minced parsley
2 eggs	200 g fresh mushrooms
25 g cheese	

Sprinkle the prepared fish with salt and pepper. Roll in flour and brown in butter. Fry the mushrooms, and the pared, washed and sliced potatoes (1/2 cm thick). Put the fish in the frying pan and top each piece with sliced hard-cooked eggs and mushrooms. Put the fried potatoes around the fish and pour over strained sour cream sauce. Sprinkle with grated cheese, pour over the melted butter and bake for 5 or 6 minutes until brown. Before serving sprinkle with minced green parsley.

Sour Cream Sauce

Bring the sour cream to a boil. Stir in one teaspoonful of flour which has been blended with one teaspoonful of butter. Stirring constantly boil for 1 or 2 minutes and then salt to taste.

Codfish Baked in Egg and Milk

500 g codfish	2 eggs
2 1/2 tblsps flour	1 1/2 cupsful milk
80 g boiled butter	600 g fried potatoes
80 g onion	Salt, pepper

Cut the filleted codfish into portions. Sprinkle with salt and pepper and roll in flour. Fry in boiled butter and then lay in a baking pan. Put the fried potatoes around the fish. Add slightly browned onion. Beat the eggs, add the milk and flour and mix. Pour over the other ingredients and bake until crust is golden yellow.

Codfish Baked in Milk Sauce

500 g codfish	25 g cheese
40 g vegetables and	600 g potatoes
spices for savoury stock	500 g milk sauce
60 g boiled butter	Salt, pepper
80 g onion	

Spread a layer of boiled or mashed potatoes on the bottom of a buttered baking dish. Over this lay portions of codfish cooked in a savoury stock. Make thin milk sauce (see p. 88). Add to it slightly browned minced onion and boil. Taste to correct seasoning. Pour the sauce over the fish, sprinkle with grated cheese and dot with butter. Brown in the oven. Serve in baking dish.

Zander Baked in Sour Cream Sauce

500 g filleted zander	500 g sauce
25 g flour	1 tsp salt
60 g boiled butter	Pepper
200 g mushrooms	Minced dill or parsley
25 g cheese	

Wash, cut up and fry champignon (meadow) or morel mushrooms. Flour the portions of filleted fish and fry. Transfer to a baking dish, surround with fried mushrooms and pour over the sour cream sauce (see p. 81). Sprinkle with grated cheese and dot with butter. Bake till the crust is golden brown. Before serving sprinkle with the minced dill or parsley.

Codfish, Pike, Catfish, Bass or Burbot Baked in Sour Cream Sauce

Substitute any of these fish in the above recipe.

Pike Baked in Onion Sauce with Mushrooms

500 g pike	20 g dry bread crumbs
40 g vegetables and	600 g potatoes
spices for savoury stock	500 g sauce
30 g butter	Salt, pepper

Boil the portions of filleted pike in a savoury stock. Lay the fish in a frying pan and surround with the sliced boiled potatoes. Pour over the onion sauce with mushrooms. Sprinkle with bread crumbs and butter. Bake to a golden brown. Serve in a baking dish.

Codfish, Zander, Catfish or Burbot in Onion Sauce with Mushrooms

Substitute any of these fish in the above recipe.

Sturgeon Baked with Potatoes and Onions

500 g sturgeon	60 g vegetable oil,
600 g potatoes	butter, margarine or
80 g onion	boiled butter
600 g sauce	Pepper, salt
20 g dry bread crumbs	Minced green parsley

Cut the fish into portions and lay in a buttered casserole. Sprinkle with salt and

pepper. Add finely cut and slightly browned onions. Cover with slices of boiled or raw potatoes. Pour over thin white sauce. Sprinkle with dry bread crumbs and dot with butter. Bake till done. Sprinkle with the minced parsley. Serve in casserole.

Sevruga, Beluga, Sole or Halibut Baked with Potatoes and Onions

Substitute any of these fish in the above recipe.

Sturgeon Baked with Tomatoes

600 g sturgeon	25 g cheese
400 g tomatoes	20 g butter or butter
120 g mushrooms	margarine
40 g crabmeat	1 tsp salt
600 g tomato sauce	Minced parsley or dill

Steam the fish and place in a baking pan. Surround with halves of browned tomatoes. Top with cooked mushrooms and crabmeat. Pour over tomato sauce (see p. 88) with the mushrooms and vegetables. Sprinkle with grated cheese and butter. Bake till brown. Sprinkle with the minced parsley or dill and serve in the baking dish.

Sevruga, Beluga, Sole or Halibut Baked with Tomatoes

Substitute any of these fish in the above recipe.

Sole or Halibut Baked with Kasha[18]

1 kg sole or halibut	20 g cheese
25 g flour	600 g prepared kasha
80 g butter, butter	500 g sour cream sauce
margarine or	Minced dill or parsley
vegetable oil	

Prepare the fish. Dredge with flour and fry in vegetable oil. Put fluffy buckwheat, rice or wheat kasha in a frying pan. Lay the fried fish on the kasha. Pour over the sour cream sauce (see p. 81), sprinkle with grated cheese and dot with butter. Brown in the oven. Sprinkle with minced parsley or dill before serving.

Sole or Halibut Baked in Milk Sauce

600 g sole or halibut	40 g crabmeat
20 g onion	4 oysters
20 g parsley	400 g milk sauce
40 g dry white wine	4 egg yolks
60 g mushrooms	40 g butter
25 g cheese	Salt

Steam the fish in a stock to which the white wine, parsley and onion have been added. Lay the fish on a platter and garnish with cooked mushrooms, crabmeat and oysters. Add the fish liquor to the milk sauce, bring to a boil and remove from the heat. Add the raw egg yolk and mix. Taste to correct seasoning. Pour the sauce over the fish. Sprinkle with grated cheese and butter. Brown in a hot oven and serve immediately.

Sole or Halibut with Spinach

Clean and wash the fish. Steam in a stock to which white wine has been added. Steam the spinach in butter and spread it on a platter. Put the fish on the spinach. Pour over milk sauce, sprinkle with grated cheese and butter. Brown quickly in a hot oven.

Fish with Sauerkraut
(Fish Solyanka)

500 g filleted fish	1 cupful fish liquor
2 tblsps butter	(or water)
2 tblsps tomato puree	50 g capers
2 tblsps dry bread crumbs	50 g olives
2 pickled cucumbers	2 onions
2 bay leaves	Salt, pepper

Stewed Sauerkraut (or Cabbage)

1 kg sauerkraut (or cabbage)	2 tblsps tomato puree
2 1/2 tblsps butter or drippings	1 onion
	1 tblsp sugar
	1 tblsp flour

Prepare the sauerkraut (or cabbage) as directed in the recipe for solyanka (see p. 93).
Clean the fish (sturgeon, sevruga or sterlet) and cut into 40- to 50-gram pieces. Put the fish in a separate saucepan and sprinkle with salt and pepper. Add the capers, peeled and sliced pickled cucumbers from which the seeds have been removed, tomato puree, sliced onions slightly sautéed in butter, the fish liquor (or water) and bay leaves. Mix these ingredients, cover with a lid and simmer for 15 to 20 minutes. Taking care not to break up the pieces of fish, stir in the flour which has been combined with a teaspoonful of butter. Boil for 10 minutes.
Spread one third of the stewed sauerkraut in an even layer on the bottom of a frying pan. Put the fish mixture on top, pour over the fish juice and cover with the rest of the sauerkraut. Smooth the top, sprinkle with dry bread crumbs and dot with butter. Heat thoroughly in the

oven for 8 to 10 minutes. Garnish the solyanka with olives, lemon slices, pickled cherries, grapes, plums or red bilberries and green parsley.

Navaga Baked with Spinach in Milk Sauce

600 g filleted navaga	25 g cheese
20 g parsley	40 g butter
20 g onion	400 g milk sauce
800 g fresh spinach	Pepper, salt

Parboil the spinach and drain off all extra moisture. Cut it up and heat in butter. Season with salt and pepper. Parboil the filleted navaga in the stock to which parsley and onion have been added. Make milk sauce (see p. 88) of medium thickness and add to it the fish stock. Bring to a boil and strain. Put the seasoned spinach on a platter and lay the fish on it. Pour over the milk sauce, sprinkle with grated cheese and dot with butter. Brown in the oven.

Codfish, Pike, Burbot or Catfish Baked with Spinach in Milk Sauce

Any of these fish may be substituted in the above recipe.

Sprat Pudding

500 g sprats	25 g cheese
60 g salt pork	30 g butter
600 g potatoes	1 tsp salt
320 g milk	Minced greens
1 egg	40 g flour
100 g onion	

Prepare the sprats. Cover the bottom of the frying or baking tin with thinly sliced salt pork. Add an even layer of potatoes sliced 1/2 cm thick and put the sprats over the potatoes. Top with another layer of sliced potatoes. Pour over the milk which has been combined with the flour, beaten egg and finely chopped onion. Sprinkle with grated cheese or dried bread crumbs. Bake in oven till done. Before serving pour over melted butter and sprinkle with minced parsley.

Sprat Roll

400 g filleted sprats	30 g butter
1 egg yolk	Lemon rind
120 g onion	20 g dried bread
80 g bread	crumbs
20 g table margarine	Salt, pepper

Fillet the sprats and put them through the food chopper twice. Add white bread crumbs and egg yolk, chopped onion, salt, a little grated lemon rind, and freshly ground pepper to taste. Mix thoroughly. Fold in the egg whites beaten stiff. Shape into a loaf and transfer to a buttered baking pan. Sprinkle with the dried bread crumbs, dot with butter and bake. Garnish with mashed potatoes or green peas in milk sauce.

Fresh Herring Baked with Egg

400 g herring	80 g onion or green
25 g flour	onions
40 g vegetable oil	Salt, pepper
4 eggs	Minced greens
80 g sour cream	

Sprinkle salt and pepper over the filleted fresh herring. Flour and fry the fillets in vegetable oil or boiled butter. Lay the fried fish in an oval metal platter or baking dish. Beat the eggs and mix with sour cream and chopped raw onion or minced green onions. Add salt. Pour over the herring and bake.

Before serving sprinkle with the minced greens.

Herring Forshmak

400 g salt herring	40 g vegetable oil
300 g dry bread	120 g sour cream
300 g milk	20 g dry bread crumbs
80 g onion	Nutmeg, pepper

Soak the salt herring in cold water for 24 to 30 hours. Clean, fillet and skin the herring. Put the fillets through the meat chopper together with the dry white bread (without crust) which has been soaked in milk or cream. Finely mince the onion and sauté slightly in vegetable oil. Add to the minced herring. Season with pepper, nutmeg and salt to taste. Put the mixture into a buttered baking pan dusted with dry bread crumbs. Smooth the top, brush with sour cream, sprinkle with bread crumbs, butter and bake until it leaves the sides of the pan. Before serving pour over sour cream.

Herring Pudding
(Herring Zapekanka)

400 g salt herring	1 tblsp sour cream
200 g bread	20 g dry bread crumbs
200 g milk	300 g sauce or 120 g
200 g potatoes	sour cream
2 eggs	Minced greens
80 g onion	Salt
20 g butter	Pepper

Fillet and skin the soaked salt herring. Mix the fillets with the white bread which has been soaked in milk or cream, boiled potatoes and a raw egg and put through

the meat grinder. Add grated or finely chopped onion and salt and pepper to taste. Mix thoroughly. Butter a baking pan and dust it with dry bread crumbs. Spread the mixture in the baking pan in a layer 3 cm thick and even off the top. Brush with raw egg combined with sour cream. Bake until the top has a crust and the bottom is crisp. Cut the zapekanka into portions. Before serving pour over sour cream sauce, tomato sauce, or sour cream. Sprinkle with finely minced parsley or dill.

Baked Anchovies

250 g anchovies	600 g mashed
30 g flour	potatoes
60 g vegetable oil	20 g cheese
80 g onion	15 g dry bread
200 g red or tomato	crumbs
sauce	Minced greens

Clean and wash fresh anchovies. Fry as directed in the recipe for fried sprats with onion (see p. 78). Lay the fried anchovies in a frying pan, pour over red or tomato sauce (see p. 88) and cover with a layer of mashed potatoes. Sprinkle with dry bread crumbs mixed with grated cheese, and dot with butter. Bake until the crust is golden brown. Before serving sprinkle with minced parsley or green onions.

Baked Sardelles or Sprats

Either of these may be substituted in the above recipe.

Baked Salt Sardelles

250 g sardelles	60 g vegetable oil
600 g potatoes	20 g dry bread crumbs
80 g onion	Minced dill or parsley
200 g white sauce	

Line a buttered baking pan with half the sliced boiled potatoes. Put the fish and slightly browned onion on the potatoes and cover with the remaining potatoes. Pour over boiled fish sauce. Sprinkle with dry bread crumbs and dot with butter. Bake for 15 to 20 minutes. Before serving pour over melted butter and sprinkle with the minced parsley or dill.

Baked Salt Anchovies or Sprats

Either of these may be substituted in the above recipe.

Fish Stuffed with Kasha[18]

750 g fish (whole)	1 onion
100 g buckwheat	1 tblsp flour
kasha[18]	3 tblsps butter
2 hard-cooked eggs	Salt, pepper
1 cupful sour cream	

Clean the fish (carp or crucian carp). Cut off the head near the fins. Remove the intestines without cutting open the belly. Wash the fish thoroughly, wipe inside and out with a cloth. Rub with salt. Prepare the buckwheat kasha (see p. 133), mix it with fried onion and hard-cooked eggs and stuff the fish. Sprinkle with pepper and roll in flour. Brown in butter on a frying pan and bake for 5 or 6 minutes. Pour over sour cream and return to the oven for another 3 to 5 minutes. Baste with pan juices. Baking time will depend on oven heat and the size of the fish. Serve in the baking dish or transfer to a hot platter together with the sauce. Pass cucumbers, vegetables, fruit salad or pickled apples.

Crayfish and Crabs

Crayfish
(Plain)

10 crayfish	Sprigs of dill
1 carrot	1 tblsp salt
1 onion	Bay leaf
Sprigs of parsley	

Wash the crayfish and put them in a saucepan. Add the sliced carrot and onion, parsley, dill, bay leaf and salt. Cover with 4 or 5 cupsful of boiling water and cook for 10 minutes. Serve the crayfish in the saucepan together with the liquor, or in a deep bowl with liquor and vegetables poured over.

Crayfish in Beer

Cook as directed in the above recipe substituting beer for half the amount of water used.

Crayfish in White Wine

10 crayfish	2 tblsps butter
1 cupful white wine	Salt, pepper
1 tsp flour	2 bay leaves
1/4 tsp caraway seeds	

Wash the crayfish. Melt the butter in a saucepan. Put in the crayfish and fry until scarlet. Sprinkle with salt, pepper and ground caraway seeds. Add the bay leaves and white wine. Cover with a lid and boil for 10 minutes. Serve in a bowl or on a platter with a cover. Pass sauce separately.

Sauce

Strain the liquor into a saucepan; heat and stir in the flour which has been combined with a teaspoonful of butter. Boil for 1 or 2 minutes and remove from the heat. Add the rest of the butter and stir until it melts and blends with the sauce.

Crabmeat with Egg-and-Butter Sauce

1 can (225 g) crabmeat
600 g potatoes
Salt
1/2 cupful white table wine
3/4 cupful egg-and-butter sauce

Put the crabmeat in a saucepan. Add the wine and cover with a lid. Simmer for 5 minutes. Pare and cut the potatoes in half and cook in salt water. Lay the crabmeat in the centre of a hot round platter. Put the boiled potatoes around the crabmeat. Pour the liquor over the crabmeat. Garnish with parsley leaves. Pass egg-and-butter sauce (see below), fresh salted cucumbers or green salad.

Crabmeat Baked in Milk Sauce

1 can (225 g) crabmeat
1 cupful milk sauce
25 g grated cheese
200 g fresh mushrooms
2 tblsps butter

Pick the crabmeat and put it in a saucepan together with the juice. Add the mushrooms which have been cooked and cut and a teaspoonful of butter. Cover with a lid and simmer for 5 minutes. Transfer to a buttered baking dish. Add the grated cheese to the milk sauce of medium thickness and pour over. Reserve some of the grated cheese to sprinkle over the top. Dot with butter and bake for 5 or 6 minutes to brown. Serve immediately.

Sauces Suitable for Use with Fish

Sauce is a basic element of fish dishes for it helps vary the flavours. Many of these sauces are made with the fish stock or liquor made specially by cooking the heads (without gills), bones and trimmings. To make this liquor, wash the latter thoroughly, cover with 2 1/2 to 3 cupsful of cold water, add 1 onion and 1 parsley finely sliced. Bring to a boil, cook for 1 hour and then strain through a sieve.

Egg-and-Butter Sauce
(For use with boiled fish)

Chop up finely two hard-cooked eggs. Melt 100 g butter, add the eggs, minced parsley and juice of 1/4 lemon. Salt to taste. Combine thoroughly and pour over fish or serve in a sauceboat.

Boiled Fish Sauce
(For use with boiled or steamed fish and fish in brine)

In a saucepan brown one tablespoonful of flour combined with one tablespoonful of butter. Stirring constantly add two cupsful of fish stock and boil for 7 to 10 minutes. Salt to taste and remove from heat. Add lemon juice and a lump of butter. Stir until the butter and sauce are thoroughly blended, then strain. If the sauce is to be used with fish in brine, substitute 1 or 2 tblsps pickle brine for the lemon juice.

White Wine Sauce

(For use with steamed fish)

Clean, wash and slice thinly 1 parsley and 1 onion (medium size). Sauté in a saucepan with one tablespoonful of butter and one tablespoonful of flour. When browned, stir in 2 cupsful of fish stock. Add salt. Simmer for 7 to 10 minutes and then remove from heat. Slightly beat one egg yolk and combine thoroughly with one tablespoonful of butter. Stir into the sauce. Mix thoroughly and strain. Add 1 or 2 tablespoonsful of white table wine (or lemon juice).

Red Sauce

Combine and brown 1 tblsp flour and 1 tblsp butter. Add 1 tblsp tomato puree and then stir in 2 cupsful fish stock. Add 1 diced carrot, parsley root and 1 minced onion which have been slightly sautéed. Simmer 20-30 minutes. Add salt to taste and 1 or 2 tblsps Madeira or port wine.

Milk Sauce

Thin. Heat 1 tblsp flour. Gradually stir in 400 g hot milk, add salt and boil 5-7 minutes, then add 1 tblsp butter.
Medium. Use 400 g milk, 1 1/2 tblsps flour, 1 1/2 tblsps butter and proceed as in the recipe above.
Thick. Use 350 g milk, 2 tblsps flour, 2 tblsps butter and proceed as in the recipe above.

Tomato Sauce with Vegetables

Finely dice 100 g carrots, 1 onion and 15 g parsley root. Heat in 1 tablespoonful butter margarine in a low saucepan, then add 1 bay leaf and 3 peppercorns. Pour in 1 tablespoonful dry white wine and simmer 7-8 minutes. When 1/3 of the bulk remains, combine with tomato sauce (one half the amount made according to the above recipe) and bring to the boil. Add salt to taste and 1/2 teaspoonful lemon juice. Stir in 1 tablespoonful butter.

Tomato Sauce

(For use with boiled or steamed fish)

Clean, wash and cut up fine 1/2 carrot, 1/2 parsley and 1/2 onion. Sauté in a saucepan together with 1 tablespoonful of butter and 1 tablespoonful of flour. Add 3 tablespoonsful of tomato puree and stir in 2 cupsful fish stock. Add salt to taste. Simmer for 8 to 10 minutes and then remove from the heat. Add one tablespoonful butter, stir until thoroughly blended. Strain through a sieve.

MEAT

1 onion

1 cupful beans

parsley

200g tomatoes

lamb and beans

500g lamb

Meat is one of the most nourishing foods. It contains complete proteins, fats and extractives that help digestion. When meat is boiled it loses about 40% of its weight. The weight loss due to frying or roasting is 35-38%. In other words, one kilogram of raw meat will yield 620-650 grams of roast or fried meat.

The wide variety of packaged and ready-to-cook meat products available in the shops are great time savers and should be taken advantage of.

Beef, pork, mutton and lamb may be obtained in the form of crumbed or plain steaks, chops, escalope, forcemeat, various types of cutlets and marinated meat for shashlyk[19].

The variety of canned meat is even greater for it includes venison and the sundries and organs such as kidneys, brains and liver which can all be used in various ways.

Boiled Meat

Boiled Beef with Horseradish Sauce

500 g meat (boned)	30-40 g celery,
800 g potatoes	parsley or pasternak
2 carrots	(optional)
1 leek	5-8 peppercorns
1 turnip	(or 5-10 g whole red
Salt to taste	pepper)
2 bay leaves	

Prepare a whole piece of meat (round, rump, sirloin or brisket). Wash and pour over boiling water to cover. Close with a lid and bring to a boil, remove the scum, reduce the heat and simmer for

1 1/2 to 2 hours. Add the cleaned and sliced carrots, turnip, the white of the leek (or onion), the seasoning and, if desired add the celery, parsley or pasternak. Cook for another 1/2 hour. When the meat and vegetables are tender, drain off the stock. Cover the meat and vegetables. Use the stock to make the horseradish sauce (see p. 108). Before serving slice the meat, garnish with the vegetables and boiled potatoes. Pour over the sauce.

Corned Beef with Horseradish Sauce

500 g corned beef	1 onion
800 g potatoes	1 parsley
1 carrot	2 tblsps butter

Soak the corned beef and put the whole piece in a saucepan with cold water to cover. Bring to a boil and remove the scum. Add the onion and vegetable roots. Simmer for 2 to 3 hours. When tender slice the meat, pour over horseradish sauce. Garnish with a puree of potatoes or peas, or boiled potatoes.

Boiled Lamb in White Stock Sauce

500 g lamb	2 carrots
600 g potatoes	1 tblsp flour
1 onion	1 tblsp butter
1 turnip	Salt

Wash the meat (loin, breast or shoulder), put it in a saucepan and add boiling water to barely cover. Close with a lid and cook over low heat. When the water begins to boil skim and then simmer for 30 to 40 minutes. Add the vegetables and salt. Simmer for another 30 to 40 minutes. When done, remove the meat and vegetables from the broth. Slice the lamb thin. Garnish with boiled potatoes and sliced vegetables. Pour over the sauce made with the flour, butter and broth.

Lamb and Beans

500 g lamb	2 tblsps butter
1 cupful beans	Salt, pepper
1 onion	Minced parsley
200 g tomatoes	

Cut the meat into small pieces. Brush with salt and pepper and sauté in butter. Put the browned meat in a shallow saucepan, add the beans which have been soaked for 1 1/2 h. Pour in 2 1/2 to 3 cupsful of water and simmer for about an hour. Add the onion which has been slightly sautéed, and the sliced tomatoes. Braise for 30 to 40 minutes. Before serving, sprinkle with minced parsley.

Tongue in White Stock Sauce with Raisins

1 ox tongue	100 g raisins
1 carrot	1 tblsp flour
1 parsnip	Salt
1 onion	Lemon juice
2 tblsps butter	

Place the tongue in a saucepan together with the sliced vegetables. Season with salt. Add hot water to cover and cook for 2 to 3 hours. When the tongue is tender, rinse in cold water and immediately skin. Make a sauce with the liquor. Combine the flour with one tablespoonful of butter and brown slightly. Stir in 1 1/4 cupful of strained liquor and bring it to a boil. Add the raisins and simmer for 5 to 10 minutes. Remove from the heat, add salt and lemon juice to taste and beat in butter. Before serving slice the tongue, garnish with green peas, macaroni, stewed cabbage, puree of potatoes or peas. Pour the sauce over. Pork tongue may be cooked in the same manner (cooking time should be 1 to 2 hours).

Corned Tongue with Garnishing

Scrub the tongue, place it in a saucepan and add cold water to cover. Add vegetable roots and onion. Boil for 3 to 3 1/2 hours over low heat. When the tongue is tender, remove it from the saucepan, rinse in cold water and immediately skin. Slice the tongue and pour over 2 or 3 tblsps of the liquor and melted butter. Garnish with buttered peas, stewed cabbage, puree of potatoes or peas.

Boiled Tripe

Wash the tripe thoroughly, scald, scrape with a knife and rinse in cold water. Cut into large squares or roll up and tie with string. Add cold water and bring to a boil. Add salt, pepper, bay leaf, one carrot, one parsley and one onion. Simmer for 4 to 5 hours.
Cut the cooked tripe into noodle-like strips. Pour over white stock sauce made with the liquor. If desired, tomato paste may be added to the sauce. Tripe may be served cold; separately pass horseradish and vinegar sauce, cucumbers or pickles, tomato salad or coleslaw.

Casseroled Meat

Beef Stew

500 g round, rump or	1 parsley
sirloin of beef (boned)	2 or 3 bay leaves
1 tblsp tomato puree	2 tblsps butter
1 carrot	8-10 peppercorns or
1 onion	sliver of hot pepper
1 tblsp flour	Salt

Wash, wipe dry and salt a whole piece of meat. Sear in a skillet or frying pan until brown. Transfer to a casserole. Add the tomato puree, washed and sliced vegetables and seasoning. Cover with 3-4 cupsful of stock or hot water. Close with a lid and braise for 2 to 2 1/2 hours. Stir in the flour which has been combined with 1 tblsp butter and a little stock. Continue to cook for another 30 to 40 minutes over low heat. Slice the meat before serving. Strain and season the gravy with salt. Pour over the meat. Serve with a garnishing of fried potatoes, baked apples, stewed cabbage. Pass cucumbers, salad or pickled fruit or berries.

Beef Stew with Onions and Potatoes

500 g round or rump	1 bay leaf
of beef	2 cloves
800 g potatoes	5 or 6 peppercorns (or
2 or 3 onions	sliver of hot pepper)
1 tblsp flour	Salt, pepper
2 tblsps butter	Minced parsley or dill

Wash and cut the meat into pieces (80-150 g each). Dredge each piece with salt and pepper and roll in flour. Brown on all sides. Put the meat in a casserole. Pour one cupful of water into the skillet, bring to a boil and strain into the casserole. Add 2 more cupsful of boiling water, cover with a lid and simmer for 2 to 2 1/2 hours on a slow fire. Add chopped and sautéed onion, browned chunks of potatoes and seasoning. Braise the meat for another half an hour. Before serving sprinkle with minced parsley or dill. Pass cucumbers, green or tomato salad.

Casserole of Beef

(Zharkoye)

600 g beef	60 g tomato puree or
20 g rendered fat	200 g sour cream
400 g potatoes	15 g flour
200 g carrots	Bay leaf, pepper,
200 g turnips	cloves, cinnamon, mint
120 g onion	

Cut the meat into portions, pound slightly and sauté together with onion. Slice the carrots, turnips and potatoes. Put the seared meat into a stoneware pot or casserole, add the meat juices, a little stock, seasoning and vegetables. Cover tightly. Braise until done. Drain off part of the juices, stir into browned flour and pour back into casserole. Add tomato puree or sour cream. Cook the meat till tender.

Casserole of Beef with Kvass[14]

600 g beef	2 1/2 cupsful kvass[14]
40 g rendered fat	80 g bread crumbs
120 g onion	Salt, pepper and other
150 g carrots	spices
60 g tomato puree	

Cut the meat into portions, finely slice the carrots and onions. Sauté the meat, onions and carrots. Sprinkle with salt and pepper. When browned, add tomato puree. Transfer to a stoneware pot or casserole, add kvass, bread crumbs and spices. Braise until done. Serve garnished with boiled potatoes.

Meat Stew with Sauerkraut
(Solyanka)

200 g boiled or canned meat, minced ham or sausage	1 kg sauerkraut
	2 pickled cucumbers
	2 onions
3 tblsps tomato puree	Vinegar, sugar, salt
1 tblsp bread crumbs	Bay leaf, pepper
1 tblsp flour	1/2 cupful meat stock
1 tblsp capers	(or water)
2-3 tblsps butter	

Add to the sauerkraut 1 tblsp butter and meat stock and braise for 40 minutes. Then add one fried onion, tomato puree, vinegar, sugar, salt, bay leaf and pepper and simmer for another 10 minutes. Stir in the flour which has been browned in butter. Mix and bring to a boil. Cut the meat into small cubes, sauté together with onion to a light yellow, add sliced pickles, capers, and 2 or 3 tblsps meat stock. Cover with a lid and boil for several minutes.

Spread half the prepared sauerkraut in a casserole. Lay the meat and garnishing on it and cover with the remaining sauerkraut. Level and sprinkle with bread crumbs and dot with butter. Bake for 10 to 15 minutes to brown. Garnish with sprigs of parsley, olives or bilberries.

Country Beef Stew, Georgian Manner

400-500 g tenderloin, short loin or rump of beef	1/4 cupful grape wine
	2 or 3 tblsps butter
	Clove of garlic
2 onions	Salt
2 pickled cucumbers	Minced parsley
2 tblsps tomato puree	

Wash the meat. Remove the tendons and cut into small pieces. Add finely cut onion and sauté in butter. Transfer to a shallow saucepan. Add tomato puree, peeled and sliced pickled cucumbers, clove of garlic, salt, wine and two or three tablespoonsful of meat stock. Cover with a lid and simmer for 30 to 40 minutes. Serve sprinkled with minced parsley.

Beef Stew with Quince

400 g tenderloin, rump or round of beef (boned)	2 tblsps butter
	Salt
	Pepper
40 g quince	Minced parsley or dill
1 onion	

Wash and cut the meat into pieces (3 or 4 per portion). Brown in butter in a shallow saucepan. Add water to cover and braise for about an hour. Pare and core the quince; cut into wedges and add to the meat along with sautéed onion, salt and pepper. Continue to cook until the meat is tender. Serve on a hot platter. Sprinkle with minced parsley or dill.

Stuffed Veal
(Veal Zrazy)

500 g veal (boned)	1/2 cupful milk
1 large onion	3 tblsps butter
100 g dry bread (without crust)	Salt, pepper
	Tomato sauce

Cut the veal into thin slices the size of the palm of your hand and pound lightly. Put a tablespoonful of stuffing on each piece of meat, roll it up, tie with a thread and sprinkle with salt. Heat the butter in a skillet, put in the zrazy and turn to brown evenly over high heat. Then turn down the heat and add 1 cupful of meat stock and 2 tblsps tomato puree. Simmer until tender (40-50 minutes). Remove the strings and pour over gravy before serving. Pass savoury tomato sauce.

Stuffing

Shred the onion and sauté in butter; soak the bread in milk and squeeze dry. Combine these ingredients, season with salt and pepper and mix thoroughly. Fry in butter over low heat until slightly browned.

Lamb Stew

(Ushnoye)

I

600 g lamb	250 g carrots
40 g fat	15 g flour
200 g onion	3-4 cloves of garlic
200 g turnips	Salt, pepper

Cut the lamb into 25-30-g pieces, dredge with salt and pepper and sear. Put the meat and sliced vegetables in a casserole, cover tightly with a lid and cook until tender. Add the garlic. Drain off part of the juice and stir into flour which has been browned. Pour this sauce into the casserole.

II

600 g lamb	120 g carrots
40 g fat	120 g turnips
40 g onion	1 tsp flour
500 g potatoes	3-4 cloves of garlic

Prepare as directed above, adding the potatoes along with the other vegetables.

Casserole of Lamb with Pickled Cucumbers or Mushrooms

600 g lamb	150 g pickled cucumbers
60 g fat	or 120 g pickled
400 g potatoes	mushrooms
200 g carrots	3-4 cloves of garlic
40 g onion	Seasoning
120 g turnips	

Cut the meat into portions and sauté with onion and carrots cut fine. Put them in a stoneware pot or casserole. Add meat juice, sliced carrots, turnips, potatoes and meat stock. Cook until the vegetables are almost done. Add the pickles or mushrooms, which have been shredded, and garlic. Season to taste and cook until done. Pickled mushrooms must be washed in hot water before using.

Braised Lamb, Georgian Manner

(Chanakhi)

500 g lamb	200 g string beans
750 g potatoes	1 onion
200 g tomatoes	Salt, pepper
300 g eggplant	Parsley or kindza[10]

Wash the meat and cut into pieces (2 or 3 per portion). If available, use a 2- or 3-litre stoneware casserole. Add finely sliced onion, chunks of potato, tomatoes cut in half, string beans from which the strings have been removed, diced eggplant, parsley greens or kindza[10]. Season with salt and pepper. Add two cupsful of water. Cover with a lid and bake for 1 1/2 to 2 hours. Serve in the casserole.

Braised Lamb with String Beans

500 g lamb	2 or 3 tblsps butter
400 g string beans	Salt, pepper
1 onion	Minced parsley or dill

Wash the meat, cut into pieces (3 or 4 per portion) and brown in butter in a shallow saucepan. Add water to cover, close tightly with a lid and braise for 30 to 40 minutes. Add the sautéed onion and cut string beans from which the strings have been removed. Season with pepper and salt. Braise until the meat is tender. Serve on a hot platter. Sprinkle with minced parsley or dill.

Veal or Lamb Kidneys in Wine Sauce

500 g veal or lamb kidneys	1 cupful meat stock
200 g boiled and sliced mushrooms	2 tblsps butter
	Minced parsley
1 tblsp flour	Salt
1/4 cupful wine (Madeira)	Pepper
	Boiled potatoes

Remove the fat and membrane, split the kidneys in half lengthwise and slice; add the mushrooms, dredge with salt and pepper and sauté in butter. Sprinkle with flour and brown for 1 or 2 minutes longer stirring constantly. Stir in the wine and meat stock. Cook for 3 or 4 minutes. Serve on a hot platter. Sprinkle with parsley. Serve buttered boiled potatoes separately.

Beef Kidney Stew, Russian Manner

500 g beef kidneys	2 or 3 tblsps butter
600 g potatoes	1 or 2 bay leaves
1 onion	5 to 8 peppercorns
3 or 4 pickled cucumbers	(or sliver of hot pepper)
1 tblsp flour	

Cut away the fat and membrane, cover with cold water and bring to a boil. Discard the water, rinse the kidneys, add fresh water and boil. Simmer until tender (about 1 to 1 1/2 hours). Make the sauce by browning the flour in one tablespoonful of butter. Stir in 1 1/2 cupsful of the hot liquor the kidneys have been cooked in and boil over low heat for 5 to 10 minutes. Cut the kidneys into pieces and mix with the onions which have been sautéed. Fry together for 2 or 3 minutes longer and transfer to a shallow saucepan. Add the potatoes which have been cut into chunks and fried, separately boiled sliced pickles and seasoning. Pour over the sauce which has been strained, cover with a lid and braise for 25 to 30 minutes. Serve on a hot platter with garnishing. Sprinkle with minced parsley or dill.

Stewed Pork Kidneys

Substitute pork kidneys in the above recipe but do not boil before frying.

Beef Heart Stew

500 g beef heart	1 tsp sugar
1 tblsp flour	2 tblsps butter
1 onion	2 bay leaves
2 tblsps tomato puree	Salt
2 tblsps vinegar	

Wash and dry the heart with a napkin or cloth. Cut into medium-sized pieces, dredge with salt and brown in butter. Before the meat is completely browned, sprinkle with flour and brown for 1 or 2 minutes longer. Transfer the meat to a shallow saucepan. Pour about 1/2 cupful of meat stock or water into the skillet, bring to a boil, make the sauce and strain into the saucepan. Add another 1 1/2 cupsful of stock or water, cover with a lid and simmer over low heat for 2 to 3 hours. Sauté the onion separately in butter in a skillet, add the tomato puree, vinegar, sugar and bay leaves, and bring to a boil. After adding to the meat, cook for another 20 to 30 minutes. Taste to correct seasoning. Serve with a garnishing of buckwheat kasha[18], boiled rice, fried or boiled potatoes.

Beef heart may also be prepared according to the directions for beef stew.

Braised Lung

500 g lung	1 tblsp butter
1 onion	1 bay leaf
1 tblsp tomato puree	Salt, pepper
1 tblsp flour	

Wash the meat and put it in hot water. Simmer for 1 1/2 to 2 hours then cut into medium sized pieces. Dredge with salt and pepper and brown in butter. Sprinkle with flour, add the finely chopped onion and fry a few minutes longer. Transfer the meat to a saucepan, add 2 to 2 1/2 cupsful of the meat stock, tomato puree and a bay leaf. Cover with a lid and simmer for another 10 to 15 minutes. Serve garnished with boiled or fried potatoes.

Braised Beef Heart or Udder

500 g beef heart or udder	1 tblsp tomato puree
	1 onion
1 tblsp flour	1 bay leaf
1 tblsp butter	Salt, pepper

Wash the meat. Cut into cubes weighing 30 to 40 g and wash again. Dredge with salt and pepper and brown in butter together with a finely shredded onion. Sprinkle with flour and brown a few minutes more. Transfer to a saucepan and add hot water to cover. Add tomato puree and a bay leaf. Cover with a lid and simmer for 1 to 1 1/2 hours. Serve with a garnishing of fried or boiled potatoes.

Cabbage Leaves Stuffed with Meat (Golubtsy)

300 g meat (boned)	2 tblsps tomato puree
800 g plain cabbage	2 tblsps sour cream
1/2 cupful cereal (rice, millet, or barley)	2 tblsps butter
	Salt, pepper
1 onion	Minced parsley or dill
1 tblsp flour	

Put the meat through the food chopper. Cook and cool the cereal. Mix together the cereal, ground meat, slightly browned onion, salt and pepper. Parboil whole cabbage leaves for 5 to 7 minutes and then cool. Chop off the stems. Put some of the meat, cereal and onion mixture on each leaf and roll up sausage-like closing the ends by folding the leaf inward. Brown in butter in a frying pan and transfer to a saucepan. Combine the sour cream, tomato puree and one cupful of water in a frying pan, add the flour, bring to a boil and salt to taste. Pour this sauce over the golubtsy, bring to a boil and cover. Simmer over low heat (or bake uncovered) for 30 to 40 minutes. Serve with the sauce. Sprinkle with minced dill or parsley.

Stuffed Grape Leaves (Dolma)

500 g lamb (boned)	400 g grape leaves
1/2 cupful rice	1 tblsp butter
1 onion	Minced dill
1 cupful stock	Salt, pepper

Put the meat through the food chopper, add the boiled rice, minced onion and dill. Season with salt and pepper. Wash the grape leaves, cut off hard stems and spread the leaves on the table in pairs.

Put a bit of stuffing on the wide end of the leaves, fold the edges inward and roll into a sausage shape. Sprinkle with salt and place the dolmas in rows in a shallow casserole. Pour over butter and the bone stock. Cover tightly and simmer over low heat for about an hour. Serve the dolmas on a platter. Pass sour milk mixed with grated garlic and salt, or cinnamon mixed with powdered sugar.

Fillet of Beef in Sour Cream with Onions

500 g fillet of beef	1 tblsp flour
1 kg potatoes	1 tblsp Yuzhny sauce[1]
1/2 cupful sour cream	3 tblsps butter
1 onion	Salt, pepper

Wash and trim the meat; allow one or two pieces per portion. Pound slightly, dredge with salt and pepper. Fry in butter over high heat, turning as soon as browned. In a separate frying pan, sauté a finely chopped onion, then add flour and continue to brown a little longer. Add the sour cream and meat juice. Cook this sauce for 3 to 5 minutes, add the Yuzhny sauce and taste to correct seasoning. Serve with sauce poured over. Garnish with fried potatoes.

Beef Stroganoff

500 g fillet, rump or	2 onions
short loin of beef	1 tblsp flour
3/4 cupful sour cream	3 tblsps butter
1 kg potatoes	Salt, pepper
1 tblsp Yuzhny sauce[1]	

Wash and trim the meat. Slice into medium-sized pieces and pound or beat to flatten. Then cut into shoestrings. Shred the onion and sauté in butter. When the onion is golden brown, add the meat which has been dredged with salt and pepper. Fry for 5 or 6 minutes stirring constantly with a fork. Sprinkle flour over the meat, stir and fry for another 2 or 3 minutes. Add the sour cream, stir and cook for 2 to 3 minutes more. Add Yuzhny sauce. Taste to correct seasoning. Garnish with fried potatoes. The meat and potatoes may be sprinkled with minced dill or parsley.

Grilled, Fried and Roast Meat

Basturma
(Grilled Beef Fillet, Armenian Manner)

500 g fillet of beef	200 g tomatoes
2 onions	1/2 lemon
1 tblsp grape vinegar	Salt, pepper
100 g green onions	

Trim the meat and cut into 40-50-g pieces. Marinate in a crockery basin. Dredge with salt and pepper, pour over vinegar, add the finely sliced onion and mix. Cover and set aside in a cool place for 2 to 3 hours. Skewer the meat and grill for 8 to 10 minutes turning frequently. Remove the basturma from the skewer and serve on a hot platter garnished with tomatoes, green onions and lemon slices.

Shashlyk
(Grilled Lamb, Caucasian Manner)

500 g best loin of lamb	100 g green onions
2 onions	200 g tomatoes

1 tblsp oil	1/2 lemon
Salt, pepper	1 tblsp vinegar

Cut the meat into pieces about 5 cm square and mix with salt, pepper, finely sliced onion and vinegar (or teaspoonful lemon juice). Cover with a lid and set aside in a cool place for 2 or 3 hours to marinate. About 15 to 20 minutes before serving, skewer the pieces of meat, alternating with sliced onion. Grill the shashlyk over a charcoal fire turning frequently until tender. Take the meat off the skewer. Pour over butter and garnish with green onions, tomatoes and lemon slices. Boiled rice may be served. Pass ground dry barberries or pomegranate juice, Yuzhny[1] or sour plum sauce.

Shashlyk, Kara Manner

500 g best loin of lamb	1 tblsp vinegar
2 kidneys	1/2 lemon
1 onion	Salt, pepper
100 g green onions	Minced parsley

Cut the best loin of lamb into 250 g portions, trim and make incisions so that the meat does not gather. Cut the kidneys in half. Put the meat and kidneys in a basin, dredge with salt and pepper, add the finely sliced onion, minced parsley and pour over vinegar (or lemon juice). Mix and set aside to marinate in the refrigerator for 2 to 3 hours. Skewer the piece of lamb putting half a kidney at each end. Grill the shashlyk over charcoal turning frequently till evenly done. Remove from the skewer and serve in one portion together with the kidneys. Garnish with sliced lemon. Sprinkle with green onions and minced parsley. Pass Yuzhny sauce[1].

Fried Kidneys

Prepare the veal kidney and dry it with a cloth. Do not remove the fat. Slice into rounds crosswise. Dredge each slice with salt and pepper and flour. Heat butter in a skillet and fry the kidneys on both sides for 5 or 6 minutes. When done sprinkle with minced green parsley, pour over lemon juice and serve in the frying pan. Separately serve fried shoestring or cubed potatoes and quarter pieces of lemon.

Liver in Sour Cream

500 g beef, lamb or	1 cupful meat stock
pork liver	(or water)
1/2 cupful sour	1 onion
cream	2 tblsps butter
1 tblsp flour	Salt, pepper

Wash the liver. Remove the skin and any ducts and cut in strips. Season with salt and pepper, dust with flour and fry in hot butter on both sides. Put the liver in a casserole. Add sautéed finely sliced onion, the sour cream, pan juices and one cupful of meat stock or water. Cover with a lid and simmer for 25 to 40 minutes. When the liver is done put it on a platter. Salt the gravy to taste, pour over liver. Sprinkle with minced parsley. Serve with a garnishing of fried or boiled potatoes.

Braised Liver with Mushrooms

600 g calf liver	200 g fat or boiled
100 g dried mushrooms	butter
400 g potatoes	200 g sour cream
200 g onion	Salt, pepper

Cut the liver into pieces (3 or 4 per portion) and sauté. Cut up the mushrooms which have been soaked and then boiled.

Sauté the mushrooms together with the onions sliced into rings. Put the liver, mushrooms and onions in a casserole. Pour over the mushroom liquor, sour cream and, if desired, tomato paste. Put the fried potatoes on top. Braise until done.

Fried Brains

1 set of brains	2 or 3 bay leaves
1 tblsp flour	1 to 1 1/2 tblsps
1/2 lemon	vinegar (3%)
5 or 6 peppercorns (or	Salt, pepper
slice of hot pepper)	Minced parsley or dill
2 tblsps butter	

Soak the brains in cold water for 30 to 40 minutes. Drain and remove the membrane. Put the brains in a saucepan, add water to cover. Add vinegar (or lemon juice), salt, bay leaves and peppercorns. Bring to a boil and then simmer for 25 to 30 minutes. Drain and dry slightly. Cut each part in half, season with salt and pepper, dredge with flour. Fry in butter, browning the both sides. When done pour over butter and lemon juice. Sprinkle with minced parsley or dill. Serve with garnishing of fried or mashed potatoes, potatoes in milk, peas, string beans, carrots or any other vegetables.

Sautéed Veal Knuckles or Pig's Trotters

4 veal knuckles or pig's	1 carrot
trotters	1 parsley
2 eggs	1 onion
1/2 cupful flour	3 or 4 tblsps butter
1 cupful dry bread	Salt, pepper
crumbs	

Scald the knuckles, dry, then dust with flour and singe to remove any possible hairs. Rinse the hocks again and then separate the meat from the bones. Put the meat and bones in a saucepan, cover with cold water, add the vegetables and salt. Bring to the boil and simmer for 3 to 4 hours. Drain and remove any meat on the knuckles, season with salt and pepper, dredge in flour, dip in eggs, and then in bread crumbs. Sauté in butter. Serve with a garnishing of mashed potatoes, green peas, pickles.

Boiled Veal Knuckles

Prepare the knuckles as directed above. Instead of frying, serve the boiled meat with white stock sauce seasoned with vegetables (see p. 108). Garnish with mashed potatoes, peas or turnips.

Ham with Tomatoes

500 g ham	3 tblsps butter
400 g tomatoes	Salt, pepper
1 tsp lemon juice	Minced greens

Slice and sauté the ham in butter. At the same time separately sauté the tomatoes cut in half and seasoned with salt and pepper. When done, put the tomatoes on the slices of ham, sprinkle with minced greens, pour over the lemon juice and serve at once in the pan.

Roast Sucking Pig* with Buckwheat Kasha[18]

1 kg sucking pig	1/2 kg buckwheat
25 g sour cream	kasha[18]
120 g fat	2 eggs
120 g onion	100 g brains

* Roast sucking pig is prepared for traditional holiday feasts.

Have the sucking pig split open lengthwise. Chop the back and pelvic bones on the inside of the creature; wash and wipe it. Dredge the inside with the salt; flatten out the creature and brush the skin with sour cream. Cover the ears with dough so that they do not burn. Roast, basting frequently. Remove the dough from the ears after roasting for 20 to 30 minutes. When done, carve lengthwise first then cut into pieces crosswise and put together again on a platter. Serve with buckwheat kasha mixed with fried onion, chopped hard-cooked eggs and pieces of slightly browned boiled brains. Pour over the pan juices.

Fried Tripe with Buckwheat Kasha[18]

500 g tripe	Salt, pepper
1 onion	1 cupful buckwheat
3 tblsps butter	groats

Prepare and cook the tripe according to the directions in the recipe for boiled tripe. Put the tripe through the food chopper, season with salt and pepper and sauté in butter. Add finely chopped and separately sautéed onion and fluffy buckwheat kasha[18] prepared from one cupful of buckwheat groats. Mix together and fry for another 3 to 5 minutes.

Forcemeat

The cheaper cuts of beef, pork, lamb or veal are usually used for forcemeat. The meat, however, should not be too lean.

Put the meat through the food chopper, season with salt and mix. Add dry bread (without crust) which has been soaked in water or milk and squeezed dry. Put through the food chopper again once or twice. Pepper and raw or slightly sautéed onion may be added.

Cutlets and Round Patties

500 g meat (boned)	3/4 cupful milk or water
125 g white bread	2 tblsps butter
1/2 cupful bread crumbs	Salt, pepper

Prepare the meat following the directions given above. Shape into cutlets or round patties, dredge in bread crumbs and smooth with a knife. Fry the cutlets or patties in hot butter on both sides for 8 to 10 minutes. Pour butter, sour cream, red or tomato sauce, Yuzhny or Lyubitelsky sauce[1] may be passed. Garnish with fried or boiled potatoes, kasha[18], noodles or vegetables.

Meat Balls in Tomato Sauce

(Tefteli in Tomato Sauce)

500 g meat (boned)	2 tblsps flour
100 g green onions or	2 tblsps butter
1 dry onion	1 cupful meat stock
1/2 cupful tomato puree	1 or 2 bay leaves
100 g white bread	5 or 6 peppercorns or
2 or 3 cloves of garlic	a sliver of hot pepper
1 tsp savoury tomato	Salt
sauce	Minced parsley

Prepare the forcemeat, add minced green onions or grated dry onion and mix thoroughly. Divide the mixture and roll into balls 20 to 30 grams each. Roll in flour, fry in butter and transfer to a casserole. Add the tomato puree, stock, spices and also the crushed garlic rubbed together with salt. Cover with a lid and simmer for 10 to 20 minutes. Season with salt and savoury tomato sauce, sprinkle with minced parsley. Serve with boiled rice, buckwheat kasha[18], fried or mashed potatoes.

Meat Roll Stuffed with Buckwheat Kasha[18]

500 g meat (boned)	1 cupful red sauce
100 g white bread	3 tblsps butter
2 hard-cooked eggs,	1 1/2 cupsful prepared
1 raw egg	buckwheat kasha[18]
1 onion	or rice
1 tblsp bread crumbs	Salt, pepper

Prepare the forcemeat as directed above.

Mix the cold buckwheat kasha with chopped hard-cooked eggs and minced onion sautéed in butter; taste to correct seasoning. Spread a cold-wet cloth on the table. Mold the forcemeat into an oblong shape 1 1/2 cm thick. Along the centre spread the cold buckwheat kasha mixture. Fold over the edges of the meat to cover the stuffing. Carefully move the roll to a buttered baking dish. Brush with a beaten egg, dust with bread crumbs and pour over butter. Puncture the top layer in two or three places and bake for 30 to 40 minutes. When done, transfer to a platter, cut into portions and pour over red sauce.

POULTRY AND WILDFOWL

roast duck stuffed with apples

1 duck

2 tbsps butter

750 g apples

Boiled Chicken with Cornel

1/2 chicken (500-600 g)	50 g raisins
100 g fresh cornel	1 tblsp sugar

Boil the chicken until tender, drain and cut into portions. Wash the raisins and cornel (seeded). Pour in just enough broth to cover the berries, add sugar and cover the saucepan with a lid, cook for 5 to 10 minutes. Serve the chicken with cornel gravy poured over.

Fried Chicken with Tomatoes and Squash

1 "spring" chicken	Salt, pepper
2 tblsps sour cream	Tomatoes
Minced parsley or dill	Squash

Cut the prepared chicken into four portions. Slash or remove the sinews or tendons in the leg and wing joints and pound slightly. Season with salt and pepper. Heat butter in a shallow saucepan and put the chicken in skin down. Brown on both sides. Pour over the sour cream, cover the pan and simmer for 10 to 15 minutes. In a separate skillet fry the tomatoes cut into halves and round slices of squash. Serve the chicken garnished with the tomatoes and squash. Pour over strained pan juices. Sprinkle with minced parsley or dill.

Fried Chicken, Georgian Manner

(Tsyplenok-Tabaka)

1 chicken	Freshly ground pepper
30 g butter	Garlic to taste
Salt	

Clean, wash and cut the bird lengthwise along the breast. Spread out the bird and rub it with garlic and salt on both sides. Heat the butter in a skillet and when hot put in the bird and cover with a flat lid. Put a heavy weight on the lid to keep the bird pressed flat to the bottom of the skillet. Fry until golden brown, turn it over and cook over medium heat for another 30 minutes.

This fried chicken may be served with or without a garnishing. If garnishing is desired, serve fried potatoes, tomatoes, boiled rice, cucumbers, etc. Separately pass a tart tomato or walnut sauce.

Broiled Chicken with Tkemali Sauce

Choose a medium-sized chicken. Dredge with salt and pepper and skewer diagonally from leg to wing. Broil over hot charcoals for 20 to 30 minutes, turning and basting regularly with butter until evenly browned. Remove the chicken from the skewer and serve garnished with lettuce, fresh salted cucumbers and tomatoes. Pass "tkemali" sauce (see below).

"Tkemali" Sauce

(Tart Plum Sauce)

200 g dried tart plums	Minced kindza[10] or dill
1 crushed clove of garlic	Salt, pepper

Wash and stew the plums until soft. Remove the seeds and rub through a strainer. Add plum liquor until the paste is as thick as sour cream. Mix in the seasoning, bring to a boil and then cool. This sauce may also be served with shashlyk[19] and other grilled meats.

Chicken Chakhokhbili
(Casseroled Chicken, Georgian Manner)

1 chicken	2 or 3 tblsps butter
2 onions	Salt
2 tblsps tomato puree	Pepper
1 tblsp vinegar	Tomatoes
1/2 cupful meat stock	Minced greens
2 tblsps Madeira or	Lemon slices
Port wine	

Prepare the chicken, wash and joint it into medium-size pieces, brown in hot butter in a shallow casserole. Add finely minced onion, tomato puree, vinegar, wine, meat stock and seasoning. Cover the casserole with a lid and simmer for 1 1/2 hours. Add sliced tomatoes and cook for another 5 to 7 minutes. Serve the chicken with a slice of lemon on each piece of chicken. Sprinkle with minced greens.

Lamb Chakhokhbili

Substitute 500 g lamb for the chicken in the above recipe. Cut the meat to have 3 or 4 pieces per portion.

Cutlets, Kiev Manner

One 70 g chicken	1/4 egg
breast per portion	25 g bread crumbs
30 g butter	Fat for deep frying

Separate the small breast fillet from the large one and remove the wishbone. Remove the skin and flesh from the wing bone, chop off the thick part of what might be termed the shoulder joint and then chop off part of the wing bone at a slant. Remove the membrane on the large and small fillets with a sharp knife, wetting it from time to time with cold water. Lay the large fillet flat on a dry carving board (this will keep the fillet from slipping) inside upward. Hold the fillet down with the left hand and with a knife cut away the outer sinew leaving no flesh on it. On the inside, slit the fillet through the middle from top to bottom on each side of the tendon. Cut the tendon in two or three places with a tap of the point of the knife. Pound the fillet slightly. Next remove the sinew from the small fillet as follows: hold down the sinew with the end of the knife blade nearest the handle and with the left hand pull the flesh away and pound slightly.

Combine the butter, egg yolk and salt, shape into a sausage and chill. When firm put the roll of butter in the middle of the large fillet and cover it with the small one. Fold over the edges of the large fillet and shape like a cigar. Roll the cutlet in flour, dip in egging, crumb it then again dip it in egg and bread crumbs. Fry in deep fat until golden yellow, remove from the frying kettle and set it in a moderate oven for a few minutes. Serve the garnishing in tartlets.

Roast Goose or Duck Stuffed with Apples

1 goose	(750 g apples for
1-1 1/2 kg antonovka	1 duck)
or other tart	2 tblsps butter for
apples	garnishing

Prepare the goose or duck and stuff with pared apples cut in quarters. Sew up the vent and roast in the usual way pouring 1/2 cupful of water into the roasting pan. Baste the bird with pan juices. Roasting time for a goose or duck is 1 1/2 to 2 hours. The goose or duck may be garnished with baked apples, stewed cabbage, buckwheat kasha[34] or potatoes.

Casseroled Giblets

500 g giblets	1 onion
600 g potatoes	1/2 cupful tomato puree
2 carrots	1 tblsp flour
1 parsley root	2 tblsps butter
2 cupsful stock	Salt, pepper, bay leaf

Prepare and wash the poultry giblets. Dredge with salt, sauté slightly, sprinkle with flour and fry a few minutes longer. Transfer to a shallow casserole, add the stock (or water), tomato puree, cover with a lid and simmer for 1/2 hour. Then add the potatoes which have been cut into chunks and fried, the vegetables and seasoning. Stir together carefully and cook for another 1/2 hour.

Pozharsky Cutlets

This is one of the few dishes whose author is definitely known. Pozharsky was an innkeeper in the old Russian town of Torzhok. The former inn building now bears a plaque with an inscription to the effect that the poet Alexander Pushkin was known to have frequented this inn and recommended to his friends "the cutlets fried at Pozharsky's".

1 chicken (1 kg)	2 tblsps dry bread
100 g white bread	cubes
1/2 cupful milk or	4-5 tblsps butter
cream	Egg

Bone the chicken and put the meat through the food chopper. Add the bread which has been soaked in milk (or cream) and squeezed dry. Put through the food chopper again. Stir in the creamed butter. Season and mix thoroughly. Divide and shape into cutlets, dip them in the beaten egg and milk and roll in dry bread cubes.

Fry until golden brown. Serve garnished with carrots or turnips in white milk sauce. Parboil the finely diced vegetables in stock, add milk and taste to correct seasoning with sugar and salt. Drain off the stock and stir it into flour blended with an equal amount of butter. Pour over vegetables and bring to a boil. Cook until tender.

Casseroled Hare with Sour Cream

1 hare (about 3 kg)	2 cupsful sour cream
2 carrots	2 tblsps flour
2 parsley roots	3 tblsps butter
2 onions	Salt
1 cupful vinegar	Minced parsley or dill

I

Chop the prepared hare into three pieces (loin, rump and shoulder), cut away the membranes. Cover the meat with 1 litre of water to which one cupful of vinegar has been added. Set aside to marinate for 2 or 3 hours. Drain, season with salt, put on a baking pan together with sliced vegetables, pour butter over and bake in a hot oven until golden brown. Baste regularly with pan juices. When the meat is tender, chop into portions and put into a shallow casserole. Make a sauce by combining the pan juices and the sour cream. Bring to a boil and pour over the carved hare. Cover with a lid and bake for 25 to 30 minutes.

II

Chop the prepared hare into portions and soak in marinade for 1 to 1 1/2 hours. Drain and fry in butter and put the pieces in a saucepan. In a separate saucepan mix, season with salt and bring to a boil the meat juices and sour cream. Stir in the flour which has been combined with creamed butter and one cupful of stock (or water). Stirring constantly, cook for 3 or 4 minutes. Strain and pour over the hare. Sprinkle with minced parsley or dill. Garnish with boiled or fried potatoes.

Sauces

Red Sauce

(Suitable for use with forcemeat cutlets, rolls, roast meat, tongue, etc.)

1 tblsp flour	1 1/2 tblsps butter
1 medium-sized carrot	1-2 tblsps Madeira or
1 medium-sized onion	port wine
1 medium-sized	2 cupsful meat stock
parsley root	Salt, pepper
1 tblsp tomato puree	

Brown the flour in one tablespoonful of butter then add the tomato puree. Stir in the meat stock. Add the sliced and slightly browned root vegetables and onion. Simmer for 20 to 30 minutes. Stir in 1 or 2 tablespoonsful of wine and strain.

Spiced Onion Sauce

(Suitable for use with roast or casseroled meat, liver or forcemeat cutlets)

1 tblsp flour	2 gherkins
2 tblsps butter	2 tblsps tomato puree
2 cupsful stock	2-3 tblsps vinegar
2 onions	Salt, pepper

Combine flour with 1 tblsp butter and

brown. Stir in meat stock. Sauté the finely chopped onions in butter then add tomato puree, salt and pepper and continue to brown. Add vinegar and cook until thick as sour cream. Chop up and add the gherkins. Combine all the ingredients with the sauce and boil for 5 minutes.

White Stock Sauce

(To be served with boiled rabbit, veal, lamb or chicken)

1 tblsp flour	2 tblsps butter
1 1/3 cupsful stock	Salt
1 egg yolk	

Cream 1 tblsp butter and flour, stir in stock (rabbit, chicken, lamb or veal). Simmer for 5 to 10 minutes. Remove the sauce from the heat. Beat the egg yolk and add to it a little of the sauce, season with salt and butter and combine with the rest of the sauce.

White Stock Sauce with Capers

(To be served with boiled veal, lamb, rabbit or chicken)

Prepare the white stock sauce as directed above and add to it 1 1/2 tblsps small capers.

Horseradish Sauce

(To be served with boiled beef, corned beef, lamb, pork or tongue)

1 tblsp flour	2 tblsps vinegar
2 tblsps grated	3 tblsps butter
horseradish	2 tblsps water or stock
1/3 cupful sour cream	5-8 peppercorns (or
1 bay leaf	sliver of hot pepper)
1 cupful meat stock	Salt

Cream 1 tblsp butter with flour. Stir in meat stock, add sour cream and simmer for 5 to 10 minutes. At the same time, in a separate saucepan slightly brown grated horseradish in 2 tblsps butter. Add 1 or 2 tblsps vinegar (depending on the strength) and an equal amount of water or stock. Season and heat to evaporate the moisture. Add the horseradish to the sauce, bring to a boil, remove from the heat, season with salt, add a lump of butter and mix thoroughly.

Sour Cream Sauce

(Suitable for use with forcemeat cutlets, liver or roast fowl)

1/2 cupful sour cream	1 cupful meat or
1 tblsp flour	vegetable stock
1 tblsp butter	Salt

Cream butter and flour; stir in the hot stock and add the sour cream. Simmer for 5 to 10 minutes. Season with salt and a lump of butter (additional). Mix thoroughly.

Sour Cream Sauce with Onion

(Suitable for use with liver or forcemeat cutlets)

1/2 cupful sour cream	1/2 tblsp Yuzhny or
1 tblsp flour	Lubitelsky sauce[1]
1 onion	1 1/2 tblsps butter
1 cupful stock	Salt

Blend 1 tblsp butter and flour in a saucepan till light yellow. Stir in hot stock, add the sour cream and simmer for 5 to 10 minutes. In a separate frying pan sauté the finely chopped onion in butter and add to the sauce. Cook for 3-4 minutes,

remove from the heat, season with salt and Yuzhny or Lubitelsky sauce.

Turnip Sauce

(Suitable for use with roast or casseroled meat, wildfowl or poultry)

300 g turnips	1 egg white beaten
1 tblsp sugar	stiff
2 tblsps butter	1 tblsp lemon juice
	Lemon rind

Boil the turnips till tender and sift through a strainer. Add sugar and butter and cook until thick. Cool the mixture, add the egg white and beat until well combined and fluffy; add lemon juice and the rind of 1/4 lemon. Mix thoroughly.

Tomato Sauce

(Georgian)

500 g ripe tomatoes	3 sprigs of parsley and
1/2 cupful boiled water	dill
3-4 cloves of garlic	1 onion
3-4 sprigs of kindza[10]	1 chili pepper
	Salt to taste

Wash, cut and cook the tomatoes in a saucepan for 10 minutes. Strain the tomatoes, gradually adding the boiled water. Pound the garlic and salt, add to the puree and cook for 10 minutes. Add the crushed chili pepper, mince and add the greens and onion. Combine thoroughly.

Walnut Sauce

(Georgian)

3/4 cupful shelled walnuts
1 tsp coriander seeds

Grape vinegar, chili
pepper and salt to
taste
2-3 cloves of garlic

Crush the nutmeats and garlic and rub together with salt, then add ground chili pepper and coriander seeds. Pour in grape vinegar and 1 cupful of cold boiled water.

Garlic Sauce
(Georgian)

6-8 cloves of
garlic

3/4 cupful stock
or water
Salt to taste

Crush the garlic with salt until a paste forms. Transfer to a sauceboat and pour over stock or chilled boiled water. Combine. Serve with cold snacks, turkey, chicken, fish or boiled lamb.

PELMENI

siberian pelmeni

1 onion

1 egg

1 beef

flour

salt, pepper
1/2 cupful sour
cream
2 tblsps butter

When one says "pelmeni" he thinks of the traditional Siberian pelmeni with a meat filling and frozen before they are cooked. Frozen pelmeni are also traditional in the northern regions of Russia. Freezing gives them a peculiar sapid flavour. When the frosts set in, pelmeni are made in quantities running into the thousands. They are laid on floured boards, carried outside to freeze, then packed in large sacks and stored away until needed.

Siberian Pelmeni
(Poached Pasties)

Dough

320 g flour	120 g water
1/2 to 1 egg	7 g salt

Sift the flour onto the doughboard, make a hollow in the centre of the flour, break in the egg, add milk (or water) and salt. Knead into a heavy dough; cover and set aside for half an hour. Roll the dough thin and cut into 5-6 cm rounds. Put a ball of filling (about the size of a small walnut) on one half of the round and fold over making a half moon. Pinch the edges, draw the two points together making a little purse.

Lay the pelmeni in 4 litres boiling water to which 40 g salt have been added. Continue to boil until the pelmeni rise to the surface. Remove with a skimmer. Serve with butter, butter and vinegar, sour cream, pungent grated cheese or mustard. Yield: 1 kg pelmeni or four portions.

Filling

200 g beef (boned)	28 g onion
240 g pork (boned)	9 g salt, pepper

160 g milk (water or stock)	20 g flour (to flour board)
	Garlic

Put the beef, fat pork, garlic and onion through the meat chopper, add the pepper, salt and milk (or stock). Mix thoroughly.

Cabbage Filling

350 g pork (boned)	180 g cabbage
40 g onion	50 g water
9 g salt	Pepper

Trim the meat. Put it through the meat chopper together with the onion. Add salt, pepper, water and finely chopped cabbage. Mix thoroughly.
These pelmeni are made in the eastern areas of Russia. They are shaped as usual or in the form of a "knot". Serve with butter, butter and vinegar, sour cream or green onions.

Mushroom Filling

150 g boiled rice	50 g butter
40 g dried mushrooms	Salt
50 g onion	

Soak the mushrooms, then cook. Chop up and sauté the mushrooms and add the sautéed onion. Combine with parboiled rice and mix thoroughly. Serve pelmeni garnished with sour cream.

Mushroom and Egg Filling

10 eggs	50 g butter
40 g dried mushrooms	Salt, pepper
50 g onion	

Prepare the mushrooms and onion as directed above. Add chopped hard-cooked eggs, salt and pepper. Mix thoroughly. Serve pelmeni garnished with sour cream.

Radish Filling

450 g radishes	50 g butter
50 g onion	Salt

Peel and shred the radishes on a grater. Sauté and add fried onion and salt. Serve pelmeni garnished with sour cream.

Fish Filling

450 g fillet of fish	50 g butter
75 g onion	Salt, pepper

The fillet of any fish may be used. Put it twice through the food chopper together with the raw onion. Add salt, pepper and butter. Mix thoroughly. Serve pelmeni with butter poured over.

Far Eastern Filling

275 g fillet of fish	1 egg
250 g fat pork	60 g water
50 g onion	Salt, pepper

Put the fillet of salmon or other fish through the meat chopper twice together with the pork and raw onion. Add the egg, pepper, salt and water and mix thoroughly. Pelmeni made with this filling are cooked or fried in butter. Garnish with butter or vinegar.

Fried Pelmeni

10 Pelmeni	20 g sour cream
15 g butter	

Heat the butter in a frying pan and put in the frozen home-made or commercial pelmeni. When browned on one side turn them over and brown the other side. Serve in an individual portion frying pan with sour cream poured over. Serves one.

Baked Pelmeni

10 pelmeni	5 g cheese
30 g sour cream	2 g butter

Put the poached or fried pelmeni in an individual portion frying pan, pour over sour cream, sprinkle with grated cheese and butter and brown in the oven. Serves one.

Manty
(Uzbek Steamed Pasties)

500 g fat mutton	3–4 tblsps butter
3–4 onions	Salt and pepper to
50 g fat of lamb tail	taste
150 g sour cream	

Chop the mutton into pieces the size of a pea, shred the onion thin, add ground red pepper and salt and combine thoroughly. Finely dice the lamb tail fat. Roll dough into a large thin cake and cut 10×10 cm squares. Place a tablespoonful of farce and diced tail fat on each square. Fold diagonally and pinch corners and edges so that the manty are oblong in shape. Butter the plate of a kettle for steaming and arrange the manty on it. Sprinkle them with cold water and steam for 45 minutes. Remove the manty with a metal paddle or spatula and brush with butter. Serve in hot meat broth.

Make the dough as follows: sift 500 g flour; beat 2 eggs, add 1 cupful of water and salt to taste; work this mixture into the flour and knead until smooth. Cover and set aside for 10 minutes.

Vareniki

(Ukrainian Pelmeni)

Vareniki are preferred in the southern regions of Russia. They are larger than pelmeni and shaped as a half-moon. Pelmeni are never made with a fruit filling whereas vareniki are. In the Ukraine the meat filling is sometimes fried; pelmeni are made with raw meat only.

Although the same dough may be used for vareniki as for pelmeni, the addition of a little butter is sometimes preferred.

Dough

280 g flour	10 g sugar
110 g milk	18 g butter
1 1/2 egg	5 g salt

Make the dough as directed for pelmeni.

Curd or Cottage Cheese Filling

480 g curds (cottage cheese)	1 egg
50 g sugar	Salt

Rub the curds through a sieve, add sugar, egg and salt to taste. Mix thoroughly. Make the vareniki. Cook in boiling salt water. Drain and garnish with butter and sour cream. Serves four.

The cooked vareniki may be placed in an earthenware pot or frying pan, pour over butter and sour cream; bring to a boil and serve immediately.

Old Russian Filling

100 g heart	25 g onion
200 g lung	25 g butter
10 g dried mushrooms	

Wash the heart and lung in cold water. Cook until tender, then put through the food chopper. Shred the onion and sauté in butter, add to the ground pluck and sauté slightly. Cook the dried mushrooms, chop up fine, sauté and add to the filling. Garnish these vareniki with butter.

"Lazy" Vareniki with Curds

140 g curds	15 g sugar
20 g flour	10 g butter
1 1/2 egg	Salt

Rub the curds through a sieve, add salt, sugar, the egg and flour. Knead until smooth. Make a roll about 1 cm thick, cut into pieces and cook as vareniki. Serve with butter and sour cream. Serves one.

Vareniki with Sour Cherries

600 g sour cherries	1 cupful flour
200 g sugar (additional)	20 g sugar
1/2 cupful water	1 egg
	Salt

Pit the cherries, mix with 200 g sugar and set aside while making the dough. Mix the flour with the salt and sugar (20 g) and make a stiff dough with the water and egg. Cover the dough and let it stand for 20 minutes. Roll the dough thin (2-3 mm), cut into small squares. Place several cherries on each square, brush the edges with beaten egg (additional), fold over to form a triangle and pinch the edges. Chill for 1 hour in the refrigerator before cooking. Drop the vareniki into boiling salt water and cook until they rise to the top.

Serve with sour cream.

Armenian Meat Pasties
(Mantapur)

250 g beef	1 egg
30 g onion	100 g matsun (sour
20 g boiled butter	milk)
100 g flour	Salt, pepper, parsley
Garlic to taste	

Prepare a broth with bones. Put the meat through the grinder twice and add to it sautéed onion, minced parsley and garlic. Sift the flour, make a well, pour into it the beaten egg and water. Quickly make the dough and divide. Roll out rounds 1-2 mm thick. Place 8-10 g filling 1-2 cm from the edge. Brush the edge with beaten egg, cover the filling with a round of dough, cut the edges with a round cutter and then pinch them. Drop the pasties into hot broth and boil gently until the pasties rise to the surface. Crush the garlic and mix with the sour milk. Serve the pasties with this mixture poured over. Separately serve the meat broth.

Chebureki
(Central Asian and Caucasian Deep Fried Pasties)

3 cupsful flour	3/4 cupful water for
400 g lamb (boned)	dough
100 g fat	200 g rendered fat for
1 egg	frying
50 g rice	Pepper, salt (to taste)
Minced parsley	

Filling

Put the meat, fat (preferably tail fat) and onion through the food chopper or chop up fine with a knife. Add salt, pepper and minced parsley. Mix thoroughly with a paddle and stir in 2 or 3 tblsps cold water.

Dough

Sift the flour, make a well and pour in the beaten egg, water and 1/2 tsp salt. Knead into a dough as for noodles. Roll out until about 1 mm thick; cut into rounds the size of a saucer. Put the filling on one half and fold over into a halfmoon shape. Brush the edges with beaten raw egg and pinch. Deep fry the chebureki and serve immediately.

VEGETABLE
DISHES

onion

fried
egg plant
with onion

1/2 cupful sour cream   3 tblsps flour
1 tblsps tomato paste

egg plant 1 tblsps butter

Fried Potatoes with Eggs

1 kg boiled potatoes	2 tblsps butter
3 eggs	Salt
1 cupful milk	

Slice and fry the potatoes in butter. Beat the eggs, add milk, salt and mix thoroughly. Pour the mixture over the fried potatoes and bake till golden.

Potato Patties with Mushroom Filling

1 kg potatoes	crumbs
100 g dried mushrooms	4 tblsps butter
2 onions	Sour cream or tomato
2 eggs	puree
1/2 cupful bread	Salt, pepper

Pare the potatoes, boil till tender and drain thoroughly. Mash the potatoes while hot. Add 1 tblsp butter and the egg yolks. Mix thoroughly. Mould into flat cakes. Put the filling on each cake, fold over, shape into a half moon and press the edges together. Brush with egg and dust with bread crumbs. Fry in hot butter. In a sauceboat pass sauce made with the mushroom liquor adding sour cream or tomato puree. These patties may be made with any vegetable filling.

Mushroom Filling

Wash and cook the dried mushrooms. When tender, chop fine and sauté in butter together with finely minced onion. Season with salt and pepper. Mix thoroughly.

Potatoes Stewed in Sour Cream

700 g potatoes	40 g butter
250 g sour cream	1 tsp flour

Pare and cut the potatoes into chunks. Put them in a skillet (or shallow saucepan), add the butter and sauté slightly. Transfer the potatoes to a saucepan or a stoneware pot, pour over the sour cream which has been blended with the flour and salt. Cover tightly with a lid and simmer until tender. Before serving sprinkle with herbs.

Pumpkin with Rice and Eggs

Cut 1 kg pumpkin into small pieces, add 1/2 cupful of water and cook until tender; stir in 1 litre milk and 1/2 cupful of rice. Cook for 30 minutes. Cool the pumpkin and rice, beat in 4 eggs, add 3-4 tablespoonsful of butter and stir in 1/2 cupful of sugar. Transfer to a buttered baking mould and brown in the oven.

Potato Cakes
(Potato Oladyi)

500 g potatoes	1/4 cupful water
1/2 cupful flour	1 egg
25 g yeast	Salt

Pare and grate the potatoes. Add the yeast previously mixed in water, salt, flour and an egg. Mix thoroughly and set aside to rise. Cook on a very hot oiled griddle. Serve with sour cream or butter.

Fried Eggplant with Onion

2 eggplants	1 tblsp tomato puree
2 onions	3 tblsps butter
3 tblsps flour	Salt
1/2 cupful sour cream	

Wash and slice the eggplant fine, sprinkle with salt and flour and fry in butter. Mince the onion and fry in butter. Top the eggplant with the fried onion. Pour the sour cream and tomato puree into the pan the eggplant has been fried in, mix and bring to a boil. Serve with sauce poured over the eggplant.

Potato Pudding

(Potato Zapekanka)

1 kg potatoes	1 cupful milk
2 eggs	3 tblsps butter
3 onions	Salt

Boil, drain and mash the potatoes. Stir in hot milk, beaten raw eggs, salt and creamed butter. Combine thoroughly. Spread half the mixture in a buttered baking pan. Put sliced and sautéed onion on the potatoes and cover with the rest of the potato mixture. Brush the top with butter or sour cream and bake for 20 to 25 minutes. Serve with milk, sour cream or mushroom sauce.

Vegetable Cutlets

200 g carrots	1/2 cupful semolina
200 g turnips	3 eggs
300 g pumpkin or marrow	1/2 cupful dried bread crumbs
300 g cabbage	1 tsp sugar
1 1/2 cupsful milk	3 tblsps butter

Pare and shred the carrot and turnip, add hot milk and a tablespoonful of butter, sugar and salt. Simmer for 15 minutes and then add the shredded cabbage and then the diced pumpkin or marrow. Cook until tender (15-20 minutes). Add the semolina and cook for 8-10 minutes stirring constantly. Remove the saucepan from the stove, add the eggs and salt. Blend thoroughly, set aside to cool and then shape into cutlets, brush with egg whites, roll in dry crumbs and fry on both sides. Serve with sour cream or milk sauce.

Potato and Meat Pudding

300 g meat (boned)	1/4 cupful milk
500 g potatoes	2 tblsps butter
3 eggs	Salt, pepper, minced parsley
1-2 onions	
1 tblsp tomato puree	

Put the meat through the food chopper and sauté slightly. Add finely sliced and sautéed onion, tomato puree, salt and pepper. Moisten with stock or water, cover with a lid and simmer for 15 to 20 minutes. Separately fry sliced potatoes; season with salt. Spread the potatoes on the bottom of a baking pan, cover with a layer of ground meat mixture and level. Beat the eggs, combine with milk and pour over the meat. Bake in hot oven for 5 to 10 minutes. Before serving sprinkle with minced parsley.

Squash Stuffed with Meat

200 g meat (boned)	2 tblsps tomato puree
2 squashes	1 tblsp flour
1/3 cupful rice or millet	1 tblsp butter
1 onion	Salt
2 tblsps sour cream	Minced dill

Prepare the forcemeat as for golubtsy[26] (see p. 97). Pare and cut the squash crosswise into 4 or 5 slices. Scoop out the seeds and pack filling into the squash, rounding it on top. Combine and bring the tomato puree and butter to a boil. Add the sour cream and a cupful of water mixed with flour. Salt the squash and pour the mixture over and bake in a medium-hot oven for 30-40 minutes. Before serving sprinkle with dill.

Casseroled Potatoes with Fresh Mushrooms

750 g potatoes	1/2 cupful sour cream
500 g fresh mushrooms	3 tblsps butter
1 or 2 onions	1 bay leaf
1 or 2 sprigs of parsley	Salt, pepper

Clean, wash and scald the mushrooms. Sauté together with the sliced onion. Slice and brown the potatoes. Put the mushrooms and potatoes in a casserole. Pour in water to cover. Add salt, a bay leaf, pepper and parsley. Cover the casserole and simmer for 25 to 30 minutes. Add the sour cream. Remove the parsley and the bay leaf. Serve sprinkled with minced greens.

Casseroled Potatoes with Dried Mushrooms

Substitute dried mushrooms in the above recipe. Dried mushrooms must be cooked beforehand then cut into strips and fried with onion. Part of the mushroom liquor may be used instead of water in the casserole.

Casseroled Cabbage

1 kg cabbage	1 tblsp flour
2 onions	3 tblsps butter
2 tblsps tomato puree	1/2 cupful meat stock
1 tblsp vinegar	(or water)
1 bay leaf	Salt, pepper
1 tblsp sugar	

Clean, wash and shred the cabbage. Put it in a casserole, add 1 tblsp butter and stock. Cover and simmer for 40 minutes. Then add browned onion, tomato puree, vinegar and other seasoning. Simmer until tender (about 10 minutes). Stir in the flour which has been combined with the butter and slightly browned and bring to a boil. Sauerkraut may be substituted for fresh cabbage, in which case vinegar need not be added.

Casseroled Beetroot with Sour Cream

500 g beetroots	1 cupful sour cream
1 carrot	1 tblsp flour
1 parsley root or	2 tblsps butter
celeriac	Salt
1 tsp vinegar	1 bay leaf
1 tsp sugar	

Clean and wash the beetroots, carrot and parsley. Cut into shoestrings. Mix together with butter, vinegar and a little water. Cover and braise in a casserole until tender (from 45 minutes to 1 hour). Stir from time to time. Stir in flour which has been combined with the sour cream, salt and sugar. Add a bay leaf. Mix and boil for another 10 minutes.

Eggplant with Walnut Sauce
(Georgian)

8 small eggplants	Garlic
1 cupful shelled walnuts	Grape vinegar or
50 g butter	pomegranate juice
2-3 sprigs of kindza[10]	Salt to taste
Chili pepper	

Wash but do not peel the eggplants. Cut lengthwise into slices 1-1 1/2 cm thick, sprinkle with salt and fry in butter one layer deep. Turn to brown on both sides. Crush the nutmeats or put them through the meat chopper together with the garlic and kindza. Add the salt, chili pepper and grape vinegar or pomegranate juice to taste. Combine thoroughly and then stir in 2 cupsful of chilled boiled water. Arrange the fried eggplant in a platter and pour over the walnut sauce.

Casseroled Eggplant with Sour Cream

Eggplant	2 tblsps butter
1 tblsp flour	Salt
1 cupful sour cream	Minced parsley or dill

Wash and peel the eggplant. Cut into chunks and parboil in hot salt water for 5 minutes. Drain thoroughly, dredge with flour and brown in butter. Put the browned eggplant in a saucepan, pour over the sour cream and simmer for 30 to 40 minutes. Before serving sprinkle with minced parsley or dill.

Stuffed Vegetables

Various kinds of vegetables may be stuffed with different meat, cereal, mushroom or vegetable fillings. Stuffed vegetables are usually cooked in a casserole or baking dish. They are served with butter or sour cream poured over or with a suitable milk, sour cream or tomato sauce.

Meat Stuffing*

500 g meat (boned)	Salt, pepper
1 or 2 onions	Minced parsley
3 tblsps butter	or dill

I

Cut up the raw meat, put it through the food chopper and sauté in butter. Put it through the food chopper once more. Add the sautéed minced onion, the meat juice from the frying pan, salt, pepper and minced parsley or dill. Mix thoroughly.

* The quantities indicated in these recipes are sufficient to stuff approximately 1kg of vegetables.

II

Put through the food chopper boiled meat. Sauté the onion separately, add one teaspoonful of flour and continue to brown. Stir in 2 or 3 tablespoonsful of stock and bring to a boil. Combine the onion with the meat. Season with salt and pepper and add minced parsley or dill.

Meat and Rice Stuffing

500 g meat (boned)	3 tblsps butter
1/2 cupful rice	Salt, pepper
1 onion	

Put the meat through the food chopper. Combine with drained, fluffy boiled rice and sautéed minced onion. Season with salt and pepper to taste.

Rice and Mushroom Stuffing

1 cupful rice	500 g fresh mushrooms
2 onions	or 50 g dried
3 tblsps butter	mushrooms
Salt, pepper	

Boil the rice till tender then drain. Clean and wash the mushrooms; plunge them into boiling water for 5 minutes, then drain, rinse, chop up and sauté in butter. If dried mushrooms are used, cook them beforehand and then proceed as with fresh mushrooms. Mix together the rice and mushrooms. Add fried onion and season with salt and pepper.

Mushroom Stuffing

500 g fresh mushrooms	3 tblsps butter
2 onions	Salt, pepper
2 tblsps tomato puree	

Clean the mushrooms, then wash them and pour boiling water to cover. Set aside the mushrooms for 5 minutes, then drain and rinse. Chop up and sauté in butter. Add the tomato puree, bring to a boil and mix with finely chopped sautéed onion. Season with salt and pepper.

Vegetable Stuffing

5 carrots	2 tomatoes
3 onions	3 tblsps butter
1 parsley or celery root	Salt, pepper
	Minced parsley greens

Shred the vegetables and sauté in butter. Add sliced tomatoes and sauté for another five minutes. Season with salt and pepper. Add minced parsley.

Stuffed Cabbage

1 medium-sized head cabbage	1 cupful sour cream
500 g meat (boned)	3 tblsps butter
125 g white bread	Salt
3/4 cupful milk	Stock

Discard unsuitable cabbage leaves and cut out the runt. Parboil in salt water until the leaves no longer break; drain in a colander. After the cabbage cools, spread out the leaves, sprinkle with salt and press the stuffing between the leaves. Gather up the leaves, reshape into a head (tie if necessary) and place on a baking dish. Pour over butter and meat stock (or water). Bake for 45 minutes. Pour sour cream over the cabbage and bake for another 15 to 20 minutes. Transfer the head of cabbage to a platter, cut it and pour over strained pan juices.

Stuffing

Put the meat through the food chopper. Mix with the bread which has been soaked in milk and squeezed dry; put through the food chopper again. Add melted butter and seasoning; mix thoroughly.

Cabbage Stuffed with Rice and Mushrooms

In the above recipe, substitute rice and mushrooms stuffing to which 2 beaten eggs have been added.

Stuffed Green Peppers

Wash the green peppers, cut off the tops and remove the seeds and inner ribs. Plunge the peppers into boiling salt water and parboil for 2 or 3 minutes; drain in a colander. Fill the peppers with meat, rice or vegetable stuffing, stand them on end one or two high in a casserole, pour in meat stock, butter and tomato paste or puree. Cover and bake or cook from 30 to 40 minutes. Before serving pour over sour cream sauce.

If the peppers are to be served cold, vegetable oil should be substituted for butter.

Stuffed Beetroot

Wash and then bake the beetroots. Cool and pare them. Scoop out the hearts with a teaspoon. Fill the beets with meat and rice stuffing, stand them on end in a buttered pan and bake for 10 to 20 minutes. Before serving, pour over sour cream and bake for a few minutes longer; transfer the beets to a platter and pour over the pan juices.

Stuffed Marrow

Select medium-sized marrow squash, peel, cut off the ends and scoop out the seeds. Wash and fill with a stuffing of meat, cereal, mushrooms or vegetables. Brown evenly in butter and place in a deep saucepan. Pour over meat stock or sour cream, cover with a lid and braise for 30 to 40 minutes. Slice before serving and pour over pan juices.

Cabbage Rolls Stuffed with Vegetables

(Golubtsy with Vegetables)

1 kg cabbage	2 tomatoes
3 or 4 carrots	1 cupful sour cream
2 or 3 onions	2 tblsps tomato puree
1 parsley root	2 tblsps butter
1 celeriac	Salt

Clean the cabbage and cut out the runt. Plunge the whole head into boiling water and parboil for 10 to 20 minutes. Drain in a colander, separate the leaves and spread them on the table. Pound the leaf stem to soften it or cut it out. Put the prepared vegetable stuffing on each leaf, fold in the ends and roll it up like a cigarette. Brown each of the golubtsy in butter and transfer to a shallow casserole. Pour over the sour cream and tomato puree. Cover and braise over low heat or bake for 30 to 40 minutes. Serve with pan juices poured over.

Stuffed Eggplant

Wash the eggplants and make a small lengthwise slit. Scoop out the seeds with a teaspoon. Plunge the eggplants into boiling salt water for 5 minutes, drain and then fill with vegetable or mushroom stuffing. Lay the stuffed eggplants in a buttered baking dish, pour over sour cream and bake for about an hour.

Turnip Stuffed with Mannacroup[9]

10 turnips (average size)	1 tblsp sugar
1/4 cupful mannacroup[9]	25 g cheese
1 cupful milk	3 tblsps butter
	Salt

Peel and wash the turnips, pour over hot water and cook until half done. Scoop out and cook the hearts until soft. Press them through a strainer and mix with the mannacroup which has been cooked in milk. Season with sugar, salt and butter. Fill the turnips with this stuffing, place them in a buttered baking dish, brush with butter, sprinkle with grated cheese and bake for 20 to 25 minutes.

Turnips may also be filled with meat stuffing.

Tomatoes Stuffed with Meat

8 medium-sized tomatoes	1 onion
200 g meat (boned)	2 or 3 tblsps butter
1/4 cupful rice	Salt, pepper

Wash the tomatoes in cold water, cut off the tops and scoop out the hearts and seeds without damaging the tomato shell. Dredge with salt and pepper and fill with stuffing.

Stuffing

Put the meat through the food chopper. Mix with sautéed finely minced onion. Season with salt and pepper. Put the stuffed tomatoes in a buttered pan. If desired, they may be sprinkled with grated cheese. Dot with butter and bake for 15 to 20 minutes, then pour over sour cream sauce and serve sprinkled with minced parsley or dill.

Potatoes Stuffed with Meat

Choose 1 kg large potatoes. Wash and cook in salt water until half done. Peel the potatoes, slice off one side and scoop out the inside. Mince 300 g meat together with the potato hearts. Combine with one raw egg and add minced dill. Season with salt and ground allspice. Mix thoroughly. Fill the hollowed potatoes with this stuffing and cover with the slices that have been cut off. Pack the potatoes tightly in a saucepan, pour in stock or water and braise until done. Thicken with tomato paste, flour and sour cream rubbed together.

Potatoes Stuffed with Herring

Prepare 1 kg potatoes as directed above. Scoop out the inside, mince with herring fillets and add 2 finely chopped onions, ground allspice and a bay leaf, a raw egg and 1/2 cupful of sour cream; beat these ingredients together thoroughly. Fill the potatoes with this stuffing, brown them in butter, pour over sour cream and bake in a hot oven.

Turnip Stuffed with Boletus Mushrooms

Bake and peel 1 kg of turnips. Scoop out and mash the inside. Wash 300 g spiced boletus mushrooms, cut them up and sauté in butter together with two finely minced onions. Add the mushrooms to the mashed turnip and mix. Stuff the hollowed out turnips with the mixture and place them in a casserole. Pour over butter, cover with a lid and bake in a hot oven for 30 minutes. Pour over one cupful of thick sour cream and brown.

Sauces

Milk Sauce

(Suitable for use with cabbage or carrot cutlets and other dishes)

1 tblsp flour	1 1/2 cupful milk
1 tblsp butter	Salt

Heat and blend the flour and butter. Gradually stir in the hot milk. Cook for 10 minutes stirring constantly. Season with salt.

Sour Cream Sauce

(Suitable for use with potato, cabbage or carrot cutlets and various kinds of zapekanka[21])

1 cupful sour cream	1/2 cupful vegetable
1 tblsp flour	stock
1 tblsp butter	Salt

Heat and blend the flour and butter. Stir in the vegetable stock and sour cream. Boil for 5 minutes, season with salt and strain.

Mushroom Sauce

(Suitable for use with potato cutlets and zapekanka[21])

50 g dried mushrooms	2 tblsps butter
1 tblsp flour	Salt
1 onion	

Wash the mushrooms in warm water and soak in 3 cupsful of cold water for 2 or 3 hours. Cook in the same water; do not salt. Blend the flour with one tablespoonful of butter and brown slightly. Stir in

2 cupsful of hot strained mushroom stock. Bring the sauce to a boil and simmer for 15 to 20 minutes. Cut the onion finely and brown in butter. Add the shredded boiled mushrooms, brown slightly and add to the sauce. Taste to correct seasoning and bring to a boil.

Tomato Sauce

(Suitable for use with potato pirozhki[6], stuffed vegetables, etc.)

1/2 cupful tomato puree	1 tblsp butter
1/2 tblsp flour	1 cupful stock (or
1/2 carrot	water)
1/2 parsley root	Salt
1/2 onion	

Cut the vegetables finely and sauté in butter. Add the flour and continue to brown. Stir in the tomato puree and the stock. Simmer for 5 to 10 minutes. When done strain the sauce and vegetables through a sieve. Add salt to taste and stir in a small lump of butter.

Egg Sauce

1 tblsp flour	1 tblsp butter
1 egg	1/4 cupful stock or milk

Heat and blend the butter and flour. Stir in stock and boil for 10 to 15 minutes. Beat the egg yolk and mix in a little stock or milk and add to the sauce. Blend thoroughly. If desired, a chopped hard-cooked egg may be added instead of the yolk.

Egg-and-Butter Sauce

In a saucepan or in the top part of a double boiler beat together with a whisk 2 tablespoonsful of cold water, two egg yolks and salt. Put the saucepan in a water bath and heat. Stirring constantly, gradually add small lumps of butter. Do not allow the sauce to boil or become too hot. Add 75 g of butter for each egg yolk. As soon as the sauce thickens, add lemon juice to taste.

MUSHROOMS

sautéed brown mushrooms
with sour cream

3 tbsps butter
salt, pepper

dill

1 onion

500 g mushrooms

The most fragrant and tastiest mushrooms are the edible boletus, the brown cap boletus, the aspen mushroom, the champignon (common meadow mushroom), the morel, the butter mushroom, the chanterelle and the honey agaric.

Cut the caps of the boletus mushrooms from the stems and scald them; peel the stems. The caps of the champignon mushrooms need not be cut from the stems but they must be peeled; drop them into cold water to which a little lemon juice (or acetic acid) has been added. This will prevent them from turning dark. Drain, pour over hot water, add lemon juice and boil for 20 minutes.

Morels and chanterelles must be cleaned and carefully washed to remove the soil. Boil them for 10 minutes, wash the stems once more and remove the membrane from the caps; rinse, cut and fry.

Mushrooms in Sour Cream

500 g mushrooms	2 tblsps butter
1/2 cupful sour cream	Salt
25 g cheese	Minced parsley or dill
1 tsp flour	

Clean, wash and scald the mushrooms. Drain in a strainer, slice, season with salt and sauté in butter. Just before they are done, sprinkle with flour and mix. Add the sour cream and boil. Sprinkle with grated cheese and bake. Sprinkle with minced parsley or dill before serving.

Morels in Sour Cream

500 g morels	2 tblsps butter
1 cupful sour cream	Salt
25 g cheese	Minced parsley
1 tsp flour	

Having cleaned the soil off the stems, wash the mushrooms carefully. Plunge them into hot water and boil for 10 minutes, then drain and rinse in cold water. Slice the mushrooms, season with salt and sauté in butter. Sprinkle with flour, sauté a little longer, add the sour cream and bring to a boil. Sprinkle with grated cheese, dot with butter and bake. When done garnish with minced parsley.

Sautéed Brown Mushrooms* with Sour Cream

500 g mushrooms	1/4 cupful sour cream
3 tblsps butter	Salt, pepper
1 onion	Minced dill

Clean and wash the mushrooms carefully and then drain thoroughly. Sauté in half the butter. Mince the onion, add butter and sauté. Mix the onion and mushrooms and continue to sauté for 40 to 50 minutes. Add the sour cream and simmer for 10 to 15 minutes. Season with salt and pepper. Serve sprinkled with dill.

Fried Edible Boletus with Onion Sauce

1 kg mushrooms	1 cupful sour cream
(young)	Salt
20 g onion	

Wash the mushrooms and wipe the caps dry. Season with salt and sauté for 15 minutes in very hot butter, stirring frequently. Shred the onion, season with salt and sauté in butter till tender. Add sour cream, bring to a boil and pour over mushrooms.

---

* Brown mushroom (Lactarius deliciosus)

Braised Mushrooms

500 g chanterelle, honey agaric, or brown-spored edible meadow mushrooms	3 tblsps butter 3 tblsps meat stock Salt Minced greens

Clean, wash carefully and boil the mushrooms in salt water. Drain thoroughly. Add hot butter and pour in the stock, cover and cook for about 30 minutes. Before serving sprinkle with minced greens.

Mushrooms Braised in Cream

500 g edible aspen or brown cap boletus 1 cupful cream 1 tblsp butter	Salt, dill, cinnamon, parsley, bay leaf, clove and peppercorns

Clean, wash and scald the fresh mushrooms. Slice, season with salt and sauté slightly. Transfer the mushrooms to a saucepan or casserole and add boiling cream. Add the herbs which have been tied together and a bag of spices. Salt to taste. Cover and bake for about an hour. When the mushrooms are tender, remove the herbs and spices. Serve in the casserole.

Mushroom Casserole

Casseroled morels are especially good but other mushrooms may also be prepared in this way. Clean and carefully wash the mushrooms. Plunge them into boiling water for 5 or 10 minutes. Drain and rinse in cold water. (This stock is unedible.) Slice the mushrooms and sauté them in hot butter in a baking dish. When slightly browned, sprinkle with flour, mix them and add sour cream. Bring to a boil, sprinkle with butter (grated cheese, if desired) and bake. Serve the mushrooms in the casserole or baking dish.

Mushrooms with Sauerkraut

(Country Manner)

500 g mushrooms 1 kg sauerkraut 1 pickled cucumber 1 onion 1-2 tsps sugar	2 tblsps butter 1 bay leaf Salt, pepper 2 tblsps tomato puree

Add a little water and butter to the sauerkraut and braise for about 45 minutes. Add tomato puree, sugar, pepper, a bay leaf and salt. Braise for another 15 to 20 minutes.

Any of the boletus mushrooms may be used. Wash and cook them in boiling water for 10 to 15 minutes. Drain, slice and sauté in butter. Transfer the mushrooms to a bowl and sauté the onions in the same frying pan. Add the sliced pickle, salt and pepper.

Spread half the braised cabbage in a baking dish, cover with the mushroom mixture and put the remaining cabbage over the mushrooms. Sprinkle with bread crumbs, dot with butter and bake. Before serving, garnish with lemon slices or olives.

This dish may also be made with fresh cabbage, adding vinegar to taste. Pickled or dried mushrooms may be substituted for fresh mushrooms.

CEREALS AND PUDDINGS

buckwheat kasha
with mushrooms
and onion

2-3 tbsps butter

2 1/2 cupfuls
buckwheat groats

1 tsp salt

50 g mushrooms

1 onion

Cereals make a variety of dishes that range from common porridge or gruel to Uzbek pilau (plov). Whether cooked plain or steamed as porridge or gruel, whether steamed and baked till it is puffy and fluffy, cereal in Russia is known as **kasha.** Puffy and fluffy kasha is prepared of whole-grain or cracked cereal (rice, pearl barley, buckwheat). The porridge or gruel type of kasha may be made of any cereal, usually with milk.

In cooking kasha the proportions given in the recipe must be strictly observed. The proportion for a fluffy kasha is always the same, but for porridge-like kasha varies depending on the thickness desired. Before cooking, millet, rice or pearl barley must be washed in cold water which should be changed several times. Millet must be especially thoroughly washed to rinse out the meal that renders it bitter. Cooking time will be saved if pearl barley is soaked for 3 or 4 hours. If the right quantity of water is used, the cereal will swell and be fluffy; otherwise it will be either too dry or soggy.

As a rule, kasha is cooked in a double boiler in the following way. Bring the required amount of salt water to a boil and then rapidly add the cereal, stirring it from time to time; cook the kasha over a low heat until it thickens. Then cover the pot tightly and place it over the lower part of the double boiler, in the oven or keep it on the hob until done. If the oven is too hot, set the pot in a water bath to prevent burning. If the cereal is to be cooked in milk, add less salt than it is needed for cooking in water. When cooking sweet kasha, a minimum amount of salt (to taste) is added.

Buckwheat Kasha with Butter

2 cupsful buckwheat groats	3 cupsful water
1 tsp salt	2 tblsps butter

Add the salt to the water and bring to boiling point. Stir in the cereal and boil for 15 to 20 minutes. When the cereal thickens, cover tightly and keep on the hob for 3 or 4 hours (or cook in a double boiler). Serve with butter.

Buckwheat Kasha Made of Cereal Fried in Butter

2 1/2 cupsful whole buckwheat groats	2 or 3 tblsps butter
3 1/2 cupsful water	1 tsp salt

Melt 1 tblsp butter in a frying pan, add the cereal and mix. Stirring the cereal allow it to roast over a low heat or in the oven. When brown, transfer to a casserole or double-boiler top, pour in the boiling water and season with salt. Boil rapidly until it thickens, close tightly and set over the lower part of the double boiler, in the oven or on the hob for 1 to 1 1/2 hours.

Buckwheat Kasha with Milk

Cook the kasha as directed above. Cool and serve with cold milk poured over.

Buckwheat Kasha with Salt Pork and Onions

Cook the kasha as directed above. Cut the pork into little cubes and sauté together with sliced onions. Mix the sautéed pork and onions together with the kasha.

Buckwheat Kasha with Brains

2 1/2 cupsful buckwheat groats	1 tsp vinegar
300 g brains	2 or 3 tblsps butter
1 1/2 tsps salt	1 bay leaf
	Pepper

Make buckwheat kasha as directed above. Soak the brains in cold water for 15 minutes, drain and remove the membrane. Put the brains in a saucepan with just enough water to cover, add salt, a bay leaf, pepper and vinegar. Bring to boiling point and remove from the heat. Allow the brains to soak for 10 to 15 minutes. Drain, slice thinly and sauté in butter. Mix with the kasha and heat in the frying pan for several minutes.

Buckwheat Kasha with Eggs

2 1/2 cupsful buckwheat groats	1 tsp salt
2 hard-cooked eggs	2 or 3 tblsps butter

Prepare the buckwheat kasha as directed above. Cut the eggs in half lengthwise and then slice finely. Mix the sliced eggs, butter and buckwheat kasha together and serve.

Buckwheat Kasha with Pluck

2 1/2 cupsful buckwheat groats	1 tsp salt
300 g lungs	2 or 3 tblsps butter
1 or 2 onions	Pepper

Prepare the kasha as directed above. Wash the pluck, cover with cold water, add salt and simmer until tender (1 to 1 1/2 h). Cool the pluck and put through a food chopper or cut it up finely with a knife. Slice and sauté the onion in butter. Add 1 or 2 tablespoonsful of butter (additional) and the minced pluck. Season with salt and pepper to taste. After frying the pluck and onions, mix with the hot buckwheat kasha.

Buckwheat Kasha with Mushrooms and Onions

2 1/2 cupsful buckwheat groats	2 onions
50 g dried boletus mushrooms	1 tsp salt
	2 or 3 tblsps butter (or vegetable oil)

Wash the mushrooms and soak in 3 cupsful of cold water for 1 to 1 1/2 hours. When the mushrooms swell, cut them into fine strips and return to the same water. Season with salt and bring to a boil, then add the groats which have been roasted. When the cereal thickens keep on the hob or in the oven for 1 to 1 1/2 hours. Mince the onion and sauté in butter, then mix with the kasha.

Buckwheat Kasha with Yellow Turnip

500 g young turnips	Sugar, salt
300 g buckwheat groats	2 tblsps butter
1 litre milk	

Pare, wash and grate the turnips, sauté in butter stirring frequently. Wash the groats, drain, add to the turnips, mix and then transfer to a casserole. Pour over the milk and cook. When the cereal thickens, add butter. Season with sugar and salt to taste. Cover with a lid and bake in a hot oven for 2 hours. Before serving stir to mash any lumps of turnip. Pour over hot butter.

Millet Porridge with Butter

2 cupsful millet   1 tsp salt
4 cupsful water   2 or 3 tblsps butter

I

Add butter and salt to the water and bring to a boil. Pour in the cereal which has been washed and cook until it thickens. Steam on the hob for 50 to 60 minutes. When the cereal is done stir in 1 or 2 tblsps butter.

II

7 to 8 cupsful water   1 tblsp butter
2 cupsful millet   1 tsp salt

Add salt to the water and bring to boiling point. Pour in the washed millet and cook for 10 to 15 minutes. Drain off the water and stir in the butter. Steam on the hob for 40 to 50 minutes. When the kasha is done mix in 1 or 2 tablespoonsful of butter.

Millet Kasha with Pumpkin

1 1/2 cupsful millet   3 cupsful water
750 g pumpkin or   1 tsp salt
winter squash

Pare the pumpkin and remove the seeds. Cut it up and cook in water for 10 to 15 minutes. Add the washed millet and continue to cook for 15 to 20 minutes. When the cereal has largely taken up the water, set it over the lower part of the double-boiler and steam for 25 to 30 minutes. Pass butter when serving.

Millet Kasha with Milk

1 cupful millet   1 tblsp sugar
4 cupsful milk   1/4 tsp salt

Bring the milk to boiling point and add the washed millet. Stir frequently and cook over a low heat for 30 minutes. Add the sugar and salt, mix and set over the lower part of the double-boiler or keep it on the hob to steam for 15 or 20 minutes.

Millet Kasha with Milk and Pumpkin

1 cupful millet   500 g pumpkin or
3 cupsful milk   winter squash
1 tsp sugar   1/2 tsp salt

Pare the pumpkin, remove the seeds and cut into small pieces. Heat the milk in a casserole, add the pumpkin and cook for 10 to 15 minutes. Stir in the washed millet, add salt. Mix and cook for another 15 to 20 minutes till the cereal takes up the milk. Put the casserole in a water bath in the oven; steam for 25 to 30 minutes.

Crushed Wheat Kasha

2 cupsful crushed wheat   1 tsp salt
4 cupsful water

Bring the salt water to a boil and add the cereal which has been washed (if not too fine). Stirring constantly, cook for 15 to 20 minutes. When the cereal takes up the water, cover with a lid and keep it on the hob (or cook in a double-boiler) for 40 to 50 minutes. Serve with butter or condensed milk.

Crushed Wheat Porridge

Follow the above directions using 5 cupsful of water.

Whole Wheat Porridge

2 cupsful whole wheat	5 to 6 cupsful water Salt

Bring the salt water to a boil and pour in the washed cereal. Cover with a lid, cook for 25 to 30 minutes stirring from time to time. Steam for 1 1/2 to 2 hours.

Barley or Cracked Oat Porridge

2 1/2 cupsful cereal	2 or 3 tblsps butter
1 tsp salt	4 1/2 cupsful water

Bring the salt water and butter to a boil. Add the cereal and cook until it has taken up the water, then keep it on the hob to steam for 30 to 40 minutes. Serve with butter.

Barley Porridge with Pork or Mutton Suet

2 1/2 cupsful barley	100 g raw pork or
1 tsp salt	mutton suet

Prepare the barley porridge according to the directions in the preceding recipe. Put the suet through the food chopper or cut up fine with a knife. Render until the cracklings are browned. Add the rendered fat and cracklings to the porridge, mix and keep it on the hob to steam for 30 to 40 minutes.

Pearl Barley Kasha with Butter

2 cupsful pearl barley	2 or 3 tblsps
1 tsp salt	butter

Pour the barley into boiling water and boil for 5 minutes. Drain the barley thoroughly in a sieve. Put 3 1/2 cupsful of water in the upper part of a double-boiler, add one tablespoonful of butter and salt. Bring to a boil. Pour in the cereal and cook until it thickens. Set it over the lower part of the double-boiler or on the hob to steam for 1 1/2 hours. When the kasha is done, mix in 1 or 2 tablespoonsful of butter.

Pearl Barley Porridge with Milk

1 cupful pearl barley	1/2 tblsp sugar
4 cupsful milk	1/4 tsp salt

Wash the barley, cook in boiling water for 10 to 15 minutes, then drain in a sieve. Bring the milk to a boil and add the drained barley. Cook over low heat for 15 minutes stirring from time to time. Add the sugar and salt, and mix. Cover with a lid and set over the lower part of a double-boiler for 10 to 15 minutes.

Guryevskaya Kasha

3/4 cupful mannacroup[9]	50 g almonds
2 eggs	1/2 vanilla powder
1/2 cupful sugar	1/2 can fruit
2 cupsful milk	Salt
2 tblsps butter	

Bring the milk to a boil, add sugar, salt and vanilla. Gradually stir in the mannacroup and cook for 10 minutes stirring continuously. Add the butter and raw eggs. Mix thoroughly and transfer to a buttered baking pan. Sprinkle with sugar and bake until the crust is golden brown. Serve garnished with cooked fruit and sweet sauce. Sprinkle with roasted almonds. This kasha may be served for dessert.

Puddings and Cakes (Zapekanka and Bitochki)

The cereals most commonly used for za-pekanka and bitochki are millet, rice and mannacroup (semolina). Zapekanka is made of thick porridge (1 cupful of cereal and 3 cupsful of milk or water) baked in a buttered pan dusted with bread crumbs. The top is sprinkled with bread crumbs and dotted with butter. It is baked for 15 to 20 minutes or until the crust is golden brown.

Mannacroup Pudding with Fruit

(Zapekanka with Fruit)

1 cupful cereal	2 or 3 tblsps sugar
4 cupsful milk	2 eggs
1/2 tsp salt	2 or 3 tblsps butter
100 g fruit various	

Cook the cereal in the milk. When done add the sugar, eggs, salt and butter and mix thoroughly. Pour into a buttered baking pan, level off the top and sprinkle with sugar. Bake until the crust is golden brown. Before serving put fresh, cooked or canned fruit on each piece and pour sweet fruit or berry sauce over.

Millet, Rice, Barley or Oat Pudding

(Zapekanka)

1 cupful cereal	1 tblsp bread crumbs
3 cupsful milk	1/4 tsp salt
1 tblsp sugar	2 tblsps butter

Bring the milk to a boil, add the cereal and cook until thick. Season with salt and sugar and mix thoroughly. Put the cereal in a baking pan which has been buttered and sprinkled with bread crumbs. Bake until browned, unmould and cut into 5 or 6 portions. Before serving pour butter over. Instead of butter, hot berry kissel[30] sprinkled with sugar, or sour cream may be poured over.

Millet Pudding with Raisins

Make a millet porridge with milk or water as directed. Add a raw egg and raisins that have been washed in cold water. Mix thoroughly. Butter a baking pan and dust with bread crumbs. Spread the porridge in the baking dish and bake until golden brown.

Buckwheat Porridge Pudding with Curds

1 cupful buckwheat groats	1/2 tsp salt
200 g curds or cottage cheese	2 tblsps butter
2 eggs	2 tblsps sugar
2 cupsful milk	1/2 cupful sour cream
	Bread crumbs

Bring the milk to a boil, add the groats and cook until thick as porridge. Add curds which have been pressed through a strainer or passed through a food chopper. Stir in sour cream and mix. Then add the raw eggs, salt and sugar. Combine thoroughly, pour into buttered baking pan which has been dusted with bread crumbs. Brush with sour cream and pour over a tablespoonful of melted butter. Bake for 40 to 50 minutes. Serve with butter or sour cream poured over.

Buckwheat Kasha[18] Pudding with Curds

1 cupful buckwheat groats	2 eggs
200 g curds or cottage cheese	2 tblsps sugar
	1/2 tsp salt
1/2 cupful sour cream	2 tblsps butter
	Bread crumbs

Cook a fluffy buckwheat kasha. Add the curds which have been pressed through a strainer or put through a food chopper, sour cream, eggs, sugar and salt. Mix thoroughly and spread in an even layer in a buttered baking pan that has been sprinkled with bread crumbs. Level the top, brush with sour cream and bake in a hot oven for 30 to 40 minutes. Serve with melted butter or sour cream poured over.

Buckwheat Pudding with Fresh Mushrooms

1 cupful buckwheat groats	1/2 cupful sour cream
500 g fresh mushrooms	2 tblsps butter

Make a buckwheat kasha as directed. When done, add the mushrooms, butter and sour cream. Mix thoroughly. Transfer to a casserole or baking pan and bake for 20 to 30 minutes.

Millet Cakes

2 cupsful millet	1/2 cupful bread crumbs
5 cupsful water or milk	
1 tblsp sugar	2 or 3 tblsps butter
1 tsp salt	

Add salt, sugar and washed millet to boiling water (or milk). Cook for 15 to 20 minutes stirring constantly. Cover tightly and steam for 25 to 30 minutes, then cool. When cool enough to handle, wet the palms of your hands in cold water and shape the cooked millet into round cakes. Dip in bread crumbs or flour and fry in butter. Serve with kissel[12], sour cream, butter or milk sauce.

Buckwheat Cakes

1 cupful buckwheat groats	1/2 cupful bread crumbs
100 g curds or cottage cheese	1/2 tsp salt
	2 tblsps butter
1 tsp sugar	2 eggs

Add salt to 1 1/2 cupsful of water and bring to a boil. Add the cereal and cook for 30 to 35 minutes. When the cereal thickens, add the curds which have been pressed through a strainer or put through a food chopper, eggs and sugar; mix thoroughly. Shape into cakes. Dip in bread crumbs and fry till brown. Serve garnished with sour cream. Without sour cream these cakes may be served with borshch[17] or rassolnik[22].

Plov (Pilau)

Plov is a rice dish cooked in a special way. The different plov derivatives have been known to include such a variety of ingredients as roast or stewed lamb, poultry, fish, eggs, cooked or dried fruits, nuts and vegetables.

The usual procedure for making plov is

to wash and soak the rice for an hour in warm water, drain it thoroughly in a strainer and then cook it in one of the two following ways:

I

Plunge the washed rice into boiling salt water and cook until the grains are soft, but still firm on the inside. Drain in a strainer and then pour over cold water to cool. Melt fat in a deep casserole, put in the rice and pour over the rest of fat. Cover tightly with a lid and keep it on the hob for 40 to 45 minutes. To prevent the rice from stocking to the casserole, put a thin flat cake of noodle dough on the bottom. The cake is served along with the plov.

II

Bring to a boil two cupsful of salt water, add half the butter or rendered fat and throw in one cupful of rice. Boil gently without stirring. When the rice absorbs the water, pour in the remaining fat, cover the casserole tightly and cook for 30 to 40 minutes longer.

Plov with Lamb

1/2 cupful rice	1/2 cupful boiled
500 g lamb	butter
2 onions	Salt
2 medium-sized	Pepper
pomegranates	

Cut the meat into small pieces and dredge with salt and pepper. Sauté in butter or drippings together with finely sliced onion. As soon as the onion and meat are browned, add water to cover and the pomegranate kernels. Cover with a lid and braise until tender. Serve the meat together with the pan juices. Heap the hot plov on top. Cook the plov as directed in Recipe I.

Georgian Plov

2 cupsful rice	150 g honey
150 g raisins	1/2 cupful boiled butter

Prepare the plov as directed in Recipe I. Mix the honey with an equal amount of hot water and add the raisins. Pour this sauce over the plov and cook for 10 minutes.

Uzbek Plov

400 g fatty mutton	200 g mutton (beef)
2 or 3 cupsful rice	fat or vegetable oil
200 to 300 g carrots	Salt, pepper
150 to 200 g onion	

Cut the mutton into small pieces and brown in a kettle (preferably of cast iron) in hot fat. Add the shredded onion and then the shredded carrots and brown together with the mutton. Pour over 4 cupsful of water, season with salt and pepper and bring to a boil. Wash the rice, add it to the meat and smooth off on top. When the water is absorbed, with a paddle make several vertical pipe holes through the plov to the bottom of the kettle. Pour 1 or 2 tablespoonful of water into the holes to keep the plov from burning. Cover the kettle tightly with a lid and cook for 25 to 30 minutes over low heat. Serve heaped on a platter with the mutton on top. Garnish with sliced raw onion.

Plov with Pumpkin and Fruit

1 1/2 cupsful rice	100 g quinces
500 g pumpkin	100 g raisins
200 g apples	1/2 cupful butter

Pare and core fresh apples and quinces; dice finely and mix with raisins. Melt part of the butter in a casserole and line the bottom with a layer of pumpkin. Put 1/3 of the rice over the pumpkin and a layer of mixed fruit over the rice. Add two more alternating layers of rice and fruit. Pour over the remaining butter and add water to cover the top layer of the rice. Cover the casserole tightly and cook over low heat for one hour.

Plov "Ararat"

(Armenian)

1.7 kg rice	200 g raisins
800 g apples	100 g shelled almonds
900 g quinces	100 g dried apricots
300 g butter	50-100 g alcohol

Prepare the plov as in the preceding recipe and heap it in an oblong platter. Place around the plov rows of baked apples and quinces, raisins and dried apricots fried as in the above recipe and the shelled almonds. Hollow out two raw apples and pour alcohol into them. Place an apple at each end of the platter. Turn out the lights, ignite the alcohol in the apples and serve.

Ukrainian Dumplings

(Galushki)

2 1/2 cupsful flour	100 g butter or boiled
2 eggs	butter
1/2 cupful water	1 tsp salt (scant)
1/2 cupful sour cream	2 tblsps melted butter

Sift the flour. Beat the eggs, add the salt and combine with water and melted butter. Work this mixture into the flour and knead to a smooth elastic dough. Roll out till 1/2 cm thick and cut into any desired shape. Lay the galushki in boiling salt water and cook at boiling point for 10 minutes. When the galushki rise to the top they are done. Remove them with a skimmer. After draining thoroughly in a colander or strainer, brown in melted butter in a casserole or frying pan. Serve hot with sour cream poured over. Pork fat or salt pork may be substituted for butter. Dice the pork finely and render; pour over the galushki together with the cracklings.

Noodle Pudding

(Lapshevnik)

250 g noodles	2 tblsps bread crumbs
1 egg	1 tblsp butter
1 cupful milk	1/2 tsp salt
2 tblsps sugar	

Cook and drain the noodles. Put them in a buttered baking pan and pour over the milk, raw egg, sugar and salt which have been combined. Sprinkle with bread crumbs and butter. Bake for 15 to 20 minutes or until browned. Serve sprinkled with sugar or butter.

Noodle Pudding with Curds

250 g noodles	2 tblsps bread crumbs
2 eggs	1/2 tsp salt
1 cupful curds	1 tblsp butter
2 tblsps sugar	

Cook the noodles, drain and mix with beaten eggs, salt and sugar. Rub the curds through a strainer or put them through the food chopper. Add the curds to the noodles and mix. Put into a buttered pan, sprinkle with bread crumbs, and butter. Bake for 15 to 20 minutes. Sprinkle with sugar before serving.

Noodle Pudding with Meat

250 g noodles	2 tblsps bread crumbs
250 g meat (boned)	1 tblsp butter
1 egg	1 onion (optional)
1/2 tsp salt	Pepper

Cook and then drain the noodles. Put the meat (beef, lamb or pork) through the food chopper, season with salt and pepper and sauté in butter over low heat. When the meat is tender, put it through the food chopper again. Add 2 tblsps stock or water drained from the noodles. Mix thoroughly. If desired, add sautéed onion to the meat. Cooked meat may be substituted for raw meat. Add a raw egg and salt to the noodles and mix. Put a layer of noodles in a buttered baking pan, spread the meat over the noodles and cover with another layer of noodles. Level off the top, dust with bread crumbs and sprinkle with butter. Bake for 15 to 20 minutes.

Beans, Peas and Lentils

Beans and Walnuts

(Lobio)

1 cupful beans	1 onion or 75 g green
50 g shelled walnuts	onions
Salt	Pepper

Wash and soak the beans in cold water for 3 or 4 hours. Drain, add cold water to cover and cook until tender; add the minced onion and bring to boiling point. Add crushed walnuts to the beans. Season with salt and pepper. Mix with a wooden spoon. Serve hot or cold sprinkled with minced greens.

String Beans with Walnut Sauce

Wash and remove the strings of the beans. Cut and cook in boiling salt water for 15 to 20 minutes. Drain in a strainer, transfer to a salad bowl and pour over walnut sauce.

Walnut Sauce

100 g shelled walnuts	1/4 cupful vinegar
100 g dry or green	1 clove of garlic
onions	Salt, red pepper
50 g kindza[10] or	
parsley greens	

Grind the nut meat and garlic. Add salt, red pepper, minced onion and minced kindza. Combine thoroughly and stir in the vinegar.

Lentils and Dried Apricots

1 cupful lentils	2 or 3 tblsps vegetable
50 g dried apricots	oil
1 or 2 onions	Salt, pepper
25 g shelled walnuts	Minced kindza[10]

Wash and put the lentils in 2 1/2 cupful of cold water. Bring to a boil and cook for 1 to 1 1/2 hours. Soak the dried apricots for 15 minutes in warm water, then drain. Sauté the apricots and minced onion in the oil. Season with salt and pepper. Add to the lentils the chopped walnuts. Cook for 10 to 15 minutes. Serve sprinkled with finely minced kindza.

White Beans Paste
(Armenian Manner)

320 g white beans	2 tsps vegetable oil
80 g seedless raisins	Lemon slices
120 g shelled almonds	Salt
	Parsley

Wash, cook, drain and then press the beans through a sieve. Remove the skins from the almonds which have been soaked, chop them up and add to the bean paste along with the raisins. Transfer the mixture to a baking pan that has been greased with vegetable oil and cook over low heat for 10 to 15 minutes. Serve garnished with lemon slices and parsley.

DAIRY
DISHES

cottage-cheese
pancakes

1/2 cupful sour cream

1/2 cupful flour
2 tblsps butter
2 tblsps sugar

500 g cottage
cheese

1 egg

Cottage Cheese and Curds

Thin Pancakes with Cottage Cheese

2 cupsful flour	500 g cottage cheese
3 cupsful milk	3/4 cupful sour cream
2 eggs	2 tblsps butter
3/4 cupful sugar	Salt

Beat one egg in a mixing bowl. Add 1 tblsp sugar, 1/3 tsp salt and 1 cupful of cold milk and blend. Gradually add the sifted flour and mix with a wooden paddle till smooth. Stir in the remaining milk and beat vigorously. Pour just enough batter onto a well-heated greased griddle or frying pan to make a thin pancake. Cook over medium heat. Brown on one side only. Quickly grease the pan and pour the batter for the next pancake. Blinchiki must be very thin. If they are thick, thin the batter with a little milk.

Cottage Cheese Filling

Rub the cottage cheese through a sieve, add beaten egg yolk, sugar, 1/2 tsp salt, a little grated lemon or orange rind and 1 tblsp boiled butter. Blend the ingredients thoroughly. Raisins may be added.

Put a heaping tablespoonful of cottage cheese mixture on the browned side of the pancake and fold up like an envelope. Brush with egg white the edge of the pancake folded last; this will prevent it from unwrapping in the frying pan. Brown evenly in butter. Dredge with powdered sugar and serve hot. Pass sour cream in a sauceboat.

Ukrainian Cottage Cheese Dumplings (Galushki)

500 g cottage cheese	1 cupful flour
2 eggs	2 tblsps bread crumbs
3 tblsps sugar	1/2 tsp salt
3 tblsps butter	1/2 cupful sour cream

Pass the cottage cheese through a food chopper or rub through a sieve. Add beaten eggs, sugar, 1 tblsp melted butter and salt. Mix thoroughly. Work in the sifted flour and knead. Transfer to a floured dough board and divide into four parts. Shape each piece into a long sausage-like roll, flatten slightly and slice off wedge-shaped pieces about 1/2 cm thick. Lay in boiling salt water and cook until the galushki rise to the top. Drain and serve hot with boiled butter poured over and sprinkled with browned bread crumbs. Serve with sour cream. Galushki may be browned in the oven. For this they should be poured over with sour cream and dotted with butter. Then put the pan with the galushki in a water bath and bake until the crust is golden brown.

Cottage Cheese Pudding

500 g cottage cheese	100 g raisins
1 egg	1 cupful berry or fruit
3 tblsps sour cream	juice syrup
3 tblsps sugar	3 tblsps butter
1/4 vanilla powder	Salt
2 tblsps mannacroup	

Put the cottage cheese through the food chopper, add 2 tblsps boiled butter, a beaten egg and sugar, mannacroup, 1/2 tsp salt and the vanilla. Mix thoroughly with a wooden paddle; add the raisins. Transfer the mixture to a buttered pan dredged with bread crumbs. Level the top, brush with sour cream and dot with butter. Bake for 25 to 30 minutes in a hot oven. Serve hot with syrup or sour cream poured over.

Sweet Cheese Paste

500 g cottage cheese or curds
100 g butter
3 tblsps sour cream
1 cupful sugar
1/2 vanilla powder

1/4 tsp salt
Fresh or fresh-frozen berries (optional)
Roasted almonds or pistachio nuts (optional)

Cream the butter until light and fluffy. Add the sugar, vanilla and salt and blend. Gradually add and mix thoroughly the cottage cheese which has been rubbed through a sieve and the sour cream. When the paste is smooth, heap it on a plate and smoothen with a knife. Garnish with fresh or fresh-frozen berries, chopped roasted almonds or pistachio nuts. Chill before serving. If desired, any of the following may be added: 1 tblsp cocoa or powdered chocolate, 1 tsp cinnamon, finely shredded candied fruit or raisins.

FANCY
BREADS AND
PIES

green onions and
eggs filling

3-4 eggs

4 eggs

1-1½ kg
carrots

400 g green
onions

carrots
filling

flour

Pirozhki, Pirogi, Kulebyaki

Pirozhki are small closed pies, patties or turnovers of various shapes usually made of straight dough, flaky paste or a shortcake dough; they may be baked or deep fired. Ordinarily they weigh 75-80 g, and about 50 g if served with soup.

Pirogi may be briefly described as large-sized pirozhki. However, pirogi are made with either straight or sponge dough. They may be closed, covered with a lattice or open.

Kulebyaki resemble pirogi but contain more filling and less dough.

Any of these may be served as a soup accompaniment, zakuski[1] or main dishes. Their place in the menu is determined by the filling. Pirozhki, pirogi and kulebyaki have their counterparts in many countries but they can hardly compare with Russian cookery as regards variety of filling, shape, size and manner of cooking.

Straight Dough

1 kg flour	2-4 tblsps butter
30-40 g yeast	(margarine)
2 cupsful milk (or	2-3 eggs
water)	1 tblsp sugar
	1 tsp salt

A straight dough is one in which the ingredients are all blended at one time, kneaded and set aside to rise.

Rub the yeast and sugar together with the back of a spoon until the yeast becomes liquefied. Stir in the luke warm liquid and beaten eggs. Add flour and salt which have been sifted together and

knead until smooth. Add the butter (margarine) last and knead until smooth and elastic. Set aside to rise in a warm place; 2 1/2 to 3 hours will be sufficient time. This will yield dough for 38-40 pirozhki.

Sponge Method

Make a thick batter using all the required liquid, the yeast, sugar and about half the flour. Mix until smooth and stand in a warm place for 45-60 minutes. After the sponge has doubled its original bulk and begins to settle, add the remaining flour, salt, butter and eggs. Knead until smooth and elastic and form a ball, leaving the sides of the bowl clean. Set aside to rise in a warm place for 1 1/2 to 2 hours.

Shortcake Dough

I

500 g flour	2 eggs
1 cupful sour cream	1 tblsp sugar
2 tblsps butter or	1/2 tsp salt
margarine	

II

500 g flour	2 tblsps vodka or
200 g butter or	brandy
margarine	1/2 tsp salt
1 tblsp sugar	

Sift the dry ingredients together. Make a hollow in the centre. Beat together the sour cream, eggs and butter. Pour them into the hollow and quickly knead into a smooth dough. Shape into a ball, cover with a cloth and chill for 30 to 40 minutes. Roll this dough into a sheet 1/2 cm thick, cut into the desired shapes, brush with egg and put a bit of filling on each piece. Fold and pinch the edges. On the baking pan space the pirozhki 1 1/2 to 2 cm apart. Brush with beaten egg and bake for 10 to 15 minutes. Yield: 20 to 25 pirozhki.

Flaky Paste

500 g flour	1/2 cupful water
400 g butter	1 tsp salt
Juice of 1/2 lemon	

Sift the flour. Combine one half the flour with the butter, roll into a square 1 1/2 to 2 cm thick and set aside to chill. Sift together the remaining flour and salt and make a dough with the water and lemon juice. Shape into a ball, cover with a cloth and set aside for 20 to 30 minutes. After this roll the dough out until it is twice as wide and a little longer than the piece of dough made with the butter. Put the butter and flour dough on it, fold over the sides of the bottom layer, and pinch the edges together to make a closed "envelope". Dust with flour and roll the "envelope" into a strip 20 to 25 cm wide and about 1 cm thick. Carefully fold to quarter size and chill for 30 to 40 minutes. Roll out the chilled dough, fold and chill again. After rolling and chilling the dough once more, it may be rolled and cut for pirozhki, pirogi, etc. Do not knead the cuttings, merely press them

together, chill and then roll, and cut into the desired shape for pirozhki or shells.

Curd Pie
(Vatrushka)

I

Make an yeast dough (see p. 149), divide into pieces, roll them into balls, put them on a buttered baking pan 2-3 cm (about an inch) apart and set aside in a warm place. When the balls rise, make a depression in each with the bottom of a small glass and fill it with curd (cottage cheese). Brush the vatrushka with egg and bake for 10-15 minutes.
These pies may also be filled with fresh berries or jam. If fresh berries like strawberries, wild strawberries and raspberries are used, put them into the depression, sprinkle with sugar and brush the edges of the dough with egg.

II

Make a shortcake dough (see p. 149), roll it out 1/2 cm thick, cut round cakes 5-6 cm across, knead the trimmings, roll and cut. Put cottage cheese (curds) or berries in the centre of each cake, pinch the edges but leave the centre open. Put the cakes on a baking pan or sheet, brush with egg and bake in a hot oven for 10-15 minutes.

Belyash
(Kazakh Meat Pie)

500 g flour	15 g yeast
1 cupful milk	1/2 tsp salt
1 tsp sugar	

Make a yeast dough and divide it into small cakes. Put a spoonful of meat filling (see below) in the middle of each cake, pinch the edges so that part of the filling is covered by the dough. Heat fat in a frying pan and fry the belyash on both sides, open side first.

Filling

400 g meat (boned)	Salt, pepper
2-3 onions	Frying fat
3 tblsps water	

Put the meat through the meat grinder, mix with minced onion, salt and pepper.

Deep Fried Pirozhki

1 kg flour	4 tblsps sugar
2 1/2 cupsful milk	4 eggs
5 tblsps butter	1 tsp salt
30 g yeast	

Make a sponge. For this in the warm milk dissolve the yeast, add half the flour and mix until smooth. Set aside for 40-50 minutes. When the sponge rises mix in the melted butter, eggs, sugar and salt. Add the remaining flour and knead until the dough leaves the sides of the bowl. Set aside in a warm place for 1 1/2 hours. As soon as the dough rises, beat it down; after it rises again turn it onto a floured dough board.

A straight dough may also be made with these ingredients. Dissolve the yeast in milk, add the butter, eggs, sugar, salt, and all the flour, knead thoroughly, set aside and let the dough rise twice.

While the dough rises, prepare the filling to have it ready by the time the dough rises for the second time.

Cut the dough into 40-50 g pieces, roll and shape into balls. Allow them to rise a little, then roll each ball into a cake 0.5-1 cm thick. Put filling in the middle of each cake, join the edges and pinch. Lay the pies on a floured board or baking sheet and set aside in a warm place to rise.

Deep fry, browning on both sides. Preserves, jam, apples or the fillings given below may be used for these pies.

Fillings

(For dough made with 1 kg of flour)

Raw Meat

800 g beef (boned)	1 or 2 onions
2 or 3 tblsps butter	Salt, pepper
3 eggs	Minced dill or parsley

Put the raw meat through the food chopper, sauté in butter and then put it through the food chopper again. Separately sauté the minced onion, combine with the meat, chopped hard-cooked eggs, minced parsley or dill. Add salt and pepper to taste.

Cooked Meat

Put the meat through the food chopper. Sauté the minced onion, add the meat and fry for another 3 or 4 minutes. Add chopped hard-cooked eggs, minced dill, salt and pepper to taste and 1 or 2 tblsps butter. Add 1 or 2 tblsps stock if the filling is too dry.

Pluck

1 kg pluck	3 eggs
2 or 3 tblsps butter	2 onions
Minced dill or parsley	Salt, pepper

Beef, calf, lamb or pork pluck may be used. Wash in warm water and cook till tender. Cut into small pieces and put through the food chopper. Sauté slightly together with the minced onions. Add chopped hard-cooked eggs, minced dill or parsley. Season with salt and pepper.

Buckwheat Kasha[18] and Liver

300 g liver	3 eggs
1 cupful buckwheat groats	1 or 2 onions
2 or 3 tblsps butter	Salt, pepper

Wash veal, lamb or pork liver in cold water. Cut into small pieces and sauté in butter together with the minced onions. When tender, finely chop the liver, season with salt and pepper, mix with buckwheat kasha made of 1 cupful of groats, and chopped hard-cooked eggs.

Fish

750 g fish (500 g fillet)	Minced dill
2 tblsps butter	Hard-cooked egg
1 or 2 onions	(optional)
Salt, pepper	

Cut the boned fillet of pike, zander, catfish or carp into small pieces. Dredge with salt and pepper and sauté in butter. Combine with sautéed minced onion and dill and mix thoroughly. Chopped hard-cooked egg may be added.

Fish and Rice

300 g fillet of fish	Salt, pepper
3/4 cupful rice	Minced dill or parsley
2 or 3 tblsps butter	

Cut the fillet into small pieces and sauté in 1 to 1 1/2 tblsps butter. Boil and drain the rice thoroughly. Add the rice, boiled butter and minced dill or parsley to the fish. Season with salt and pepper to taste.
This recipe may be varied by substituting cooked fish. If desired, minced sautéed onion may be added.

Viziga[3]

100 g viziga	3 or 4 eggs
2 or 3 tblsps butter	Salt, pepper
Boiled rice (optional)	Minced parsley or dill

Soak the viziga in cold water for 2 or 3 hours. Wash, add fresh water to cover and cook for 3 to 3 1/2 hours. When tender, drain thoroughly in a colander. Put the viziga through the food chopper or mince it with a sharp knife. Add boiled butter, chopped hard-cooked eggs and minced parsley or dill. Season with salt and pepper to taste and mix thoroughly. If desired, boiled rice, small pieces of fish and minced onion sautéed in butter may be added.

Rice and Eggs

1 1/4 cupsful rice	Minced dill
3 or 4 eggs	2 or 3 tblsps butter
Salt, pepper	

Wash the rice and boil in salt water (10 to 12 cupsful). Drain thoroughly in a strainer. Mix together the boiled rice, chopped hard-cooked eggs, butter, minced dill and salt to taste.

Buckwheat Kasha[18] and Eggs

2 cupsful buckwheat groats	2 or 3 tblsps butter or boiled butter
3 or 4 eggs	

Prepare a fluffy buckwheat kasha and mix with the chopped hard-cooked eggs and butter. Salt to taste.

Buckwheat Kasha[18] and Dried Mushrooms

2 cupsful buckwheat groats	50 g dried mushrooms, cooked and finely chopped
2 or 3 tblsps butter or boiled butter	1 onion

Prepare a fluffy buckwheat kasha and mix with the minced onion sautéed in butter and the mushrooms. Salt to taste.

Fresh Boletus Mushrooms

1 kg mushrooms	1 onion
1 or 2 tblsps butter	1/4 cupful sour cream
Minced parsley or dill	Salt

Clean, wash and cook the mushrooms till tender. Cut them into small pieces and sauté in butter. Add the sour cream, sautéed onion and salt to taste. Cover and simmer for 10 to 15 minutes. Add the parsley or dill and cool.

Pickled Mushrooms

1 kg pickled mushrooms	2 or 3 tblsps boiled butter or vegetable oil
1 or 2 onions	Pepper

Wash the mushrooms. If too pungent, soak them for an hour or two in cold water. Drain thoroughly, cut the mushrooms fine and sauté in butter. Separately sauté the minced onion and then mix with the mushrooms, add pepper to taste.

Dried Mushrooms and Rice

50 g dried mushrooms	2 or 3 tblsps butter or vegetable oil
1 cupful rice	Salt, pepper
1 or 2 onions	

Cook the mushrooms and cut them fine. Add sautéed minced onion, mix and sauté for 2 or 3 minutes. Boil the rice, drain and mix with the mushrooms. Season with salt and pepper.

Rice or Millet with Raisins

1 cupful rice or millet	2 or 3 tblsps sugar
200 g raisins	1 1/2 tblsps butter

Wash the raisins in warm water, drain thoroughly and dry on a cloth. Mix them with boiled rice or fluffy millet kasha (see p. 135), sugar and butter.

Fresh Cabbage

1 1/2 to 2 kg head of cabbage	2 or 3 tblsps butter
3 or 4 eggs	1 tsp sugar
	Salt

Clean and shred the cabbage. Scald in a colander, then rinse with cold water and drain thoroughly. Sauté in butter for 10 or 15 minutes, stirring continuously. Mix with chopped hard-cooked eggs, add sugar and salt to taste.

Sauerkraut and Mushrooms

1 kg sauerkraut	50 g dried mushrooms
3 or 4 tblsps fat	Salt, pepper
2 or 3 onions	

If the cabbage is too sour, rinse it in water and then scald. Chop up fine, add butter or vegetable oil, cover and braise until tender (for 5 hours). Separately sauté minced onion and add to it finely cut up cooked mushrooms, salt and pepper. Sauté for 3 or 4 minutes and mix with the cabbage.

Green Onions and Eggs

400 g green onions	3 or 4 tblsps butter
4 eggs	Salt, pepper

Wash and cut up the green onions. Sauté slightly and then mix with the chopped hard-cooked eggs. Season with salt and pepper to taste.

Carrots

1 — 1 1/2 kg carrots	1 tsp sugar
3 or 4 eggs	Salt
2 or 3 tblsps butter	

Scrape, wash and finely dice the carrots. Add 1/2 cupful of water, one spoonful of butter, cover with a lid and simmer until tender. Mash the carrots. Add sugar, butter and salt to taste. Add the chopped hard-cooked eggs and mix thoroughly.

Curds

(Cottage Cheese)

500 g curds	1/2 cupful sugar
1 egg	1 tblsp butter
Salt	1 tblsp flour

Rub the curds through a strainer or put them through the food chopper. Add beaten egg, flour, sugar and boiled butter, and salt to taste. Mix thoroughly. If desired, vanilla flavouring, raisins or candied fruit may be added. Should the curds be too moist, put them in a cheese cloth and squeeze out the whey.

Apples

1 kg apples
1 cupful sugar

Pare, core and cut up the apples. Add sugar and 2 or 3 tblsps water. Cook over low heat until thick and mushy.
This filling may be used for pirogi made with straight or shortcake dough, flaky, paste, for fancy bread, or deep fried dumpings.
If raw apples are used for filling, pare, chop and mix them with sugar.

Dried Apricots

400 g dried apricots
1/2 cupful sugar

Wash the dried apricots in warm water and drain. Add just enough water to cover and cook for 10 to 15 minutes. Drain the fruit in a sieve, spread it on the dough and sprinkle with sugar. Use the fruit liquor for kissel[12] or sweet sauce.

Pancakes

Bliny. Sponge Method

1 kg flour	2 tblsps sugar
4 to 5 cupsful milk	1 1/2 tsps salt
3 tblsps butter	40 g yeast
2 eggs	

Make the sponge by dissolving the yeast in 2 cupsful of warm water and adding 500 g flour. Mix until smooth, cover with a cloth and set aside in a warm place for about an hour, or until the batter becomes bubbly. Add the salt, sugar, egg yolks, melted butter (oil or margarine) and mix thoroughly. Gradually add the rest of the flour and beat until smooth. Add the warm milk gradually, cup by cup and mix the batter, thoroughly. Cover with a cloth and set aside in a warm place to rise. When the batter rises, beat it till it settles and set aside to rise again. After the batter rises, beat until it settles and then stir in beaten egg whites. As soon as the batter rises, cook the pancakes on a hot griddle. The batter should rise no less than three times.

The pancakes will be drier if buckwheat flour is substituted for half the wheat flour. Make the sponge with the wheat flour and one tablespoonful of buckwheat flour along with the other ingredients and warm milk.

Quick Pancakes

500 g flour	1/2 tsp salt
3 cupsful water	1/2 tsp baking soda
2 or 3 eggs	1/2 tsp acetic acid or
1 tblsp sugar	cream of tartar

Beat the eggs and add warm water, salt, sugar and soda. Stir in the flour and mix with a whisk until the batter is smooth. Dissolve the acetic acid or cream of tartar in a cupful of water (additional) and stir it into the batter. Mix thoroughly and cook at once as directed.

Ukrainian Pancakes

300 g millet	2 tblsps sugar
300 g buckwheat flour	1 cupful sour cream
3 or 4 tblsps butter	2 cupsful milk
2 eggs	15 g yeast

Carefully wash the millet and cook a porridge. Chill and rub through a strainer. Bring to a boil 1/2 cupful of milk and 1 tblsp butter. Stir in 1 cupful of buckwheat flour, make a thick batter and cool to room temperature. Add to the batter the yeast which has been stirred in warm water, mix and set aside to rise. Then add the sifted porridge, the rest of the buckwheat flour, the egg yolks which have been rubbed together with the sugar, salt and warm milk. Mix thoroughly and set aside to rise again. Cook on a hot griddle. Before serving pour melted butter over. Serve sour cream separately.

Thick Pancakes

(Oladyi)

500 g flour	3-4 tblsps butter or
2 cupsful milk or water	vegetable oil
2 eggs	1/2 tsp salt
1 1/2 tblsps sugar	25 g yeast

Dissolve the yeast in warm milk, stir in the flour and beat. Set aside in a warm place to rise. Then add the eggs, salt, sugar and 1 tblsp butter or oil. Mix the batter thoroughly and set aside. After the batter rises again, cook. Pour the batter onto the hot buttered griddle with a wet spoon. Brown on both sides and serve with sugar, honey, preserves or cottage cheese mixed with sour cream and sugar.

Pumpkin, Squash Marrow or Carrot Thick Pancakes

1 kg flour	2 tblsps vinegar
1 kg desired	1 1/2 tsps salt
vegetables	1/2 tsp soda
2 eggs	2 tblsps butter
1 or 2 tblsps sugar	

Wash, cut and cook the vegetables in a small amount of water. When tender put them through the food chopper or rub through a strainer. While the vegetable puree is still warm, beat in the eggs, add salt, vinegar (or sour milk) and stir in the flour which has been sifted together with the soda. Mix thoroughly and cook the oladyi on a hot griddle.

Pancakes with Apples

500 g flour	1 tblsp sugar
2 cupsful milk	1/2 tsp salt
(or water)	25 g yeast
2 eggs	3 or 4 apples
2 tblsps butter	

Dissolve the yeast in warm water or milk. Add the butter, eggs, sugar and salt. Mix thoroughly and gradually stir in the flour. Cover with a cloth and set aside in a warm place to rise. Pare, core and shred the apples. When the batter rises, stir in the apples. Cook the pancakes on a hot griddle. Use a wet spoon to ladle the batter onto the griddle.

Marrow Pancakes

Make a puree of 1 kg marrow. Add 3 tblsps butter, mix and cool. Add three beaten eggs, salt, 1/4 cupful sugar and mix thoroughly. Gradually stir in 2 cupsful of flour and 2 g soda. Beat until the batter begins to bubble. Cook on a hot well-greased griddle.

Thin Batter Pancakes

(Blinchiki)

250 g flour	2 tblsps boiled butter
2 1/2 cupsful milk	(to oil griddle)
3 eggs	1/4 tsp salt
2 tblsps butter	

Beat the egg yolks, add 1/2 cupful milk, salt and sugar. Gradually stir in flour and combine thoroughly. Heat and add the butter. Beat the batter until smooth. Gradually add the rest of the milk and beaten egg whites. Cook thin blinchiki on a well-oiled griddle. When done fold into quarter size and remove from the griddle to a hot plate; cover with a napkin. Pass honey or sugar.

Blinchiki with Cottage Cheese, Apple or Other Filling

250 g flour	1 tblsp boiled butter
2 1/2 cupsful milk	or margarine (to oil
3 eggs	griddle)
1/4 tsp salt	1/2 tblsp sugar

Beat the eggs, add salt, sugar and 1/2 cupful of milk. Stir in the flour and beat the batter until smooth. Then add the rest of the milk. Heat a medium-sized griddle and oil it with butter or a piece of pork. Ladle the batter with a spoon and turn the griddle so that the batter spreads evenly. Brown on one side only; sprinkle with dry bread crumbs and stack on a plate or board. When all the pancakes have been cooked, spread them out browned side up and put a tablespoonful of filling on each. Fold the thin pancakes like an envelope and brown it in a buttered frying pan. If served with cottage cheese or apple filling, the blinchiki may be dusted with powdered sugar. Blinchiki with a meat filling may be served with sour cream or tomato sauce.

Pancake Pie

Prepare the pancakes (blinchiki) as directed above. Butter a cake pan or shallow saucepan and dust it with bread crumbs. Line the bottom and sides with one layer of blinchiki, browned side in. Spread a layer of filling and cover with a pancake. Alternate layers of filling and pancakes till the pan is full. Cover the top layer of filling with a pancake, brush it with a beaten egg, dust with bread crumbs and sprinkle with butter. Bake for 30 to 40 minutes. When the pie is done, turn onto a plate. Separately pass butter. This pie may be served as a meat or chicken bouillon accompaniment.

Any kind of filling is suitable for a pancake pie. Also, several fillings may be alternated in the same pie. Minced chicken meat and white sauce make a good filling (see p. 151).

Fancy Breads

Buns
(Shanezhki)

1 kg flour	5 egg yolks
1 1/2 cupsful milk	1 1/2 cupsful sugar

300 g butter or margarine	1/2 tsp salt
	40 g yeast

Glaze

1 tblsp sour cream	1 tblsp oil
1 tblsp flour	1 to 1 1/2 tblsps sugar

Dissolve the yeast in warm milk, add half the flour and set aside till the sponge rises. When the bulk is doubled, mix in salt, egg yolks and sugar beaten together until light. Add the remainder of the flour and knead. Add the melted butter or margarine, knead until the dough leaves the walls of the pan clean and forms a ball. Dust with flour, cover with a cloth and set aside in a warm place to rise. When the dough has doubled in bulk, turn it on a special board, divide and shape into little buns. Put the buns on a buttered baking pan and set aside in a warm place to rise. Brush the buns with the glaze made by mixing sour cream, oil and flour, sprinkle with sugar.

Knotted Tea Biscuits
(Krendelki)

1 kg flour	100 to 125 g butter or
1 1/2 cupsful milk	margarine
5 eggs	1/2 tsp salt
1 cupful sugar	30 g yeast
Rind of 1/2 lemon	

Prepare the dough as directed above in the recipe for shanezhki. Add the grated lemon rind together with the eggs and sugar. After the dough rises, transfer it to the dough board, sprinkle with flour, cut and tie into a knot. Brush with butter and sprinkle with sugar. Bake for 10 to 12 minutes.

Knotted Almond Biscuits

1 kg flour	100 g almonds
1 1/3 cupsful milk	40 to 50 g yeast
12 egg yolks	1/2 vanilla powder
1 1/2 cupsful sugar	1 or 2 tblsps powdered
300 g butter or	sugar
margarine	3/4 tsp salt
200 g raisins	

Prepare a sponge by combining the yeast, milk and half the flour. Separately rub together the egg yolks, sugar and vanilla until light and then stir in the creamed butter. When the sponge is ready, add to it the prepared mixture, the salt and the rest of the flour. Knead until the dough forms a ball and leaves the sides of the bowl clean. Add washed and dried raisins, knead again, cover and set aside in a warm place to rise. This dough should be rather heavy. After it rises, turn onto a floured board, knead and roll out rope-like (thinner at the ends). Tie it nicely into a knot or bow, transfer to a baking sheet and set in a warm place for several minutes. Brush with egg yolk, sprinkle with chopped almonds and bake for 40 to 50 minutes. When done, remove the krendel from the baking sheet and lay it on several layers of paper. Before serving sprinkle with powdered sugar.

Spring Cake
(Kulich)

1 kg flour	150 g raisins
1 1/2 cupsful milk	50 g candied fruit
6 eggs	50 g almonds
300 g butter or	1/2 vanilla powder or
margarine	5-6 ground cardamom
1 1/2-2 cupsful sugar	seeds
40-50 g yeast	3/4 tsp salt

Dissolve the yeast in 1 1/2 cupsful of warm milk, stir in half the flour and mix until the dough is smooth. Cover with a cloth and set aside in a warm place to rise until spongy. When the dough is double its original bulk, add the salt, egg yolks (reserving one to brush the top) beaten together with sugar and vanilla and butter. Mix thoroughly with a whip, add the egg whites beaten stiff and the rest of the flour. The dough should not be too thick. Mix until the dough forms a ball and leaves the sides of the bowl and the whip clean. Cover with a cloth and set aside in a warm place. When the dough has doubled its bulk, add the raisins (washed and dried), the candied fruit (diced) and the chopped almonds (without skins). Mix thoroughly. Butter round pieces of paper on both sides and place them in the bottom of each mould; butter the sides of the mould and sprinkle with flour or bread crumbs. Put in just enough dough to fill only 1/3 the height of the mould. Cover with a cloth and set aside to rise. When the dough rises and fills 3/4 of the mould, brush the top with beaten egg and bake in a moderate oven for 50 to 60 minutes. Turn the kulich carefully so that it bakes evenly. Take care not to jar it.

Should the kulich brown too rapidly, cover it with a sheet of wet paper. Test it with a wooden toothpick; if it comes away clean, the kulich is sufficiently baked.

Cool the kulich and decorate with glaze

(see above) and candied fruit, berries from preserves or chocolate figures, etc.

II

Dissolve the yeast in 1 1/2 cupsful of milk, stir in 4 cupsful of flour and knead. Then add salt, sugar, egg yolks beaten light, boiled butter or margarine and egg whites beaten stiff. Knead until smooth, sprinkle with flour, cover with a cloth and set aside to rise over night in a place protected from draft. The following morning add the remaining flour and vanilla mixed with sugar. Knead as directed in I. Cover the dough with a cloth and set aside in a warm place to rise. When the dough has risen, mix in raisins, almonds and remaining ingredients. Turn into moulds and continue as directed in I.

Spring Cake with Almonds

(Almond Kulich)

1 kg flour	300 g blanched
1 1/2 cupsful milk	almonds
6 eggs	40 to 50 g yeast
300 g butter or	1/2 vanilla powder
margarine	1 1/2 to 2 cupsful sugar
3/4 tsp salt	

Prepare the dough as directed in the above recipe for kulich; knead and add 250 g shredded almonds. Before baking sprinkle the remaining almonds on top.

Spiced Drop Cookies

(Pryanichki)

1 cupful flour	5 cardamom seeds
3 eggs	1/4 vanilla powder
1 cupful sugar	Grated lemon rind

Beat egg yolks and sugar together until light. Add the ground cardamom seeds,

vanilla or a little grated lemon rind. Stir in flour and mix until smooth. Drop the batter onto a buttered cookie sheet with a teaspoon, spacing the cookies about 4 cm apart to allow for spreading. Bake in a hot oven for 7 to 10 minutes.

Honey Cake

(Kovrizhka)

2 cupsful flour	50 g almonds or other
1/2 cupful sugar	nuts
150 g honey	Ground cinnamon and
1/2 tsp baking soda	cloves
	1 egg

Beat the egg and sugar together until light. Mix in the honey, cinnamon, cloves, and baking soda. Gradually stir in the flour and beat the batter with a whip for 5 to 10 minutes. Brown 1 or 2 lumps of sugar in a small saucepan, add 1 1/2 to 2 tablespoonsful of water and bring to a boil. Add this to the batter together with the honey to make the batter brown. Pour into a buttered baking pan that has been dusted with flour. Smooth the top and sprinkle with shredded almonds or nuts. Bake in a warm oven for 15 to 20 minutes. After the kovrizhka cools, it may be cut into two layers, a filling of jam spread between them. Coat with glaze (see p. 157).

Moscow Doughnuts

(Ponchiki)

1 1/2 cupsful flour	1 egg
2 tblsps sugar	1/2 cupful milk
1 tblsp butter	1/2 tsp baking soda
1/2 tsp cinnamon	100 g frying fat

Sift together flour, soda and cinnamon. Beat together egg and sugar, stir in milk and add flour gradually. Knead and then roll 1/2 cm thick. Cut with a doughnut cutter and deep fry. Sprinkle with powdered sugar.

Rye Cookies

2 cupsful fine rye flour	2 tblsps sour cream
3 tblsps sugar	1/2 tsp baking soda
2 eggs	2 tblsps melted butter

Beat together the egg and sugar with a wooden spoon. Gradually stir in the melted butter and then chilled sour cream. Add the soda mixed with a little flour and then the rest of the flour, making a thick dough. Roll thin, brush with egg yolk. With a fork make zig-zagged lines on top and cut into any desired shapes. Bake on a buttered cookie sheet.

Biscuits

(Korzhiki)

2 cupsful flour	1 egg
2 tblsps butter	3 tblsps sugar
2/3 cupful sour cream	1/2 tsp baking soda

Sift together flour, sugar, baking soda and salt. Make a well in the middle, pour in the egg, sour cream and creamed butter and knead. Roll 1/2 cm thick and cut with a cookie cutter, then place on a buttered cookie sheet. Brush with the beaten egg and pierce with a fork. Bake in a hot oven for 10 to 15 minutes.

Tart meat solyanka (see p. 40)

Fish soup (see p. 46)

Russian pokhlebka (see p. 29)

Zharkoye (see p. 93)

Caucasian shashlyk (see p. 98)

Tsyplenok-tabaka (see p. 105)

Pelmeni (see p. 113)

Manty (see p. 114)

Kvass (see p. 169)

DESSERTS

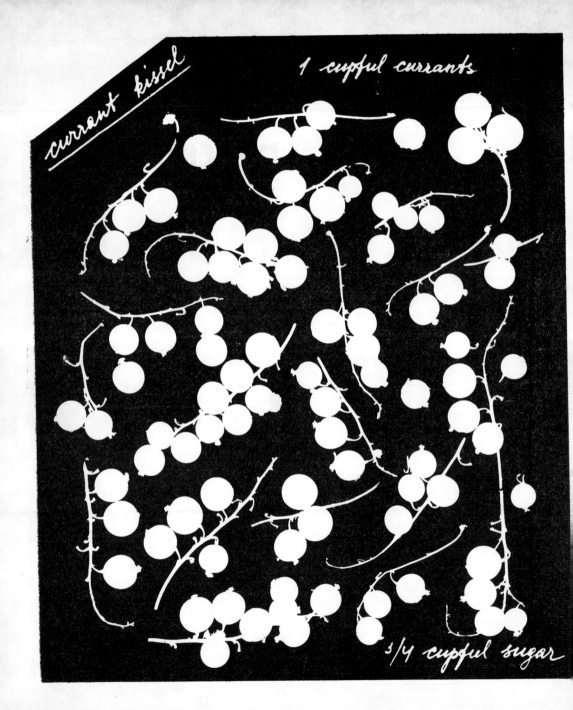

currant kissel

1 cupful currants

3/4 cupful sugar

Kissel

The name "kissel" goes back to the time when this essentially Russian dessert was made with soured cereal water known as "keesel". Potato flour began to be used as the jellying agent in the 19th century. Kissel may be made of any fresh, fresh-frozen or dried fruits or berries, rhubarb or milk. Two tablespoonsful of potato flour will make 4 cupsful of kissel of medium thickness. Dissolve the potato flour in 1 cupful of cold boiled water and immediately stir into the hot syrup. Do not boil the kissel more than 1-2 minutes or it will become thin.

Kissel is usually served cold but kissel of medium thickness may be served hot. Thick kissel, like cornstarch pudding is poured into large moulds, that have been rinsed with cold water, and then chilled. Sprinkle with sugar so that a skin does not form. Serve kissel with sugar, cold milk or cream.

Cranberry or Currant Kissel

1 cupful cranberries or currants	2 tblsps potato flour 3/4 cupful sugar

Pick over the berries, wash in hot water and crush with a wooden spoon or masher. Mix with 1/2 cupful of cold boiled water and rub the pulp through a strainer. Boil the berry skins in 2 cupsful of water for 5 minutes and then strain. Add the sugar to the water, bring to a boil and stir in the dissolved potato flour. Stirring continuously, bring to a boil again. Pour the berry juice into the kissel and blend.

Strawberry and Wild Strawberry Kissel

1 cupful strawberries or wild strawberries	2 tblsps potato flour 3/4 cupful sugar

Wash and hull the berries. Rub them through a sieve. In a saucepan dissolve the sugar in 2 1/2 cupsful of hot water. Bring this syrup to a boil, stir in the potato flour which has been dissolved in water and bring to a boil again. Add the berry puree and blend.

Raspberry or Bilberry Kissel

Substitute raspberries or bilberries in the above recipe.

Sour Cherry Kissel

1 cupful sour cherries 3/4 cupful sugar	2 tblsps potato flour

Wash the cherries in cold water, stone them, dredge with sugar and set aside for half an hour. Stir them several times. Pour off the juice. Crush the cherry stones and boil in 2 1/2 cupsful of hot water. Strain the liquor over the cherries and bring to a boil again. Stir in the dissolved potato flour and bring to a boil again. Remove from the heat. Stir in the cherry juice and blend.

Apple Kissel

500 g apples 3/4 cupful sugar	1 1/2 tblsps potato flour

Pare and slice the apples thinly and cook in 2 cupsful of water until soft. Press through a sieve and mix with liquor. Add the sugar, bring to a boil and stir in the

164

potato flour which has been dissolved in water.

Dried Apple or Apricot Kissel

100 g dried apples   2 tblsps potato flour
3/4 cupful sugar

Wash the dried apples and soak in 3 1/2 cupful of hot water for 2 or 3 hours. Bring to a boil and simmer for 30 minutes. Strain and press the apples through a sieve. Add the pulp to the liquid, stir in the sugar and bring to a boil again. Thicken with potato flour which has been dissolved in water.
Dried apricot kissel is made as directed, using 1/2 cupful of sugar.

Dried Bilberry or Sweetbrier Berry Kissel

50 g dried bilberries or   3/4 cupful sugar
sweetbrier berries   2 tblsps potato flour

Wash the dried berries in hot water and drain. Cover with 2 cupful of cold water, bring to a boil and cook for 15 to 20 minutes. When the berries are soft, strain the liquid into another saucepan. Crush the berries with a wooden spoon or masher and add 1 cupful of water. Bring to a boil, drain and squeeze the liquid out of the berries. Add the sugar, bring to a boil again and stir in the potato flour which has been dissolved in water.

Milk Kissel

4 cupsful milk   2 tblsps cornstarch or
1/2 cupful sugar   potato flour

Bring three cupsful of milk to a boil and add the sugar. Dissolve the cornstarch in 1 cupful of cold milk (or boiled water), and stirring continuously add it to the boiling milk. Boil the kissel for 5 minutes over low heat. If desired, flavour with vanilla or almond extract or with a little grated lemon or orange rind. Pour the hot kissel into cups and chill.

Rhubarb Kissel

300 g rhubarb   2 tblsps potato flour
3/4 cupful sugar

Wash the rhubarb in cold water and remove the skins if tough. Dice and soak it in cold water for 10 to 15 minutes. Boil the sugar in 2 cupful of water. Drain the rhubarb, add to the syrup and boil for 5 to 10 minutes. Thicken with the potato flour which has been dissolved in water. Chill and serve cold.

BEVERAGES

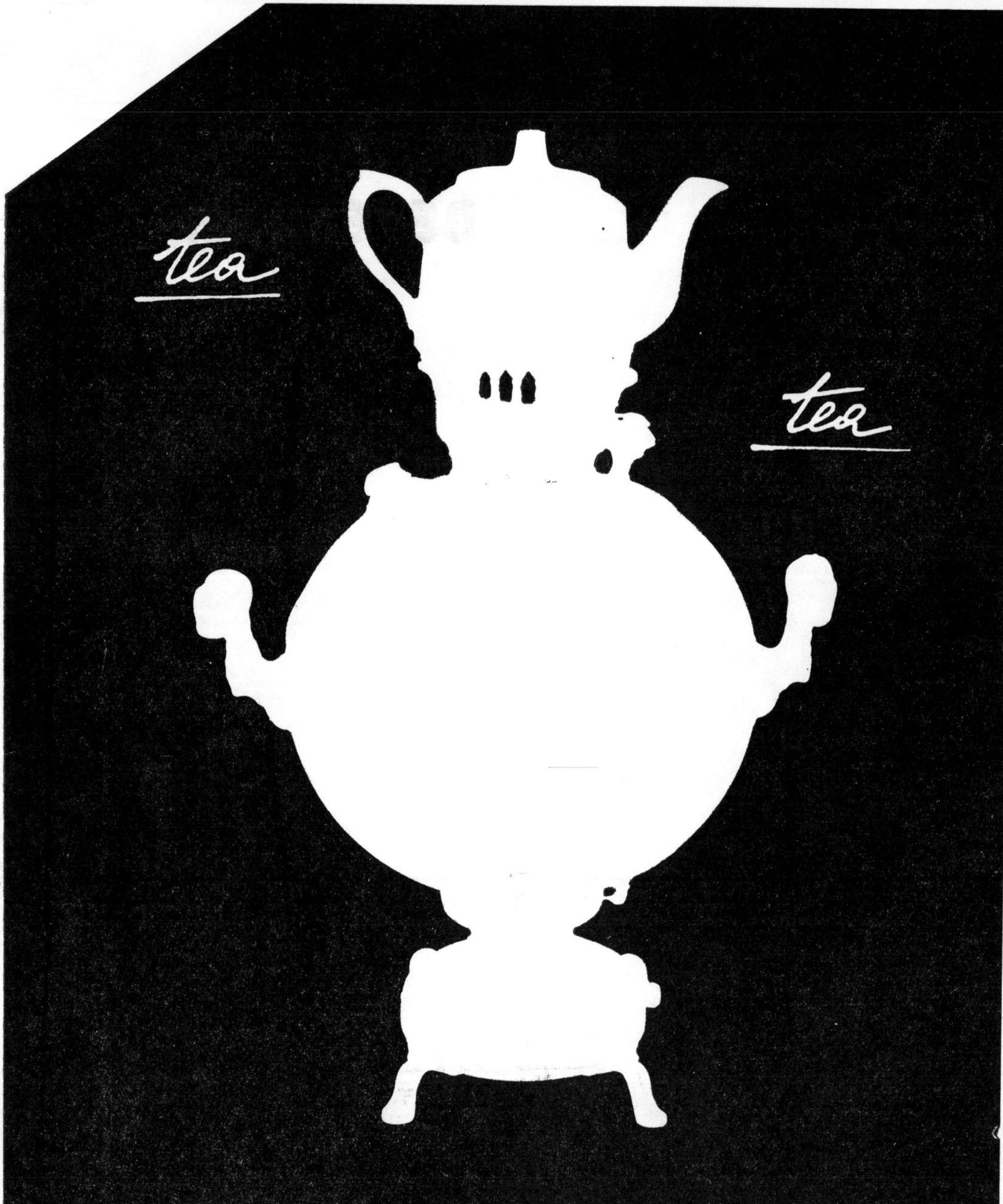
tea
tea

Tea
(Chai)

Tea was introduced in Russia in 1640. Russian ambassadors returning from the Mongol horde brought a gift of 200 packages, each weighing 500 grams. It was praised for its medicinal powers and ability to "refresh and purify the blood". It was also noted that it would keep one awake during "church services".

By the beginning of the 18th century tea was part and parcel of Russian life and had become very much a national drink.

Around the tea table family affairs were settled, opinions aired, trade negotiations carried on and contracts concluded. Thus, asking one to sit down to tea became a traditional sign of hospitality.

The brewing of tea, its service and the very manner in which it is drunk by the Russian people has a number of time-tested aspects that would today be defined as "technical" and "physiological". Tradition demanded, in the first place, that the water be boiled in a **samovar** if possible. It is difficult to establish exactly when the samovar made its appearance in Russia, but it can be established with certainty that its predecessor was a unique sort of thermos employed by vendors of **sbiten**, a hot beverage concocted of honey and spices (see p. 168). This vessel resembled a barrel with a cock at one end and a chimney pipe in the middle into which coal was stoked; this "thermos" had not bottom draft. The sbiten was not boiled, it was merely kept hot in these vessels. Then the samovars for boiling water appeared in a great variety of shapes. The traditional spheric-al, cylindrical and tapered samovars date back to the 18th century.

The samovar creates a peculiar atmosphere of coziness at the tea table. And the tea itself is usually tastier when brewed with boiling water drawn from the samovar.

The word "chai" in Russian cooking is applied to a number of hot drinks other than tea. Chai brewed of linden blossoms, raspberries, bilberries and numerous other teas are known for their medicinal properties.

Tea Brewing and Service

Tea should be brewed in an earthenware pot. Scald the pot with boiling water before measuring the tea into it. Use 20 g of tea for every half litre of water. Pour rapidly boiling water over the tea until the pot is 2/3 full. Close and cover the pot with a napkin or stand it on the samovar to draw for about 5 minutes; a tea cozy may be used instead.

Serve the tea in glasses or cups with saucers. Pour in the amount of brewed tea desired and then add boiling water. The usual proportion is one part tea, four parts water.

Ordinarily, tea is served with lump sugar, lemon, preserves, honey, fruit cooked in honey or sugar, and various other sweets.

Tea with Berries

Make the tea as directed above. Separately pass sugar, fresh cranberries, raspberries, strawberries or any other berries in season.

Sweetbrier Vitamine Tea

The sweetbrier fruit is known to be rich in vitamine C. One or two glasses of this beverage a day is sufficient for a healthy adult and one glass for children. Sugar to taste may be added.

Crush the fruit slightly so that the vitamine is more easily extracted. Use 1 table-spoonful of crushed fruit per glass of boiling water. Boil in an enamelled sauce-pan for no more than 8 to 10 minutes. Transfer the tea to a glass or earthenware vessel, cover and set aside in a warm place for several hours or overnight. Strain through a fine sieve and then squeeze the crushed fruit.

This tea must be made daily since vitamine C is highly volatile.

Bilberry Tea

1 tsp bilberry leaves
1 cupful boiling water

This tea is popular in the northern areas of Russia. Bilberry leaves are gathered in summer and dried. This tea may be drunk hot or cold. The leaves of the bilberry are known to contain arbutin, flavonoids, tannin and vitamines. Their infusion has diuretic, astringent and antiseptic effects.

Diaphoretic Tea

1 tsp raspberry, linden blossoms and aniseed
1 cupful boiling water

This tea is drunk as a cure for colds. Pour water over the mixture and boil for 5 minutes.

Sbiten

(Hot Spiced Beverage)

This old Russian beverage was especially popular in the 18th and 19th centuries. It was peddled by street vendors, or served at inns and taverns, at tea houses and other types of catering establishments. In winter street vendors carried sbiten on their backs in huge copper kettles resembling samovars covered with a heavy cloth to keep it warm; in the shops it was poured from large samovars. The sbiten vender was a figure so common in the streets of 19th century Russian towns that he became one of the characters frequently portrayed in folk drawings known as the lubok, old engravings and watercolours.

The following are two recipes for sbiten.

I

150 g sugar	5 g cinnamon
150 g honey	5 g ginger
2 g bay leaves	5 g cardamom
5 g cloves	1 litre water

II

100 g honey	0.2 g mint
50 g sugar	3 g hops
0.2 g cloves	1 litre water

Bring the water to a boil, dissolve the honey in it and add all the other ingredients. Boil for 10 to 15 minutes, set aside to draw and then strain. If desired, nutmeg may be added and molasses substituted for honey.

Fruit Drinks

Cranberry

Prepare the cranberry juice as directed in the recipe for cranberry kissel. Mix the sugar with an equal amount of water and boil for 5 minutes. Pour the fruit juice into this syrup and chill.
Per cupful of water use 3 tablespoonsful cranberry juice and 1 tablespoonful sugar.

Wild Strawberry

Add to 3/4 cupful milk 1 tablespoonful sugar, 1/4 cupful crushed berries and a pinch of salt. Whip until completely blended. Serve chilled.

Sour Cherry

Combine 1/4 cupful sour cherry juice, 1/2 tablespoonful lemon juice, add 3/4 tablespoonful sugar and a pinch of salt. Bring to a boil over low heat and cook for 5 minutes and then chill.
Add to this syrup 3/4 cupful milk and whip till blended. Serve chilled.

Meads

The preparation of this drink is as old as foraging for the honey of wild bees. "Mead" is what the ancient Greeks called the fermented drink popular among the Slavic tribes. Ancient European travellers to Russia are known to have described the cherry, currant, juniper, raspberry, bird cherry and spiced meads drunk here.

Spiced Mead

1 kg honey	10 g spices
3.5 litres water	100 g yeast

Boil the fresh honey, skim it and add pepper, ginger, cardamom, cinnamon and water. Bring to a boil and cool. Dissolve and add the yeast. Pour into large flasks and set aside in a warm place for 12 hours. Cover and age in a cool place for 2 or 3 weeks. Pour the mead into bottles and seal.

Cranberry Mead

1 kg honey	5 g spices
2.5 litres cranberry juice	100 g yeast

Add 1 litre water to the honey, bring to a boil and skim. Pour into a flask or barrel, add the cranberry juice, cinnamon, cloves and yeast and set aside to ferment for two days. Cover the flask or barrel and set aside in a cool place for about three weeks. After this pour into bottles and seal.

Kvass

Bread Kvass

1 kg rye bread	20 g mint
25 g yeast	50 g raisins
200 g sugar	5-6 litres water

Slice the bread and toast it in the oven taking care not to burn it. Put the toasted bread in a kettle or barrel, pour over boiling water, cover and set aside for 3 or 4 hours. Strain and add the yeast, rubbed together with the sugar, and the mint. Cover the barrel with a cloth and set aside to ferment for 5 or 6 hours. When foam appears, strain the kvass again and pour into bottles into which the raisins have been put. Soak the corks in boiling hot water and then seal the bottles, making sure the corks are securely fastened. Lay the bottles flat in a cool place for two or three days.

FOOD
PRESERVATION

apple preserves

1 kg apples
1 kg sugar
½ cupful water

pear preserves

1 kg pears
1½ kg sugar

173

Food Preservation

The food industry of the USSR puts on the market a large assortment of high-grade canned foods. Nevertheless, in summer when there is an abundance of fruits and vegetables many people like to put in a stock of homemade preserves, spiced and pickled vegetables, fruits and mushrooms.

Preserves

Almost any fresh fruits or berries are suitable for preserves as long as they are firm and not overripe. An equal amount of sugar (by weight) is usually used to make the syrup. Honey is sometimes substituted for all or part of the sugar. Sugaring can be prevented by adding a little molasses.

The general procedure is to measure the sugar into a wide shallow copper or aluminum preserves pan, add the required amount of water and boil until the sugar dissolves. Remove the syrup from the heat, add the fruit or berries and return the pan to the heat. Bring to boiling point over high heat, shake the pan slightly so that the fruit or berries settle into the syrup.

While cooking, skim the preserves and shake the pan slightly to keep from burning. Quality and storage time depend on the ability to judge exactly when the preserves are cooked. The following hints may be helpful: cool a drop of syrup on a saucer; if it does not run, the preserves

may be considered cooked. The fruit or berries will be evenly distributed in the syrup and in most cases transparent.

When cooked, skim the preserves, cool and transfer to a glass jar. Preserves cooked in this way need not be sealed; it is sufficient to cover them with parchment or oiled paper and then tie with a string. Store in a cool dry place.

Wild Strawberry Preserves

1 kg wild strawberries
1 kg sugar
1/2 cupful water

Hull the berries carefully so as not to crush them. Prepare the syrup as directed above. Gently lay the berries in the syrup. Shake the pan so that the berries settle into the syrup. Return the pan to the heat. Bring to boiling point and remove the scum. Cook over low heat as directed.

Strawberry Preserves

1 kg strawberries
1 kg sugar
1/2 cupful water

Hull the berries. Prepare the syrup as directed above, remove it from the heat. Lay the berries in the syrup. Carefully shake the pan so that the berries sink into the syrup and cook over low heat as directed. If the strawberries are very juicy, spread them on a platter, sprinkle with half the sugar and set aside in a cool place for 5 or 6 hours. Drain the juice into the remaining sugar and make the syrup without adding water.

Raspberry Preserves

1 kg raspberries
1 kg sugar

Carefully look over and hull the berries. Spread them on a platter and cover with half the sugar. Set aside in a cool place for 5 or 6 hours. Drain the juice into the remaining sugar and make the syrup; cool and then add the berries. Shake the pan carefully so that the berries sink into the syrup. Return to the heat and cook as directed until the syrup is of the required thickness.

Sour Cherry Preserves

1 kg sour cherries   3/4 cupful water
1 1/2 kg sugar

Look over and wash the cherries in cold water. Remove the pits. Put the sugar into the pan, add water, paddle and bring to boiling point. Add the cherries to the syrup and cook as directed.

Black Currant Preserves

1 kg black currants   1 cupful water
1 1/2 kg sugar

Stem, remove the bloom ends, wash and drain the currants. Make a thick syrup and add the currants. Bring to a boil and cook over low heat as directed for 40 to 50 minutes.

Gooseberry Preserves

1 kg gooseberries   3/4 cupful sugar
1 1/2 kg sugar   Vodka

Remove the seeds from unripe green gooseberries. Sprinkle with vodka and shake the pan to evenly dampen the berries. Refrigerate for 5 or 6 hours. Prepare the syrup. Drain the gooseberries and add them to the syrup. Cook as directed.

Apricot Preserves

1 kg apricots   2 cupsful water
1 1/2 kg sugar

Wash the apricots and pierce them in several places with a toothpick. Prepare the syrup, pour it over the apricots, and set aside for 24 hours. The next day, drain off the syrup, bring it to a boil, again pour it over the apricots and set aside for 24 hours. On the third day cook the apricots in the syrup as directed.

Quince Preserves

1 kg quinces
1 1/2 kg sugar

Pare and slice the quinces. Add cold water to cover and cook until tender. Remove the quinces with a skimmer and strain the water. Put the sugar into the preserves pan, add 1 1/2 cupful of fruit water and make a syrup. Put the quinces into the boiling syrup and bring to a boil twice. Simmer until the fruit is transparent. The peculiar quince flavour will be stronger if the parings are boiled in the water to be used to cook the fruit.

Rose Petal Preserves

1/2 kg rose petals   Juice of 1/2 lemon
1 1/2 kg sugar   1 cupful water

Cut away the white part of red or pink rose petals and then shred them. Mix with 1/2 kg sugar and set aside for two days. Add the lemon juice and water to the remaining sugar and make a syrup. Drop the sugared rose petals into the hot syrup and cook over low heat as directed.

Apple Preserves

1 kg apples   1/2 cupful water
1 kg sugar

Pare and slice a sweet variety of apples. Make a syrup, add the apples and cook until translucent. If some pieces of apple become translucent before others, carefully remove them with a spoon; return them to the pan when the rest are done. To improve the flavour of some apples a little vanilla, orange or lemon rind may be added. When making preserves with sweet apples add one cupful of cranberries per kilogram of apples.

Melon Preserves

1 kg peeled melon   2 cupsful water
1 1/2 to 2 kg sugar

Select half-ripe melons. Peel, remove the seeds and dice. Sprinkle with sugar and set aside in a cool place for 2 hours. Prepare a syrup with the remaining sugar and pour over diced melon. Set aside for 24 hours. Drain off the syrup, bring to a boil and pour over the melon. On the third day cook the melon in the syrup until translucent.

Pear Preserves

1 kg pears
1 1/2 kg sugar

Pare and slice firm ripe pears. Add just enough water to cover and boil until tender. Put the sugar in the preserves pan, add two cupsful of pear water, stir and bring to a boil. Put the pears in the hot syrup and cook as directed.

Cranberry Preserves

1 kg cranberries   1 cupful shelled
1 kg antonovka or any   walnuts
other tart apples   3 kg honey or 2 1/2 kg
                     sugar

Look over and wash the cranberries. Add 1/2 cupful of water, cover and cook until the berries are soft. Mash and press them through a fine sieve. Put the honey in the preserves pan and bring to a boil. Add the strained cranberries, pared and sliced apples and the shelled walnuts. Simmer for about one hour. Sugar may be substituted for the honey; add one cupful of water to the sugar to make a syrup. Cook as directed.

Green Walnut Preserves

100 walnuts   10 cloves
2 kg sugar   Juice of 1 lemon

Remove the outer green walnut shells and soak in cold water for 2 days. Change the water three or four times a day. On the third day drain and soak in lime water (see below) for 24 hours; paddle frequently. Drain and wash in cold water. Pierce each nut with a prong in several places. Soak in cold water for 48 hours. On the sixth day remove the nuts from the cold water and drop them into boiling water. Cook for ten minutes and then drain in a strainer.
Dissolve the sugar in two cupsful of water, bring to a boil and skim. Put the nuts into the syrup; add the cloves and lemon juice, bring to a boil, remove from the heat and cool. Bring to a boil again and cool (repeat this procedure three

times). After this the preserves may be considered cooked.

Lime water

Dissolve 500 g slacked lime in 5 litres cold water. Set aside for 3 or 4 hours to settle, then strain the water into another vessel.

Ashberry Preserves

1 kg ashberries	1 1/2 kg sugar
1 cupful water	

Pick the ashberries after the first frost. Stem, wash and soak them in cold water for 24 hours. Drain thoroughly in a strainer and soak in water again 2 or 3 times. Make the syrup with the water and while hot pour over the drained berries. Refrigerate for 24 hours, remove the berries from the syrup with a skimmer. Boil the syrup for 20 minutes, return the berries to the boiling syrup and simmer for 20 to 25 minutes or until the syrup becomes thick and the berries have a luster. Do not overcook or the berries will be dry and tasteless.

Cloudberry Preserves

Wash 1 kg cloudberries, drain in a strainer and then wash again in a stream of water and drain. Make a syrup of 1 kg sugar and 1 cupful water; stir continuously. When the syrup begins to boil, add the berries. Cook for 30 minutes. Strain and rub the berries through a fine sieve and cook for 10 minutes longer.

Apple Jam

Any apples unsuitable for preserves may be used for jam (povidlo). Cook the apples and rub them through a sieve. To each cup of puree add 3/4 cupful of sugar and cook over low heat stirring regularly. When the puree becomes thick, remove it from the heat, transfer to glass jars and seal. Store in a cool dry place.

Apple and Plum Jam

1 kg apples	1 kg sugar
1 kg plums	1 cupful water

Put the pared and sliced apples and pitted plums in a preserves pan. Pour in the water, cover with a lid and cook until tender. While hot, rub the fruit through a sieve. Add sugar to the puree and mix thoroughly. Cook over low heat until thick (about 1 1/2 hours).

Red Bilberry Preserves

1 kg red bilberries	Stick cinnamon, lemon
500 g sugar or honey	rind
	3 cloves

Look over the berries and pour over boiling water; paddle and immediately drain thoroughly in a strainer. Put the bilberries in a preserves pan, add the sugar (or honey), 1/2 cupful of water, a piece of stick cinnamon, cloves and a little grated lemon rind. Cook as directed. When cool, transfer to glass jars and cover with parchment or oiled paper. Store in a cool dry place.

Bilberries in Syrup

1 kg bilberries
300 g sugar

Look over the ripe berries, wash them in cold water and put them into a clean glass or porcelain jar. Dissolve the sugar in 2 cupsful of water, add a little lemon rind and bring to a boil. Strain and cool. Pour the cold syrup over the bilberries. Cover the jar with parchment or oiled paper and tie. Store the bilberries in a cool place. Serve with roast meat or fowl.

Pickles

Various fruits, vegetables, berries and mushrooms are preserved by pickling. In many respects the quality of the pickles depends on the kind of vinegar used. Grape vinegar or flavoured table vinegar makes especially good pickles. Strong vinegar (6%) should be diluted (1 : 1) with water; add salt, sugar, such spices as pepper, cinnamon, cloves, nutmeg and bay leaf; bring the mixture to a boil and then cool. Pack the fruit, vegetables or berries in glass jars and pour over the vinegar and spices. Pour oil on top to prevent mould from forming. Tie parchment or oil paper over the jar. Store pickles in a cool dry place.

Cucumber Pickles

1 kg cucumbers	Terragon
2 cupsful vinegar	Garlic
1 tblsp salt	1 red pepper

Select small firm cucumbers; wash and scald them. Pack the cucumbers in a glass jar putting terragon between each row. Add 2 or 3 cloves of garlic and 1 red pepper. Pour over the cold pickling mixture. Cover the jars with paper and tie.

When the cucumbers become saturated, add vinegar. Store in a cool place.

Pickled Cabbage

1 kg cabbage	10 peppercorns
1 cupful vinegar	3 bay leaves
3 cupsful water	1 tblsp salt
1 cupful sugar	

Add the vinegar, sugar, peppercorns and bay leaves to the water, boil and cool. Shred the cabbage, mix with salt and rub slightly. Squeeze and drain the juice. Pack the cabbage in jars and pour over cold pickling mixture. Cover with parchment paper and store in a cool place. Within 5 or 6 days the cabbage will be pickled.

Pickled Tomatoes

Select small tomatoes (preferably plum variety). Wash and pack in jars. Cover with pickling mixture. To each cupful of vinegar, add 1 cupful of water, 1/4 cupful of sugar, 1/2 tsp salt, cinnamon, cloves and peppercorns; boil together, cool and pour over the tomatoes. Should the brine become misty within two or three days, drain it off, boil, cool and pour over the tomatoes again.

Pickled Beets

Wash and cook whole beets. Set them aside to cool in the water. Clean, dice or slice, pack in jars and cover with vinegar mixture. To each cupful of vinegar add 1 cupful of water, 1 tblsp sugar, 1/2 tsp salt, a little pepper, cloves and a bay leaf; mix together, boil and cool before using.

Pickled Melon

Select half-ripe melons. Wash, cut them in halves, remove the seeds, peel and dice the flesh. Pack into jars and pour over cold pickling mixture. Cover the jar with parchment paper and tie. Stand the jars on a rack in a water bath with water enough to reach the level of the melon in the jars. Boil for one hour. Cool in the water bath. Store in a cold place.

Pickling Mixture

To each cupful of vinegar add 1 cupful of water, 3/4 cupful of sugar, 2 tblsps honey, 2-3 cloves, a piece of stick cinnamon, 2-3 allspice and 1/2 tsp salt. Bring to a boil in an enamel saucepan, cool and strain.

Brining

Fresh-Salted Cucumbers

Choose small cucumbers. Wash and pack into a jar along with dill and garlic. Cover with cold brine made of 2-3 tblsps salt per litre of water. The pickles will be ready to serve within 2 days.

Quick Fresh-Salted Cucumbers

Cut off the ends of the cucumbers before packing into the jar. Add dill and garlic. Pour over hot brine. The pickles will be ready to serve within a few hours.

Pickled Cucumbers

One pail water	50 g dill
600 g salt	1/2 red pepper

1 garlic	5 g terragon
300 g horseradish root	

Choose small young cucumbers preferably picked the same day. Cover the bottom of the barrel with oak, black currant or cherry leaves, dill, horseradish, terragon, garlic and 1/2 red pepper. Pack the cucumbers into the barrel tightly, stand them on end. Spread the various leaves and spices between rows. Close the upper end of the barrel and pour the brine into the barrel through the hole in the lid. Stop up the hole with a wooden peg. Cucumbers may be pickled in a wooden tub. After packing, cover the tub with a wooden lid and weight it down just enough to keep the cucumbers from floating. The brine level must be 3 or 4 cm above the cucumbers. Cover the tub with a cloth and store in a cool place.

Pickled Cucumbers with Vinegar Brine

10 litres water	1 cupful grape vinegar
500 g salt	3/4 cupful vodka

Prepare the cucumbers as directed in the recipe above. Pack the cucumbers and savoury herbs in a barrel or jar and cover with hot brine to which vodka and grape vinegar have been added. On the following day add more cold brine and seal the barrel or jar. Store in a cold place. These pickles will keep for a long time.

Pickled Tomatoes

12 litres cold boiled water	700-800 g salt

Scrub and scald the barrel. Sort the tomatoes according to ripeness; make sure they are all firm. Wash and pack the tomatoes alternately with layers of dill, terragon, savory and cherry or black currant leaves. Shake the barrel or jar from time to time so that the tomatoes settle more compactly. Fill the barrel to the top and pour in the brine. Cover with a wooden lid and weight it down. Store the tomatoes in a cool place. Pickling time is 40 to 50 days.

Fresh Soured Cabbage

Shred, wash and plunge the cabbage into boiling water. Drain in a colander and pour over cold water. Add salt. Sour according to the directions for sauerkraut. Souring time is 5 to 6 days.

Sauerkraut

Cabbage is usually soured in large wooden barrels but small quantities (5 to 10 kg) can be prepared in a glass jar or crock.
Choose firm fresh heads of cabbage, discard the green leaves. Shred and mix with salt (250 g salt per 10 kg cabbage). Sprinkle a thin layer of rye flour over the bottom of the barrel and spread whole cabbage leaves over it. Pack the shredded cabbage into the barrel tightly, cover with whole cabbage leaves. The shredded cabbage may be mixed with sliced or shredded carrots, quarter pieces of antonovka (tart) apples, bilberries or cranberries. Place a wooden lid on the top and weight it down. Within a few days a scum will appear on the top. Insert a birch pole or stick long enough to reach the bottom of the barrel. The gases formed will escape through the vent made by the pole. The disappearance of the scum is a sign that the cabbage is soured. Store in a cool place. Should mould appear on the surface of the brine, remove it carefully. Scald the wooden lid and wash it as well as the cloth and weight that cover the cabbage.

Pickled Apples

The antonovka, a tart apple, is best for pickling. Spread a layer of cherry or black currant leaves on the bottom of the barrel. Wash the apples and place them in the barrel stems upward. Alternate every few layers of apples with a layer of leaves. Cover the last layer of apples with leaves. Pour in wort or sweet water to fill the barrel.

Wort

10 litres water	2 tblsps salt
200 g rye flour	

Pour boiling hot water over the rye flour, add the salt and stir until thoroughly mixed. Set aside to settle, then strain.

Sweet Water

10 litres water	400 g sugar or
3 tblsps salt	600 g honey

Mix the ingredients together, boil and cool.
Before pouring the wort or sweet water into the barrel, move it to a cool place. Cover the apples with a wooden lid and weight it down (a clean heavy stone will serve the purpose). During the first 3 or 4 days the apples will absorb much of the liquid and it will be necessary to add

more wort or cold water. During pickling and storage, the level of the liquid must be kept 3 to 4 cm above the wooden lid. The apples will pickle within 30 to 40 days.

Preservation of Mushrooms

The best known among the edible mushrooms are the boletus, aspen, brown cap boletus, butter, milk, edible brown, chanterelle, russula and honey mushrooms. They should be gathered in the early morning.

Mushrooms spoil quickly and therefore must be cooked or preserved within 4 or 5 hours after they are picked.

Drying

Most suitable for drying are the boletus, aspen, brown cap and butter mushrooms. Do not wash them; wipe them clean with a cloth. On hot days they may be strung on a thread and hung in the sun. When dried in a Russian or ordinary oven the temperature must not exceed 70°-80°C (158°-176°F). Keep the oven door slightly open to ensure continuous air circulation and evacuation of moisture. Finish drying the mushrooms in the sun or hang them over the cooking range. Store in a dry, well-ventilated place away from any products with a pungent flavour. If they become moist, the mushrooms must be examined and redried.

Pickled Mushrooms
(Cold Method)

The edible brown, milk, volnushka (Lactarius torminosus) and russula mushrooms are best for cold pickling. Milk, volnushka and russula mushrooms must be soaked in cold water for 5 or 6 hours before pickling; edible brown mushrooms need only to be washed. Pack the mushrooms in a barrel crock or glass jar, sprinkling each layer with salt (50 g for each kilogram of milk, volnushka or russula mushrooms and 40 g for each kilogram of edible brown mushrooms). Cover with a wooden lid that fits easily into the vessel and weight it down. When the mushrooms settle, add more to keep the barrel or crock full. Check within five or six days to see if the mushrooms are covered with brine; if they are not, increase the weight on the lid. Pickling time is 1 to 1 1/2 months.

Pickled Mushrooms

(Hot Method)

Clean and sort the mushrooms. Pickle the caps and stems of the boletus, brown cap boletus and aspen mushrooms separately. If large and small caps are to be pickled together, cut the large ones into two or three pieces. Wash the mushrooms in cold water. Valui (Agaricus emeticus) must be soaked for 2 or 3 days before pickling.

Pickling Mixture for 1 kg Prepared Mushrooms

2 tblsps salt	3 cloves
1 bay leaf	5 g dill
3 peppercorns	2 black currant leaves

Add the salt to 1/2 cupful of water and bring to a boil. Put in the mushrooms. When they begin to boil carefully skim and add the spices. **Do not burn.** Cook boletus, aspen and brown cap boletus mushrooms for 20 to 25 minutes, valui, 15 to 20 minutes, and russula and volnushki, 10 to 15 minutes. When the mushrooms begin to settle and the pickling mixture becomes clear, turn into a wide saucepan, cool quickly and pack the cold mushrooms and pickling mixture in a barrel or crock and cover. The brine must comprise not more than one fifth the weight of the mushrooms. Pickling time for these mushrooms is 40 to 50 days.

Spiced Mushrooms

Select firm young boletus, brown cap boletus, aspen, butter or honey mushrooms.

Spice each kind separately. Clean and sort them according to size. Cut off the stems (peel butter mushrooms), wash in cold water and drain in a colander.

Pickling Mixture for 1 kg Mushrooms

1/2 cupful water	2 cloves
1 1/2 tblsp salt	2 or 3 g dill
1/2 cupful vinegar	3 peppercorns
1 bay leaf	Piece of stick cinnamon

Add the vinegar and salt to the water. Put in the mushrooms, bring to a boil and skim. Add the spices. Cook for 20 to 25 minutes; paddle carefully and continuously. When the mushrooms settle to the bottom remove from the heat and cool. Pack in a crock or glass jar.

182

Glossary

1. Yuzhny, Ostry, Lyubitelsky and Kubansky sauces are commercial sauces obtainable in the USSR
Yuzhny is spicy;
Ostry is tart and spicy;
Lyubitelsky is sweet and spicy
Kubansky is sweet-sour
2. Rasstegai — meat or fish patties or pies; either entirely open on top or closed, a vent hole being left in the top
3. Viziga — fish cartilage or spinal marrow of sturgeon fish. It is air dried and sold in bundles resembling skeins. Viziga contains up to 40% glutinous matter
4. Zakuska — hors d'oeuvres
5. Ukha — fish soup. Originally any clear soup was called ukha
6. Pirozhki — patties, small pies or turnovers
7. Pirogi — large patties or pies
8. Kulebyaka — large patties with more filling and less dough than pirogi
9. Mannacroup — semolina
10. Kindza — the leaves of coriander, widely used in Georgian cooking
11. Kletski — drop dumplings
12. Kissel — jellied dessert of varied thickness made with potato flour
13. Vareniki — Ukrainian poached pasties
14. Kvass — a beverage usually made from rye, yeast, sugar and mint
15. Okroshka — chilled soup made with kvass
16. Botvinnya — chilled fish-and-vegetable soup
17. Borshch — soup made with beetroot stock
18. Kasha — see p. 133
19. Shashlyk — marinated, skewered and then grilled meat of lamb
20. Solyanka — tart soup or other dish made with a large variety of ingredients usually including pickled cucumbers or sauerkraut
21. Zapekanka — pudding
22. Rassolnik — soup made with brine and pickled cucumbers
23. Bliny — pancakes
24. Blinchiki — thin pancakes
25. Oladyi — thick pancakes
26. Golubtsy — cabbage rolls stuffed with meat or vegetables
27. Telnoye — stuffed cutlet
28. Shchi — traditional cabbage soup
29. Pelmeni — poached pasties

Index

TO THE READER

Mir Publishers would be glad to have your opinion of the translation and design of this book.
We would also be pleased to receive any suggestions and proposals you care to make about future publications.
Our address is:
USSR, 129820, Moscow, I-110, GSP,
Pervy Rizhsky Pereulok, 2,
Mir Publishers